THE RED ISLAND

THE GATEKEEPER

Adil Alzarooni

Adil Alzarooni

DISCLAIMER

'The Red Island: The Gatekeeper' is a work of fiction, suitable for readers aged thirteen and older. Names, characters, businesses, events, incidents, the depiction of jinns and practices of dark magic are all products of the author's imagination. Any resemblance to actual persons, living or dead, or actual events is purely coincidental. Certain places, institutions, agencies, and historical events are mentioned, but the characters and events involved are wholly imaginary.

In context of the story, the author has included some quotes from The Clear Quran translation by Mustafa Khattab. The author has created characters of various nationalities and religions to depict a multicultural society. By doing so the author does not intend to promote any stereotypes or hurt the sentiments of any individual, religious community, sect, ethnic or political group.

The author also does not intend to discuss or provide a commentary on Islamic beliefs or philosophies or any other religions. It is not a reflection of Emirati, Arabic, or Islamic traditions or beliefs. It does not recommend or endorse any spiritual or healing practices.

The publisher and the author assume no responsibility for errors, inaccuracies, omissions, or any other inconsistencies herein.

PROLOGUE

"Allah created the heavens and the earth, and all that is between them, in six days."

(The Holy Qur'an, 7:54)

"Be," the Creator said, and the seven skies and the heavens rose, with rivers flowing through lush gardens and meadows of dazzling flowers the fruit trees laden with delicious produce.

In this peaceful and serene atmosphere, He spoke into existence heavenly beings, the angels, made of pure light and bound to obey him, and the jinns, fashioned from a smokeless fire and in possession of free will.

He separated the earth from the heavens, placing mountains on vast expanses of land, creating the sun and the moon to mark time and illuminate the earth.

As the Creator settled on His throne, he placed the fiery jinns as inhabitants of the earth. The jinns sang praises for their Lord and the miracles He had bestowed upon them.

The world echoed with *'Allah'* and harmony reigned supreme until a nascent curiosity about willpower, which set jinns apart from the angels, grew amongst a tribe of jinns.

They discovered the thrill of rebellion and were seduced by forbidden pleasures. Their once noble spirits became. They sowed discontent across the earth, spreading fear and despair, and turning the land into a pyre.

As their darkness threatened to consume the earth, the Creator, in His infinite wisdom and boundless mercy, sent down an army of His angels to restore peace.The heavens trembled as the greedy jinns refused to obey and for the first time, the universe witnessed a war.

When the angels collided with the jinns, the powers of the two opposing forces were unleashed in a dazzling display of light and fire.

The jinns, with their fiery forms and cunning intellects, conjured storms of flame. The angels fought back with unwavering resolve, each movement a testament to their *taqwah*. They pushed the jinns to the edge of the ocean, slamming the gate shut on their darkness, crushing their vile ambitions with the weight of divine justice.

The echoes of battle faded into a distant memory as the victorious angels ascended to the heavens. They took with them Azāzīl, a jinn, who had remained steadfast in his devotion to the Creator.

With his status elevated, Azāzīl walked amongst the highest-ranking angels, his heart a vessel of pure devotion for his Creator. But with his newfound standing, a seed of pride began to take root in the depths of Azāzīl's heart.

His piety was tested when the Creator sculpted the first human, Adam, from clay, and designated him to reign over the earth.

"Remember when your Lord said to the angels, 'I am going to place a successive human authority on earth.' They asked Allah, 'Will You place in it someone who will spread corruption there and shed blood while we glorify Your praises and proclaim Your holiness?' Allah responded, 'I know what you do not know."

(2:30)

When the Creator commanded the angels and Azāzīl to prostrate themselves before Adam, a wise human, a creature made of mud, Azāzīl's haughtiness and jealousy made him defy his Creator.

Joining the ranks of disbelievers, he cemented his transformation into Iblis, becoming the chief of a mischievous cult of jinns who chose *haram* over *halal*. He earned the title of *shaytan*, as he embarked on his mission to lead astray both humans and jinns, weaving webs of temptation, blind to the tragedy and destruction he had brought upon himself. He was banished from the forces of light, placed down on earth till the Day of Judgement, to forever regret the loss of divine love.

THE PRESENT
CHAPTER 1

"We will certainly test you with a touch of fear and famine and loss of property, life, and crops."

(2:155)

His face was melting. Badr inhaled and exhaled deeply, loudly, hastily, as if someone was about to cut off the Earth's oxygen supply and he needed to suck all the air in.

Visible from the corner of his left eye was a tiny crescent, surviving, yet still shining in the clear indigo sky.

He could hear the waves but could not see where the shore and the sea plunged into one another. As his eyes adjusted to the dark, his car began to quiver and quake, rattling him to the core.

"I'm imagining it," he, but there was no telling for sure. Trembling, he grasped the steering wheel.

"Am I dying or reaching the edge of sanity?" he wondered.

Then everything stopped. In the abrupt silence and stillness, Badr closed his eyes, unable to open them again, as glass shattered and a car door creaked.

A pair of strong arms hoisted him and pulled him out, with some shards stinging his exposed skin, but his eyelids remained firmly pressed against his eyeballs.

When he finally blinked, he was pleasantly surprised to find himself in the embrace of the morning sun. His eyes travelled down and locked with the sapphire-blue sea, an endless reflection of her eyes. He could always find her, every day, everywhere, especially in the myriad hues of blue.

He thought of their last phone call. Her voice had been a tangled web of immeasurable love, teary hopefulness, emotional ambivalence, and rising mistrust. That last conversation was lodged permanently in his heart's largest artery. An unhealed wound that kept him awake at the strangest hours.

"You're awake?" He was startled out of his reverie by a familiar Emirati accent.

A tall, muscular guy, clad in a *faneela* and *wizar*, was sitting cross-legged, not far from where Badr lay on the golden sands. The guy's head was shaved but he had covered it with a *ghafiya* and a *ghutra*, sans the *igal*. He looked odd without the *kandura*, like he'd forgotten to wear it.

Badr looked at his long, unkempt, salt-and-pepper beard and his rough skin. His face was not entirely unpleasant to look at. A rugged handsomeness that didn't reveal whether he was in his thirties or forties. But Badr was put off by the overpowering smell of fish and the sight of his dirty, bitten nails.

As he scrutinised the stranger, the man's eyes seemed to make incisions into his soul.

"You've never seen a man before?" He seemed furious.

Badr turned his head away, crossing his arms over his chest. Usually, he was the six-foot-one-inch tall, confident Emirati guy who didn't feel intimidated by anyone. But it was difficult to find his voice today, with sand grains layering his tongue. His body was aching, and small seashells were prickling his waist and butt.

He spat on the sand, and slid his hands down his back, throwing the seashells towards the sea.

"Where am I?" he asked, looking up at the cloudless sky.

"You don't know where you were driving to?" the strange man asked sharply, almost angrily.

Badr found it hard to respond as fatigue and exasperation were overtaking his senses. He slowly raised and rotated his head to catch sight of the various shades of brown, smudged in places. Squinting, he realised they were the eerie remnants of traditional coral stone architecture, the empty shells of courtyard homes, two-storey buildings and a mosque lying asleep not too far from the coast. There were also some intimidating watchtowers and a rather gloomy fort peering at him from a distance.

As he scanned his backdrop in its entirety, it seemed oddly familiar, like an image he might have seen on a postcard or perhaps an old photo? It all came back to him.

"Al Jazirah Al Hamra ... the Red Island," he muttered, and his companion nodded.

Badr remembered visiting this ancient ghost town with Baba when he was thirteen. He had heard many stories about this village in Ras Al Khaimah and how its inhabitants had abandoned it.

"Where did they all go, Baba?" Badr had asked, a curious teenager with an unquenchable thirst for knowledge.

"I am not sure," Baba had replied. "We don't really know why they left. Many people believe they ran away suddenly, when jinns infested this place. That probably explains why, to this day, this town is untouched by humans and urbanisation."

Like any traditional Muslim, Badr believed in jinns and how they were invisible to humans but had always co-existed with them. He wasn't a huge fan of the supernatural stories of his childhood, or he hadn't been until ... images from the past flashed before his eyes. He thought about how his two great loves had driven him to his lonely and bleak reality.

Badr quietly looked up at the mysterious man staring at him and noticed he had kind, brown eyes.

"I need to hide," he whispered.

CHAPTER 2

"Whether you speak openly or not, He certainly knows what is secret and what is even more hidden."

(20:7)

"**I** am in love."

Badr wasn't sure why he said that. A diversion tactic?

The rustle of leaves had his heart racing as he lay in a near-empty house, made of mud, rocks and coral, situated in the middle of the Red Island.

The room they were in had cracked, bronze walls, and no furniture at all, just some old mattresses and worn-out coverlets and blankets thrown around to create the illusion of a bedroom. There seemed to be no power supply. The house was built at a time when there was no air conditioning, but it had some natural cooling techniques in place, aided by a small, battery-operated, Indian, pedestal fan.

A large, dusty window was open but curtained by a huge green tree.

"That's a Sidr tree, isn't it?" Badr asked. "I've read that it can grow in the harshest environments. And that its leaves are rich in calcium, iron, and magnesium, so they are often used to treat health conditions."

"Reminds you of *Sidrat al-Muntaha*," said the mystery man.

"What?" Badr asked.

"It's mentioned at several places in the Qur'an, the tree which marks the utmost boundary in the seventh heaven that no one can cross, as the knowledge of angels stops there. Only Prophet Muhammad (PBUH) was able to see it during *Isra* and *Mi'raj*."

"This place is quite far from my vision of heaven," Badr thought, but said nothing, not wanting to antagonise his host.

The whiffs of smoke brought his focus back to their dwelling where they had been sizzling the air with Marlboro after a typical but finger-licking Emirati breakfast of *baith tamat* paired with *khameer* bread and a side of date syrup.

Badr's rescuer had arranged it from the other side of the island. He wasn't sure what he was more surprised at: having a huge appetite after all that had transpired, or this messy man's treat or smoking.

Badr never smoked, except for the occasional drive-thru *shisha*, which was more of a stimulus for socialising than a nicotine fix. But for some inexplicable reason that morning he had asked his companion for a cigarette when he lit up. Now they were resting on a sagging mattress. Perched up on their elbows, they blew smoke while looking at the tree and an intricate spiderweb near the window.

"I am not particularly fond of spiders," Badr said.

"But we are discouraged from killing them," his host replied.

"Yeah, I know. We've been told that by divine intervention Prophet Mohammad (PBUH) and his best friend were saved from assassins when a spider quickly spun a large web at the opening of a cave they hid in, leading the enemy to believe that no one could be inside that cave," Badr said, looking at the spiderweb closely for the first time and admiring the construction of the delicate silky net.

"So, what are you hiding from?" his stranger-companion asked. He had shown absolutely no interest in Badr until now. Even though Badr expected hospitality from an Emirati, given the whereabouts and circumstances, his indifference had been making Badr edgy.

"Now that he's fed me, I don't know what he'll do with me. Feed me to the jinns? If they really live in this godforsaken place," he wondered. "Or maybe he is a jinn? After all, they are shape shifters and can take the form of humans or animals, although they are said to be invisible to humans."

Pearls of sweat formed on his neck, so he said the first thing that came to his mind. "I am in love."

He was hoping to elicit some response. But his companion did not laugh or look shocked. Instead, he turned his head around slowly to look at Badr.

For the first time in months, someone hadn't questioned Badr's declaration. In fact, his expression softened; it was almost like he understood Badr.

Like a lightning bolt, it hit him. Badr knew who this man was.

"You're the crazy guy," he blurted out before he could stop himself.

A flicker in the man's right pupil told Badr he was hurt by his words. But other than that, it seemed he had been freezing his emotions for decades.

"Abdulaziz," Badr said apologetically, his face turning a hot pink, as it usually did when he felt anxious or embarrassed.

"So, I see you've heard of me," Abdulaziz said in a vacant voice.

Of course Badr had heard of him! The elders had narrated so many tales about this mad man, a distant relative, an outcast, a black sheep, a symbol of the perils of falling in love.

"He's under the spell of love," some people would say.

No one really knew the complete version of Abdulaziz's descent into madness. The abridged version was that Abdulaziz was just a regular Emirati guy who deeply loved his third cousin, Azza. But for some unknown reason Azza's father had rejected him and married her off to a friend's son. If rumours were to be believed, Abdulaziz had lost his mind following Azza's marriage and moved to an undisclosed location.

Over the years, many versions of this tale were told and retold until everyone forgot about Abdulaziz. Now he was only mentioned when someone made the mistake of falling in love and had to be cautioned with 'look what happened to Abdulaziz' stories.

It was widely believed that Abdulaziz lived with the jinns of Al Jazirah Al Hamra. Some said he had become a mystic or a Sufi saint. Others speculated he had died of heartache. But Badr didn't think the man lying next to him was a saint or a ghost; at least he hoped he was not the latter.

"Unless I died that night in my Nissan Patrol, and this is a non-fiery isolated hell. Feels like it," Badr thought.

"If you don't mind, can I ask you something personal?" he asked, trying to stop his thoughts from spiralling.

Abdulaziz did not respond or look at him. Badr wasn't sure whether to go on or shut up. He wanted to ask Abdulaziz about his love story.

Abdulaziz was probably the only person who knew exactly what had happened and Badr was eager to be the first one to learn the truth about this infamous character from his childhood. He was from a species that was going extinct as most locals in Badr's generation were turning out to be the arranged-marriages-and-listen-to-your-parents kind. But Abdulaziz didn't seem to be in a mood to indulge Badr.

"You can unpack and keep your things in the next room," he instructed.

"I don't want to unpack. I am not gonna be here for long." Badr liked feeling unsettled. He didn't want to belong to this desolate, waste of a place.

Abdulaziz gave him a doubtful look, as if he knew something about the future or this place that Badr didn't.

"Is it a swamp that sucks humans in?" Badr felt worried but shooed away his catastrophic thoughts. He'd had enough shocks recently.

"So, you live here alone?" he asked.

"No, not alone," Abdulaziz replied.

"You have a family?" Badr asked, considering the possibility that Abdulaziz had found love again. But the dark clouds forming on Abdulaziz's face quashed his innocent hopefulness.

"Do you know anything about this place?" Abdulaziz asked. He seemed a bit annoyed.

"Yes, of course, what do you mean?"

"So, you know it's not the abode of humans?"

"Th ... then?" Badr did not feel quite ready to hear his answer.

Abdulaziz was quiet as a cool breeze blew their way and the rustle of leaves got louder. He sensed some movement outside, as if someone was circling the house. The tree seemed to be shaking. The first tremors of an earthquake? Badr started to breathe heavily, but to his relief, Abdulaziz stood up and shut the window. The movements and sounds stopped as unexpectedly as they had started.

Abdulaziz turned around to look at Badr, who felt like a small, fear-filled child cowering under the man's gaze.

Abdulaziz moved towards him as Badr moved back and mentally prepared to defend himself, looking at the strong arms of his opponent nervously. But Abdulaziz's expression was neutral now, almost friendly. The dark clouds had left. Extending his hand towards Badr, he said, "Come, I will show you."

CHAPTER 3

*"Who guides you in the darkness of
the land and sea, and sends the winds
ushering in His mercy?"*

(27:63)

Badr had visited very few places like Al Jazirah Al Hamra and never had he lived in such conditions. Even during family vacations, he had stuck to the good life: the vibrant, urbanised parts of cities. Now he made his way through the dilapidated houses and dunes, guided by Abdulaziz's cyan-blue lantern and the full moon's glow.

They clambered over tumbled walls, avoiding discarded furniture and debris. Some buildings had been torn down completely, with only limited evidence of the foundation structures remaining, mostly in the form of hollow frames, bricks, and the mud squishing below their sandals.

The still-surviving buildings, laid out neatly in rows, featured ttraditional architecture constructed with local materials: coral blocks, beach rocks, woven leaves, mangrove tree beams, date palm trunks, ropes, and layers of seashells.

The buildings had several wind towers, known as *barjeel*, which rose about five metres above the roofs, open on all four sides. These towers helped catch and direct a cooler breeze into the rooms below through vertical shafts.

Badr wasn't sure where Abdulaziz was taking him, but he followed the man like a puppet on a string. He knew he could probably make a run for it and drive away, but he couldn't think of a better place to hide than this. Plus, a part of him was also curious to see if Abdulaziz was, in fact, tderanged.

Badr had seen the Arabic letter *Ain* carved twice on various tree trunks, and assumed the *Ain & Ain* stood for Abdulaziz and Azza.

"That's not crazy behaviour", he thought. He was aware of the tradition of love padlocks, inscribed with lovers' names or initials, which were locked on bridges, with the keys thrown away to epitomise eternal love. But he had also been spying on Abdulaziz to see if he posed any danger and occasionally found the man speaking to himself.

It reminded him of the time when he used to be alone in his car or bedroom, role playing how he would talk to his *habibiti*. But Abdulaziz had taken it up a notch.

When he was alone, Abdulaziz would turn into a completely different man, gentle and warm. His posture would become relaxed when he sat in a corner of his house, near a small window, a space which could only be described as a shrine for his love.

It comprised a worn-out, undyed, large *khoos* coaster, a gold *Ain* alphabet pendant, a small clay pot, an *al-sadu* bookmark featuring earthy and sea tones, a few sketches of horses and a gold *al shubuq*. Badr assumed all these objects, now resting on top of an old silk pillowcase, had once belonged to Azza.

When Abdulaziz thought Badr was napping in the other room, he would visit this shrine to express his devotion to his beloved. It seemed like a daily ritual to commemorate his love. Sometimes he even had complete conversations with her. "Azza, did you like the beach today? Did you see that I tried something new this morning?" He would also change positions and respond to his questions on Azza's behalf.

This multi-character solo performance freaked Badr out. Abdulaziz reminded him of the fictional 7th century Bedouin poet Qays ibn al-Mulawwah, popularly known as Majnun, who had gone insane after his love interest Layla was forcibly married off to a rich merchant.

If Abdulaziz was, in fact, a contemporary version of Majnun, this adventure would be nothing but a colossal waste of time, Badr thought. But he tried to suspend disbelief, bury it under the ruins, as he was hungry for answers and for a way out of this meandering mess, for a way to rescue his *habibiti*.

He followed Abdulaziz, noticing how time stood still on the island. An empty wooden boat, a broken cart with four wheels, and a small green, rusting truck were parked in the middle of nowhere, suspended in the past, as if one gloomy day, the Zaab tribesmen had jumped off the boat, emptied the cart, turned off the engine and fled from their homes for good.

"This is the first vehicle of Ras Al Khaimah," Abdulaziz said, pointing at the truck.

"It seems people left Al Jazirah Al Hamra suddenly and very quickly."

"Yes."

"Clearly, he's in bed with brevity," Badr thought.

"Our destination is close now," Abdulaziz said, signalling towards a cluster of abandoned houses.

Badr swallowed and tried to sound brave as he asked, "The jinns?"

Abdulaziz nodded.

"Do you speak to them?"

"Yes, I speak to them every day."

"I have been told that humans can't see them. At least not in human form."

"Usually, they can't, apart from the chosen few."

"Chosen few? Like you?"

Abdulaziz was quiet.

"Are there any good jinns?"

"Of course! They are the reason I am still alive and here."

"Aren't you here because you are depressed? Because of losing..." Badr caught his tongue. He didn't want to offend Abdulaziz. They had just started bonding.

Abdulaziz did not look at Badr or show any emotion,t but after a pause said, "And I never knew before I met Azza what crying was, nor what were heart aches until she departed."

Badr was familiar with the verse. It was from a poem by an Arab poet, Kuthayyir ibn 'Abd al-Rahman, about his unfulfilled love for a married woman. He had first read it in high school, but the unfulfilled love part hit too close to home now.

He looked at Abdulaziz and felt an affinity with the man. They were the same: both pining for their lost loves. But, unlike him, Badr still had hope. He wondered if he should tell Abdulaziz his love story and ask for help. But it seemed too early to trust him. Badr needed to tread carefully. Abdulaziz could be almost friendly one minute, but aloof and intimidating the next.

Not knowing how to break down the iron walls guarding Abdulaziz's secrets, Badr changed the subject and asked, "What about the bad jinns? What happens to them?"

"The same thing that happens to humans," Abdulaziz said, and then recited:

> *"Many are the Jinns and men We have made for Hell: They have hearts wherewith they understand not eyes wherewith they see not and ears wherewith they hear not. They are like cattle nay more misguided: for they are heedless (of warning)."* (7:179)

"That means jinns and humans are not that different?" Badr asked.

"Exactly. Jinns have a life, they have families, beliefs. They do good and evil. They're rewarded or punished by Allah," Abdulaziz explained, as they crossed the empty houses. Badr was surprised they were not going inside, but instead, heading towards the sea that lay adjacent to the houses.

Something grazed his leg, and he jumped. It was a white-silver, malnourished creature.

"Is that a dog?" Badr asked.

"No. A fox," Abdulaziz said.

Badr looked at it carefully and realised it was indeed a very small fox, kind of like a Canadian Marble Fox, but without the fur. He was trying to taste Badr's trousers.

"He'll find something to eat. Let's go," Abdulaziz said, moving forward as if he was on the clock.

With some difficulty, Badr disengaged from the tiny fox and left him sniffing garbage. The two men walked towards the sea and stopped close to the waves crashing on the shore, slapping their feet, throbbing in their ears. Badr loved this sound. It was his top stress reliever.

"I have never interacted with a jinn before," he said, staring at the water, waiting in suspense, perhaps for an awful rendition of the depth of Abdulaziz's insanity.

"Are you aware of the concept of *Qareen*?" Abdulaziz asked. Badr shook his head.

"Every person has a *Qareen*. He is your devil-companion, the one who tempts you to do evil and disobey Allah."

"Really? Like my personal bad jinn?"

"Yes, it's mentioned in the Qur'an:

> *"His companion will say: 'Our Lord! I did not make him transgress but he was (himself) far astray.' He will say: 'Dispute not with each other in My Presence: I had already in advance sent you Warning. The Word changes not before Me and I do not do the least injustice to My Servants.'"* (50:27-29)

"My devil-companion?" Badr repeated. "The same way we all have two angels, *Kiraman Katibin* or 'The Noble Recorders,' Raqib and Atid, the ones who rest on our shoulders and record all our good and bad deeds in the *Name A'amal*?" he asked.

"Yes, exactly," Abdulaziz said, now focusing on the sea and reciting,

> *"But verily over you (are appointed angels) to protect you*
> *Kind and honourable writing down (your deeds):*
> *They know (and understand) all that ye do."* (82:10-12)

Badr hoped his Qareen was inactive because he aspired to fly high in the afterlife as well. He began to sense a sudden change in the air but dismissed his uneasiness as the new breeze felt awesome on his sweaty torso. Abdulaziz put his lantern down and started digging a small, round hole in a mound of sand.

"What are you doing?" Badr asked.

"Just observe. Quietly, please."

"Was he a perfectionist teacher or a strict librarian in the past?" Badr wondered. Nobody had ever talked about what he did, apart from being in love.

Abdulaziz gathered rocks to make a circle around the hole. He retrieved some logs, branches, and dried small twigs, hidden between a cluster of rocks.

Badr understood what he was doing, thanks to all the barbecue and bonfire parties he had attended. Abdulaziz added the logs and other materials to the hole, using his lighter to light the kindling.

As the fire burned in front of them, Badr looked at the tide. It was transitioning from a slow and peaceful one to a high tide, threatening to become a king tide. It seemed like the ocean's giant belly was bulging. Badr felt dizzy and took many steps back, but Abdulaziz remained rooted to his spot, guarding the bonfire.

"Abdulaziz? Does the tide not scare you?" he yelled.

This seemed to be turning into a suicide mission, as if Abdulaziz had been waiting for an earthling to come witness his ceremonial drowning.

"Do I need to write the end of his tragic story? Or am I supposed to rescue him from his fate?" Badr asked himself.

"Don't punish yourself. The world needs you," Badr shouted, but his voice was lost in the harsh wind that sliced straight through them, whispering, hissing, perhaps trying to warn them of unknown perils that lay ahead. Badr tried to shield himself with his hands.

"Do you see them?" Abdulaziz asked in a calm, quiet voice, unmoved by the wind or the sea.

"See what?" Badr asked, walking back towards him.

"You are blind, Badr." Abdulaziz had called him by his name for the first time.

"Are we friends now?" The thought made Badr happy for some reason.

"Open your eyes, open your heart," Abdulaziz snapped, as if his quota of niceties had ended for the day.

"Do you mean there are jinns here?" Badr asked.

"You need to believe they exist if you are a true Muslim. Do you see them?"

"I believe they exist. But I … I don't wanna to see them. I'm scared," Badr confessed. He wanted to crawl back and hide undert their blankets.

Abdulaziz was cross, but the fear in Badr's puppy-dog eyes softened him. t

"I understand, but don't worry … they will be equally suspicious of you! They don't accept anyone quickly. Especially not an unknown man who has mysteriously landed on this island and is behaving like a fugitive," Abdulaziz said.

Badr wondered if there was a hidden question. Was Abdulaziz expecting him to divulge the details? Did he think Badr was a criminal?

"But what do they look like?" he asked, trying to redirect the conversation.

"Jinns can take different shapes and forms, but they might not reveal themselves to you, at least not right away. I just want you to feel their presence."

Badr drew a deep breath, attempting to gather his wits and tap into the sensations Abdulaziz wanted him to perceive. While he had grown increasingly convinced that his new friend hallucinated, he didn't blame the guy. After all, years of solitary existence in this desolate place would make anyone stark raving mad.

What could he possibly say to assuage the concerns of this unhinged man? He studied the sea, hoping that prolonged focus might yield some insight.

After five minutes of nothing, the chemicals in his brain started playing tricks on him. The tide was still high, but the waves, defying convention, were surging in the opposite direction, away from the shore.

Unlike the usual backwash waves, each wave was pushing higher in its retreat, pulling the sea backwards. Abdulaziz no longer needed to protect the bonfire.

Badr had never seen anything like this before, the coastline expanding, forcing the sea to recede.

"Is it just me or is the sea playing some odd games today?" he asked.

"Keep looking," Abdulaziz urged.

Badr kept staring ahead. Just as he was about to abort his mission, he discerned a few odd-shaped silhouettes retracting with the waves, mirroring their backward rhythm.

"I ... I see some shadows in the water," he said, hoping he'd passed the test.

"Excellent. You are almost there. That was fast. Perhaps because they see you're here with me. Keep trying," Abdulaziz encouraged.

"They have human-like heads and extremely slender necks. And the rest of their bodies appear distorted, blending with the undulating waves so it's hard to see their whole form," Badr said, as stress-sweat drenched him.

He watched the silhouettes meandering in the water, then disappearing into the mammoth waves. He desperately wanted their little excursion to be over.

Just then a fresh gust of wind brought a stench so revolting that Badr felt the urge to retch. He saw Abdulaziz extracted a small glass bottle of Arabic perfume from his pocket and removed its lid. The fragrance was potent and brought a wave of nostalgia.

"Musk," Badr whispered softly, recalling his childhood days nestled in *Ummi's* embrace, inhaling the scent of her lustrous, black hair.

"The angels and benevolent jinns are drawn to pleasant scents, while the devil and bad jinns prefer foul odours," Abdulaziz explained, as he sprinkled the perfume into the air and onto his fingertips. Bending down, he traced intricate patterns with his hand, akin to playing a melody on an invisible piano, inscribing *Bismillah*, the opening phrase of the Holy Qur'an, onto a sizable grey stone.

He was ambidextrous. Badr had never seen anyone use both their right and left hands so well. He knew that only one percent of the world's population could do this.

"Guess I shouldn't be too surprised because this guy is the poster child of rarity, at least in our culture," he reflected.

Abdulaziz closed his eyes, muttering something. Badr moved closer to him, trying to listen.

"And We pried into the secrets of heaven; but We found it filled with stern guards and flaming fires." (72:8)

As Abdulaziz recited *Surah* Jinn, a cloud of grey smoke rose from the water, filling up the sky. Badr's thoughts were zigzagging as he saw the monstrous cloud ate up the moon.

"This can't be happening! It's unreal!" Badr said out loud, blinking a few times. He looked at the large, grey ball of doom and gloom with a feeling of nervous trepidation, scared that it was going to nibble on him next.

"Abdul …" He wanted to seek reassurance, but froze, shocked till he was shockless. His friend was no longer there.

The *ghoul* standing near Badr had taken his *kandura* off. Badr watched with horror as the *ghoul's* bare-chested upper body grew, as if he was on steroids or had taken a magic bodybuilding pill. His hands balled into fists; a frown cutting incisions on his forehead. His body twitched, and his shoulder muscles moved like a bag full of small pebbles.

Abdulaziz's eyes turned crimson as he uttered some verses indistinctly, his hands stretching out, like a beggar asking for supplication.

"Has he been possessed by a jinn? Or is he morphing into a humanoid or a beast?" Badr tried to grasp what was happening.

"Are you going to kill me?" he shrieked.

The *ghoul* looked at him, his face turning cochineal red with primal rage. Badr knew he had to escape the wrath and ruthlessness *ghoul*-Abdulaziz was planning to unleash.

He started running backwards towards the decaying houses. Abdulaziz called out, but Badr couldn't tell if he was calling him or the dreadful cloud. All he wanted was to get away from his beastly form and the monster smoke cloud, which was now taking over the entire sky.

"Ouch!" His left foot hit something large and sharp, forcing his sandal off and He toppled over rather unheroically.

Badr lay on the ground whimpering, breathing loudly, close to the empty shells of houses. Liquid drops trickled onto his face; the tiny fox was drooling. He shut his eyes, feeling a mix of disgust and dread.

His body was trembling as he prayed for Allah's mercy. Just then, footsteps echoed, and the fox was no longer his biggest problem.

Someone was getting closer and all he could do was curve into a ball, his ability to breathe blocked.

A shadow hovered over him. Badr opened his eyes to see the menacing ghoul with his icy-cold eyes peering into his. An emotion greater than fear rose in him, like his soul was struggling to leave his body. As the ghoul's face moved towards his, Badr's world went pitch black.

CHAPTER 4

"Indeed, Allah alone has the knowledge of the Hour. He sends down the rain and knows what is in the wombs. No soul knows what it will earn for tomorrow, and no soul knows in what land it will die. Surely Allah is All-Knowing, All-Aware."

(31:34)

Badr opened his eyes to a woven date palm roof with specks of the sky visible. He lay there, watching the sky transition from black indigo to a pinkish orange. He was inside a house, huddled in a corner, a small piece of cloth tied around his aching foot.

He was relieved to see Abdulaziz, who was now back in this human form and sitting cross-legged in front of him, wide awake. Badr wondered if the man ever slept.

"Good sleep?" Abdulaziz asked sarcastically, as if Badr had been overreacting to last night's events.

"What happened?" Badr asked, breaking into a sweat again.

"Let's go for *fajr*. The sun will rise soon," Abdulaziz said casually, and Badr wondered if he had dreamed it all.

After prayers, Abdulaziz took him fishing. That's how he survived, he said, by selling fish on the other side of the island.

As they settled down with large fishing nets, Badr said, "So you're a fisherman."

"Yes, and in the winters, I'm a *ra'I Al jaseef*."

"A what?"

"A fish preserver. When there are many varieties of fish near the coast, usually in winter, like *badah, nisar, al kaseef* and *bayah*, I catch and clean them, cut them into two, remove their heads and insides, and stuff them with salt."

"Why is that?"

"Because it helps draw out any water from the flesh, increases its acidity, and prevents germs from infecting the fish. And then I hang the fish with ropes or place them on a mat on the ground in the open air. This way, I can make them last for several months and the dried fish can be eaten without cooking."

"Oh yeah. I think I've had it several times. It's delicious."

"Yes, it's very popular among locals. Also ideal for people going on long trips or those who live far from the sea. I also sell some of the fish as compost for plants."

This was the first time Abdulaziz's conversation with Badr had exceeded a few short sentences. He seemed to be getting more comfortable around Badr.

"So ... what were you doing this morning?" Badr asked.

"Oh, I was opening the gate for the jinns leaving the island, trying to ward off the bad ones with the musk," he replied, as if describing a normal workday.

"I am not really sure I saw them."

"You did ... you will get better with time."

"You ... you do this every day?"

"Yes … I have been doing this for the last fifteen years or so."

"But why?"

"It's my job."

"What's your job?"

"To keep the peace. I hold the key and guard the gate."

"What gate?" Things were getting silly again.

"The gate to the sea. It keeps them and us safe. You see, Al Jazirah Al Hamra is a gateway for three species. It is where angels, jinns and a selected group of humans meet. It's where they have their peace talks, do trade, and occasionally coexist."

"And what is it that you do?" Badr asked, arching his eyebrows.

"I usually just open the gate at sunset for the jinns to come onto the island and close it after they leave before sunrise."

"And what do they do on the island at night?"

"They trade … eat … talk …"

"So why do you watch the gate?"

"It's a long story, but the jinn who used to guard the gate … one day he left it open and ran away, which caused chaos, led to a war between the three species as the jinns could not agree on a replacement. The three tribes were in conflict."

"What three tribes?"

"There are three tribes of jinns inhabiting this island. They sought my help. I consider it my way of paying rent for cohabiting with them."

"Really?" Badr asked, thinking it all sounded beyond ridiculous. But then he remembered the nightmarish grey cloud, the freaky tide reversal, and Abdulaziz's horrifying transformation.

"Maybe there is some truth in all this," Badr thought.

"And what do you do, Badr?" Abdulaziz asked.

Badr was surprised, as the spotlight had suddenly shifted onto him. But perhaps Abdulaziz had earned some intel on him. After all, he had shared some of his secrets. Badr felt pressured to reveal something.

"I'm a pilot," he said.

Really?" Abdulaziz did not seem to believe him.

"Why? Do I not look like someone who could fly planes?" Badr asked, annoyed.

"What's a pilot doing in this abandoned town?" Abdulaziz asked.

After deliberating for a few minutes, Badr decided it was time to tell Abdulaziz the truth.

"It all started in August 1996 ..."

THE PAST
CHAPTER 5

"For your Lord has decreed that you worship none but Him. And honour your parents. If one or both of them reach old age in your care, never say to them even 'ugh,' nor yell at them. Rather, address them respectfully."

(17:23)

Badr considered 24th August 1996 as the last day of his teenage life. It was an important day that started well with *fajr* prayers at the small neighbourhood mosque. Badr said his prayers alongside a few elderly, distant relatives, wondering why they always made it to *fajr*.

Was it because they couldn't sleep or because they had committed a lot of *haram* acts during their long lives?

He strolled back home, feeling unusually exhilarated, admiring the colourful trees, the little doses of light filtering through the leaves, and all kinds of birds, the house sparrow, the common *myna*, the red vented *bulbul*, the laughing dove, and others, chirping away, happy to be alive, free, and ready to fly away.

Once home, he checked his tickets and the travel guide again while *Ummi* packed his suitcase.

"I don't know what to pack for you, Badr. It's been so long since I did this for Humaid," she said.

"Don't worry *Ummi* ... just don't send me naked, *khallas*," Badr said, making her smile, as he put his electronic diary, a yellow lava lamp, a Walkman and some cassettes in a box and labelled it 'Discard or Distribute.'

"You better not roam around in public without any clothes," *Ummi* said, pretending to scold him. "We represent our Muslim, Emirati identity no matter where we are. And don't bring back some girl with you."

"Oh, don't you worry! I'll get you a gorgeous white daughter-in-law and maybe adopt a couple of black kids," Badr said, giggling, as he passed her his I Love NY t-shirt.

"Those white women only use paper in toilets!" *Ummi* said, neatly folding properly ironed shirts and pants.

"What? I can't believe you said that! Don't say it to anyone else. People will get offended."

"It's a legitimate concern. You must be practical when it comes to marriage, Badr."

"Well, you can teach her the Muslim way to use the toilet."

"Don't get a Jew, though!" she snapped.

"Oh! I ... I forgot to mention that my Bashert will be a Jew who prays to Elohim!" Badr said, confused by the change in her tone.

"You know we have one of those in the family? Just don't kill your Baba by marrying one," she said solemnly while tucking his best-loved cargo pants in the suitcase.

"A one of what?" Badr asked while fondly looking at his new PalmPilot, a gift from *Baba*.

"A *Yahudy*."

"Really? Who? How did that ever happen?" His eyes widened. Emiratis rarely married outside the local community, let alone a Jew.

"A distant family member. And he married an American Jew! Can you believe it? She would probably have us believe that Musa *('Alay-hi 's-salam)* was white! Anyway, don't worry about them. Just focus on your training," she said dismissively, as if she'd done enough by issuing this random red alert.

Badr knew better than to probe her with questions. She didn't like to indulge in gossip. And he probably didn't care enough since he was already rolling up in big fluffy clouds and blue daytime skies.

Later that day, he clutched his tickets, kissed *Ummi's* forehead, and glided down the stairs with his suitcase.

Baba was sitting at the end of the staircase, wearing a plain white shirt, a *wizar*, and a *ghafiya*.

"Assalamu alaikum, Baba!" Badr said, surprised to see him in his night clothes.

Baba looked up at him with tears in his eyes.

"*Baba*, what's going on?" Badr asked. Amidst all the excitement, he had not anticipated an emotional farewell, especially not from his father. He had rather expected *Baba* to crack a joke about him transforming into an Americanised Arab.

"You ... you don't need to go ...," *Baba* said.

"What?" Badr was startled.

"There are good colleges in town, you know, and your grades will get you anywhere you want," *Baba* continued.

The clock ticking, but he was too taken aback to move. This was a completely new runway, and Badr didn't know how to fly out of it.

Usually, he was the well-behaved, sensible teenager who hated going to school, but loved being an A-grader. He didn't mind following rules and earning brownie points.

Peering into Baba's sad, drooping, red eyes, he said, "*Baba* ... you know I'll do anything for you."

"Then don't go," *Baba* insisted, like a petrified child. Badr wasn't sure what his fear was and patted his father's arm.

"But we did plan this together, *Baba*!" he said. "We are meant to go to the airport now!" He waved his ticket as alien emotions threatened to emerge.

"There are engineering colleges here, Badr. You don't have to go to the US for this."

"I don't want to be an engineer, *Baba*!" His voice had become unrecognisably tense.

"You know aviation engineering is the closest scholarship I've found to flying. I really want to be a pilot. I can't imagine being anything else. And you know I wanted to be a jet fighter, but *Ummi* was afraid I would get killed, so I settled for becoming a commercial pilot," he pleaded. "Once I reach the US, I know I'll be able find a way to change the scholarship to flying."

"You can start here ... in that school you told me about," *Baba* said, wiping his tears with a cotton handkerchief.

"Sure, I can," Badr said, after a pause, trying desperately to recover from this unexpected crash.

"But it would cost a lot! And ... and I would eventually need to fly to the US either way to become a commercial pilot."

"I am fine with that, Badr. We can figure that out later when you're older. You stay here for now ... please," *Baba* said softly, but decisively, tapping Badr's shoulder.

After a few minutes of silence, which felt like hours of dull melody, Badr finally managed to say, "Sure, *Baba*, whatever you want, *khallas* ... just don't cry, please."

He watched *Baba* walk away, stress leaving his shoulders, and *Ummi* following him.

That evening, Badr went to his favourite spot on the sand dunes to watch the beautiful, man-made bird fly out from behind the white domes of Sharjah International Airport. He watched his flight, his raison d'être, accelerate, ascend, and eventually disappear into the clouds.

Sitting quietly with his best friend Rashid, a psychology junkie, he listened to his friend's discourse on the 'less-talked-about heartbreak' that came with parent-child relationships. What Badr experienced in his silence, Rashid expressed in words. "The people closest to you, the ones you love the most, can hurt you the most, sometimes unconsciously, without any explanation, in the most unexpected ways."

CHAPTER 6

*"It is He who created you from a single
person and made his mate of like
nature in order that he might dwell with
her (in love)."*

(7:189)

Five years after his piloting dreams took an uneventful turn, Badr and his family squeezed together for a group photo to celebrate his graduation, summa cum laude, from the Etisalat College of Engineering.

A few days later, he drove towards a brown tower with green glass windows, topped by a golf-ball-like sphere, which people fondly called 'the bean' or 'secret chamber.'

It was his first day as a Security Engineer at a leading telecom company in Dubai. Badr quite liked his slick office with swivelling chairs, marble flooring and thick glass doors. He was confident he would do well in his job, but sitting inside air-conditioned offices and testing new technologies was not his biggest dream.

All was going well, according to his plans, when one evening Badr overheard *Ummi* and three of his sisters whispering about a picnic that was in the works. His heart sank even though he had known this day would come soon. It was not unusual for Emiratis to get married at the age of eighteen or twenty, and most marriages were fixed by the elders.

Thanks to the time he had spent buried in engineering books in a college full of men, Badr had been able to enjoy freedom for a little longer, having turned twenty-one recently.

He knew this picnic, planned with a group of relatives, would be a façade for a matchmaking episode, to nip any blossoming love story in the bud. Eligible bachelors like him would get a sneak peek at the single Emirati girls around. To feel they had some choice in the matter.

Two weeks later, he found himself reluctantly driving towards a spacious, Greek-style farmhouse in Khor Fakkan.

Omar Uncle, one of *Ummi's* four brothers, had acquired and furnished it recently. He gave everyone a tour, showing off its freshly painted white walls and lapis lazuli-coloured doors and windows that opened to majestic views; dark-chocolate-brown, rugged Hajar mountains and a crescent-shaped, glittering beach, dotted with palm trees and resilient coral reefs.

Badr was impressed by the farmhouse, its tastefully furnished bedrooms, well-equipped kitchen, big *majlis*, a dedicated area for barbecue, and a circle-oval shaped swimming pool. He wanted to build a similar house once he had become a pilot and was ready to settle down.

After the tour, all the guests settled into one of the bigger open-air seating areas. Omar Uncle's multi-generational domestic staff, who had been working for his family for decades, had laid out fresh and clean linen cloths, along with some handmade cane tables and chairs.

The spaces for men and women were separated by the main farmhouse building in the middle. It seemed that the elders were attempting a loose form of segregation, so the usual anti-mingling brigade wasn't keeping an eye on the younger generation, though they were still expected to keep a distance from the opposite sex.

This was Nada Aunty's doing. Over the last couple of months, she had become obsessed with the notion that Badr's eighteen-year-old cousin Fahad was trying to bring a foreigner-bride home, given his increasing fixation with Sharon Stone and Halle Berry, and preoccupation with ICQ.

Rumour had it that Fahad's dad, Mansur Uncle, who Badr did not really like, had said, "Do whatever you like Fahad, but keep it discreet. And don't promise marriage ... that can only happen with a local girl from one of the families we know."

Badr looked in the direction of the women's section, observing how the *abayas* and *shaylas* had changed over the years. The younger women had adorned new styles made of modern and ostentatious fabrics, embellished with rhinestones, crystals, and embroidery.

As he looked at their clothes, Badr spotted a familiar face. She was wearing an *abaya* with a cross-over front fastening that was in vogue. Badr exercised his grey cells, trying to recall where he had seen her.

"Munira," he said softly. A fourth cousin.

When Badr was young, he and Munira would often play together at family gatherings and their parents would hint at their future union.

Badr had quite liked the idea as a seven-year-old when all he wanted in a wife was adorable big eyes, thick black curls, and someone who fake-giggled at all his lame jokes. But once they had evolved into teenagers with hormones, the two were no longer allowed to socialise with each other or with anyone from the opposite sex, as dictated by local culture.

Badr had completely forgotten about Munira's existence up until this moment. She had grown into a graceful woman, with a glowing olive complexion, groomed to be the perfect housewife, if the delicate way she was pouring the *gahwa* from the *dallah* was anything to go by. Even though house help was around, she chose to serve, possibly an attempt to impress a prospective mother-in-law.

"Maybe she is aiming for *Ummi*," Badr thought. He was soon distracted by the other eligible bachelors and their deck of cards. There was intense excitement and competition in the air. Some people were even losing their tempers, cursing under their breath so that the elders would not hear them.

Badr's group of six was divided into two teams and playing *Hokm Bo Sit*, a trick taking game, in which the victorious team had to win a count of fifty-two. Fahad was on the other team and doing well. He seemed least bothered about Nada Aunty's schemes for his coupling.

"So, Fahad, I hear we'll be seeing you soon in a *bisht*?" Another cousin, Mahmud, teased him.

"Only if I lose the game today," Fahad replied.

"So, your punishment would be to lose your virginity with the blessings of your elders?" Mahmud asked.

"Who said I'm a virgin? I've been sowing my wild oats," Fahad replied and nearly fell off his chair, guffawing.

Badr realised he did not like Fahad much, especially when he was cocky and overconfident. He was also exasperated because he seemed out of luck today when it came to cards and relieved when one of the servants announced that lunch had been served.

Ummi had prepared her famous chicken *kabsa* while the others had brought homemade *harees*, *robyan mashwi* and other local dishes. Following *Sunnah*, they washed their hands, sat on a cloth laid out on the floor, said *'Bismillah'*, and then, in true Emirati style, extended their right hands to eat from a main plate.

There was no specific order of eating. Soup, salad, main courses, all had been served together, so guests could feast on whatever they fancied first, puzzling their metabolism. They used spoons only for soup and bare hands for everything else. Badr liked how his community was keeping these traditions alive.

"They're so practical," he thought.

Fahad and Mansur sat down next to Badr, whispering, but he could overhear them making plans involving European women and some quintessential Emirati experience.

He wondered what that meant exactly and if he should try to tag along. But he was done with being a college guy who wasted time over infatuations. He liked looking at pretty women but had never really fallen head over heels in love with anyone. And now he had started working, he wanted to focus on his dreams. He was going to be a kickass pilot and travel the world!

Making a mental list of all the destinations he'd like to fly to, Badr made his way to the kitchen to look for a clean cup for coffee. He was surprised to see his elder brother, Humaid, sitting alone at a rectangular, wood carved dining table.

Humaid seemed to have put on five more kilos since the last time they had met. He looked older as well. Middle age had descended early in his life, not so much biologically as psychologically. Perhaps being a human resource manager at a multinational company, a husband, and a doting father of two was not as hunky dory as people would have you believe, Badr thought.

They rarely saw each other one-on-one, briefly meeting during the family *majlis* and the occasional football match they played socially with cousins.

As they greeted and hugged each other, Humaid's porcelain-doll-like wife Najla came in. She nodded at Badr.

She often did that. Acknowledge but not really greet people, if they were younger or poor. Badr had imagined it would change as he grew older, but clearly, he was still one of the ignorable entities.

She banged a half-filled teacup on the table in front of Humaid. It seemed slightly cracked from one side.

"Isn't this broken?" Humaid asked, scowling.

"Do you want me to go get another one?" Najla asked, looking annoyed. "This is not our house."

Humaid shook his head slowly. As she was walking out, Badr thought about the forwarded email he had received that morning. A photograph of an old couple and some text about how they 'fixed' anything that was broken. He wondered if Humaid and Najla would be one of those old couples, getting accolades for making it work.

"So, what's new?" Humaid interrupted his thoughts, as he popped a pill for hypertension, clearly forgetting he was supposed to take it in the mornings.

Badr briefly explained the wedding conspiracy that was in full swing.

"So?" Humaid asked. "What were you expecting? You've managed to postpone your nuptials for longer than most of us!"

"Yes, I know. But I do sometimes wonder about the notion of romantic love? What it would be like to ride a Harley Davidson with a girl, letting the long winding roads watch us create something bigger than ourselves."

"You paint quite a picture," Humaid said, smiling. "Well, you can enjoy platonic love, build a connection, and appreciate the goodness of women as friends. Maybe at work?"

"No, no, I don't know about that. Other locals will notice. And I feel like other people are intimidated by men like me because we're all walking about like kings in our loosely fitted white *kanduras*. But then I do want to know how it would be to have a real love relationship. You know, one that is not inside a teenage internet chat room or a childhood infatuation with a half-American, half-Lebanese school canteen lady," Badr said, feeling frustrated.

"You mean the lady who beamed at you every time she gave you a box of Areej mango juice for fifty fils?" Humaid asked, trying to lighten the mood.

Badr did not say anything, so he continued, "Did you fancy any of the girls? At least you're allowed to see them. I only got to see Najla after our wedding.".

"Yes, I remember. I saw some girls. But I would have liked to talk to them, to see who I like and maybe take their phone number."

"Sadly, that's out of the question. To be honest, I have no problem with this, the world's changing. We've entered a new millennium, but it would create such a big scandal in our family, if anyone saw or found out," Humaid said.

"So, what should I do?" Badr asked.

"You know, the only way you can get to know an Emirati girl is if you ask for her hand through our parents and go through the *milcha* period, which means you guys will already be legally married, but not living together. If you ask me, it's still better than meeting her on your wedding night."

"Yes, you're right, *okhoy*," Badr said. He remembered Humaid's wedding in bits and pieces as he had been four years old at the time. But thanks to the photo albums and VHS tapes, he could fill in the details.

The wedding celebrations were, of course, segregated. The men's party had been low key, as it typically was, and held inside a traditional tent. Some of their male relatives had stood in a line, holding a thin gold cane in one of their hands. A few in the front and at the end of the line had also carried small rifles while they all danced to Emirati music.

"What are you thinking about?" Humaid interrupted Badr's walk down memory lane.

"How weddings are such a yawn-fest! Only the women seem to enjoy them," Badr said.

"Well, I get it. For them, it's a place where they can take off their *hijab* to show off their jewellery, *shnaf, tassah, bushuq*, and their glittery dresses. They can sing and dance freely and handpick the best single girls for their sons and brothers."

"Yeah, and enjoy their *henna* party, and the lavish decorations, the cakes and dessert."

"Yeah, I only like the part where they serve *luqaimat* with tea and coffee," Humaid said. He then started telling Badr about his workplace, how men and women would mix a lot professionally and socially.

Badr listened absent-mindedly as he moved towards a hand painted Moroccan style wooden mirror and checked out his hair.

Humaid's words became distant as he noticed another reflection in the mirror; strips of lilac and white that disappeared almost instantly.

"What's that?" Humaid asked, as they heard a loud thud from the next room.

"Let me check," Badr said as he parted a translucent, white curtain draping the side entrance, and stepped into a quaint lounge, left untouched by the renovators.

For a second, he felt blinded by an ethereal and shimmering presence. As his vision cleared to reveal a young, white woman picking up a small table she had knocked over. Her size reminded Badr of Polly Pocket.

"Hi, do you need any help?" he asked, startling her.

As she looked up at him, Badr found himself peering into large, almond-shaped eyes. Soulful, intelligent, evocative. With a sapphire-blue iris that sparkled and stunned him.

He felt paralysed, both physically and emotionally, as her pupils dilated in response to his. The depth in her eyes was pulling him forward, but he couldn't move or breathe. His gaze wandered, memorising her delicate features. She was hypnotically beautiful, with a playful, childlike quality he found very endearing. Her cheeks turned pink like a child's as she blushed, tugging at his heartstrings. Her shayla wasn't hiding her rich, dark coffee-brown hair properly.

As Badr looked at the strands of her hair, a peculiar sensation spread through his arms. It was not painful. In fact, he liked it.

"So probably not a heart attack," he thought. It felt like some kind of fluid, possibly a love potion, had been injected into his veins. He kept looking at her and his gut told him he was feeling all he needed to feel for a woman. He wanted to know her, to be with her, to make her his. He was surprised at the lightness and ease this thought brought to his nervous system. A sense of pleasant certainty gripped him.

"In only one-fifth of a second, the neurochemical reaction connected with feelings of love can fire off," he remembered reading in some article and thinking it was absurd.

Badr had never seen her before or anyone like her, especially not amongst the locals. He gazed at her petite, feminine form, wrapped in a lilac, petal-like *abaya*.

"How marvellous it would be to be able to gently unwrap it and become well-versed in all her secrets?" he thought and suddenly became conscious of his brazen stare.

Mirroring his self-consciousness, she moved back and looked disoriented, her posture now restless. Badr unfroze, not ready for their connection to break. He wanted to reach out, pull her towards him and hold her protectively. But before he could say or do anything, she was gone. As if a magician had snapped his fingers and made her disappear.

Badr dashed after her, checking the surrounding rooms, but they were empty. He ran outside and shielding his eyes from the sun, slowly sifted through the crowd, dodging the men who were calling him for more card games. But she was nowhere to be found.

He became aware of a strange sense of hollowness growing inside him that hadn't been there before. Like she had sliced up some vital organ and taken the most important piece away.

CHAPTER 7

*"And there are those who would
dedicate their lives to Allah's pleasure.
And Allah is Ever Gracious to His
servants."*

(2:207)

A month had passed since the picnic in Khor Fakkan. Badr was behind the steering wheel on most evenings, watching sunsets turn into cool, dark nights. His heart raced faster than the speed limits as he accelerated and braked around different neighbourhoods, hoping to catch a glimpse of her. He knew it was crazy, but he still drove through Halwan, Khazamiyah, Darrari, Shahba and Talaa, all the localities where Emiratis lived in Sharjah. He also passed by Sharjah University, the American University of Sharjah and Polytechnic, checking out the postgraduate students arriving for their evening classes. He knew she was probably too young for a master's degree.

The prognosis wasn't good, but Badr didn't know how else to find relief. He wondered if she was an expat, a friend of one of the Emirati girls at the farmhouse. Asking *Ummi* or his sisters was out of the question. He didn't want there to be complications even before he had met Blue properly.

Sometimes he questioned whether she was real, or a fantasy born out of some unrecognised desire for true love, to be found outside the confines of a typical, arranged marriage. Not that he believed there was anything wrong with arranged unions, but they seemed unimaginative. More like transactions, especially where they focused on keeping money within the family, with people getting hitched to their relatives.

"I feel like you," he told Rashid.

"Feel like me?" Rashid asked, as he put his hair up in a short ponytail.

"Yes. When you disappear in search of hashish or cocaine or whatever it is that you're addicted to!"

"Ooh. But why are you so fixated on this woman?" Rashid asked. "Just move on, man!"

"I can't," Badr said. "She magically appears in my room, my car, in the movies I watch."

"This is an obsession! Nothing but a teenage infatuation," Rashid said.

"I don't think so," Badr said, thinking how mystifying it was that he had never felt anything was missing from his life until he saw Blue. He did not consider himself much of a philosopher or a poet, but his gut was telling him that this feeling of hollowness could only be filled when he saw her again.

"Learn from me!" Rashid pestered him.

"Okay, and what would you do?" Badr asked.

"I secretly date women at work. The ones with symmetrical faces and hour-glass figures."

"But I am not in love with any of those women!" Badr protested.

"You are not in love with anyone," Rashid said.

"Okay. So, what do you do with these work women when you go out with them?" Badr asked, feeling annoyed.

"I pick one. Pursue her till she thinks she is falling in love with me."

"To score?"

"No. I'm quite nice, so we both score."

"And then?"

"I ask her to go with the flow."

"And then?"

"Then I start avoiding her."

"But you work in the same office?"

"Yeah, so if she doesn't get the message and insists on getting answers, I just make up a story, like how my parents are marrying me off to some Emirati chick and will cut me out of their will if I refuse."

"Oh God, Rashid, you're turning into Iblis!"

"Maybe. But I think Iblis is misunderstood."

"And how so?" Badr asked, rolling his eyes.

"Maybe Iblis just knew he was better," Rashid continued.

"Okay, I am off," Badr said, jumping up from the hammock in Rashid's garden.

"Where to, you lunatic? The streets of Sharjah, looking for Blue again?"

"Yes."

That night, Badr once again returned home, disappointed with his lack of success at finding Blue. He sat on his dysfunctional massage chair and switched on his favourite TV channel, MBC 2, trying not to feel dejected.

The bedroom door was slightly ajar, and Badr noticed a movement. He looked up and spotted *Ummi* standing outside his room.

"Badr how are you?" she asked, walking inside his room.

"Oh! *Assalamu alaikum, Ummi.* I didn't see you coming. Why are you still up?"

"I was talking to Sara on the phone."

"Oh," Badr said, sighing. His sister Sara had tried to talk to him about his marriage plans, but he had dodged her questions.

"Things happen when they're meant to happen," *Ummi* said, as if reassuring herself. "It's all in Allah's hands."

Badr just nodded.

"Suppose you are ready in like a couple of months is there someone you would want to marry?"

"No, not really," Badr said, wondering how he could dodge *Ummi's* questions without being disrespectful. He kept his eyes glued to the television screen.

"You don't like anyone at all?" she persisted.

Badr silently wondered how Emirati parents expected their children to like someone, given their complete segregation from the opposite sex. Maybe they were expected to sneak around.

"No," he answered.

"Are you at all curious about any girl? Not for marriage or anything, just curious?"

"Does she suspect I like someone at work?" Badr wondered. Suddenly, he realised this conversation might not be such a bad thing. It was an opportunity to find out Blue's whereabouts.

"Well," he said, clearing his throat. "I ... I once saw a girl. But I don't know if I am curious about her or not. I know nothing of her."

"And?" *Ummi* asked, sitting on the edge of his bed.

"I don't know … nothing. It's okay. I don't want anything," he said, trying to appear nonchalant.

"What is her name? Who is her father?"

"I have no idea."

"Where have you seen her?"

"You know the family picnic we went to? The one in Khor Fakkan?"

"Yes. A relative then?" She seemed excited now and visibly relieved that he was considering someone from within the community.

"Yes … maybe. I just don't know her name."

"Can you describe her to me?"

"She looks like three or four years younger than me. She has blue eyes."

Ummi's face crumbled. She seemed agitated, and Badr's heart sank.

"The daughter of the Jew. The daughter of Sultan Al Tajir, the atheist?" Badr had never seen her face turn so red.

"I … I don't know. I think she was wearing lilac."

"Yes … that's the one. I was hoping they would not show up. But that Jew doesn't give up, trying to fit in with us Muslims! Her daughter doesn't even know how to wear the *shayla* properly," she said, looking absolutely revolted.

"What's the story? Who are they and what happened?" The name Sultan Al Tajir seemed very familiar to Badr.

"I think their son was my friend in college … a nice guy, used to pray with me at the mosque," he said. "But what's the story?"

"I think Sultan met the Jewish woman when he was studying in the US. I'm not sure how. But you don't need to know their stupid love story," she said, shaking her head.

"Just avoid this family, Badr. You don't want to kill your father," she added, horror radiating from her, as if some calamity has befallen the family. Badr had rarely seen her so emotional. She looked tired suddenly, and after kissing his forehead, retired for the night.

Badr turned back towards the television screen and watched *Children of Heaven*. Tears rolled down his cheeks, and he told himself that he was sad about the Iranian children on the screen who had lost their pair of shoes.

He did not want to accept that his Blue dream had ended as abruptly as it started. He tried to suppress the yearning for Blue to lean in, wipe his tears and say, "You'll be okay."

He felt foolish and attempted to push away thoughts of her deep blue eyes, lily-white skin and slim figure. He tried to suppress the desire to taste her with a French kiss or simply melt into her cotton candy-soft lap.

Badr knew he had everything anyone could need or want in life. But these dreams and desires were *haram* for him.

CHAPTER 8

"I do not worship what you worship,
nor do you worship what I worship.
I will never worship what you worship,
nor will you ever worship what I
worship. You have your way, and I
have my way."

(109:2-6)

Struggling to divert his mind from Blue, Badr immersed himself in his pilot training. He had enrolled six months ago and was required to complete a minimum of forty hours of flying, along with a written test

He knew it would probably take at least a year, as he only had time for weekend classes.

tThe fee was quite high, AED 170 per flight hour, but he didn't mind. He was making great progress with his thirty-something Indian flying instructor, Captain Asad.

He drove to the flying school, which was in a quiet, hidden location, next to a DHL hangar inside Dubai Airport. Its reception always reminded him of some of the old, termite-infested books in his home library that he still loved. The school's walls were made of prefab artificial wood partitions and the posters on the walls had faded into an ugly yellow. But he found it comforting to be there. It was his secret kingdom where he was all-powerful, getting ready to fly away.

"Hey … how are you, buddy?" asked the twenty-year-old Pakistani receptionist.

"OK, bhai. Kesa tum?" As usual, Badr responded in Urdu, proudly showing off his shrewd old Emirati heritage.

Like most locals, he had grown up around South Asians, who worked for his family's businesses, and had enjoyed many Bollywood movie nights with the family. Even though he had picked up many words of Urdu, he was not good at it and would usually switch back to English for the rest of the conversation.

He entered the room where the ground class was underway. It was the first time he was late, and the seating area was already dark, with the projector running.

He settled down at the back corner desk adjacent to the window. There were around twenty-five students in this class, all different nationalities, with only one female student, a British expat.

Badr squinted and noticed an unfamiliar face; a bearded Arab guy with a receding hairline and glasses was sitting next to him. He was taking notes on his pink book as the instructor talked about cloud formations.

The lights were switched on soon afterwards, as it was time for a short break. Blue was still lurking somewhere at the back of Badr's mind, but he didn't want to indulge and instead turned to the bearded guy to introduce himself.

"*Salam okhoy*. I am Badr. Hope you are well," Badr said, extending his hand.

"Oh. *Hala hala* … you are local?" the soft-spoken guy asked, shaking his hand.

"Yes, I am!" Badr said with a wide smile.

"Your English is so good!"

"Yeah, it helps … all the video games I play are in English. And many English words haven't been Arabized yet!" Badr tried to break the ice.

"Oh, and you know how to dress up like westerners! You studied in the US, right?"

"No, no, all here."

"Oh? Good, *Masha Allah*." He looked very impressed.

"Thanks. So how are you finding this school? Have you been here for long?"

"The school is okay, but not like the US. It's more expensive here."

"Oh! So did you fly in the US?"

"Yes, yes. I was flying there. I only came back for some work and thought of attending some ground classes since I have my exams soon."

"Good luck! You will do well, *Insha Allah*!"

"*Insha Allah*. Pray for me."

"Of course. But tell me about the US. How is the scene and all?" Badr asked with a mischievous grin, fishing for some X-rated, savagely graphic stories.

"All *kafir Astaghfirullah*. All bastards. A man won't know his father and ladies sleep with anyone. They are nice people when you talk to them, but they are like sheep fooled by their media and the Jews. That is why they are destroying our Muslim nation," he said, his face turning red, hands trembling.

Badr's smile faded, and his face turned a bright pink. He had not been expecting this and looked around, desperately hoping no one else had overheard their conversation. He hadn't thought this man would have such radical views. He usually ignored armchair extremists. He'd met several in his college as well who would hound him with all sorts of questions.

"Badr, have you prepared for *akhirah*?" they would ask, while promising him a smooth pathway to *jannah*. Badr tried his best to avoid them, making sure he never took a course with them. But this local guy's western outfit and moderate beard had deceived him.

He wanted to disengage quickly, but the guy seemed eager to talk; he probably wanted to preach his distorted version of Islam and jihad.

"You know, Allah gives us abilities for a reason and it's what helps us serve him," he said.

"Yes, yes … that is always the case," Badr replied, not sure where this conversation would take them.

"What do you think your purpose is, *okhoy*?" the guy asked.

"This is probably going to be one long conversation," Badr thought.

"My purpose? I … I am ambitious … I want to fly *insha Allah*. Other than that, Allah will show me the way … one day … hopefully soon," he replied.

"If it was in front of you … if your purpose was in front of you, would you like to see it? Would you like to follow it?" he asked.

"Sure … sure … who wouldn't?" Badr said in a dull tone, wishing he could go back to blue pastures.

"What does he want me to say? That I am going to become the Arab-Muslim version of Übermensch?" he wondered.

"Look Badr … do you pray?"

"Of course, every day, since I was five years old. My family is very religious!"

"*Masha Allah*. It's obvious you're a man that knows Allah. You are blessed by Him by all the virtues you carry. You are meant to be something, to be someone of importance to the Islamic nation *Insha Allah*."

"*Insha Allah*," Badr said, suddenly reminded of the torturous summer camp he had been sent to as a ten-year-old to lose the thirty extra pounds his family wasn't proud of.

"Badr ... why have you been created by Allah?"

"To obey the orders of Allah?" Badr responded, realising he was not a fan of quizzes, trying to recall running tips from fat camp.

"*Subhan Allah*. May Allah bless you. And how do you obey the orders of Allah?" he continued.

"By following the Qur'an and the teachings of His Prophet, peace be upon him?" Badr sounded like an automated answering machine, but his friend seemed completely oblivious to all the sensory information signalling Badr's boredom.

"*MashaAllah*. You are a blessed young man, *okhoy*."

"I'm sorry, I don't think I got your name, *okhoy*," Badr asked.

"Oh ... no apologies needed. I am Samer Alfatwa. Please see me as your brother."

"Of course. I am honoured and thank you for all your kind words. We should stay in touch," Badr said out of courtesy and regretted it almost immediately as Samer grabbed his hands a little-too-firmly. He said, "Sure, sure ... what's your mobile number?"

Badr knew he was bound to run into Samer again, so he reluctantly exchanged contacts. Driving back home, he felt irritated as he recalled Samer's weird questions. He considered himself a practical, progressive Muslim, the kind who prayed five times a day and would fast during Ramadan, but didn't make a big deal about it. Someone who also had worldly dreams, who wanted to be a pilot and enjoyed all that life had to offer. And he really didn't care about the bigger purpose of his existence right now. It could wait. Right now, he needed to focus on his pilot training and forgetting Blue. Just then, an unknown number flashed on his phone.

CHAPTER 9

*"Glorify the Name of your Lord, the
Most High, Who created and perfectly
fashioned all, and Who ordained
precisely and inspired accordingly, and
Who brings forth green pasture."*

(87:1-4)

The call was not from Blue, as Badr had secretly hoped, but from an old college friend Misha'al, who invited him to his family's secluded farm in Khawaneej, a predominantly local, suburban, and mostly desert area with many large villas, private farms and agricultural lands owned by wealthy Emiratis.

Misha'al's farm had a big and stunningly beautiful swimming pool, like the ones seen in fancy hotels, and a large football pitch.

Badr and Rashid planned to stay overnight along with other local guys from their college. It was a nice long drive out of the city,t and Badr was glad to get away. But it seemed impossible to get thoughts of Blue completely out of his system. He was not one to question his elders. But it had been difficult, no matter how much he tried to bury himself in work or at the gym.

Walls had sprung up between him and his family members, but no one seemed to notice his distance or pain.

Sulking in his invisibility, Badr would engage in intense discussions with Blue, while lying on his large, lonely bed, or slouching in mind-numbing traffic, or feeling alone in a room full of people. She was the only one who understood,t but it was dangerous to indulge her. He asked her to leave him alone. But she was stubborn. Appeared when he least expected it.

tSometimes she disturbed him at work, making him stop midway during meetings and presentations. His supervisor had not been too pleased with him this month and a concerned American co-worker had even tried to slip him an anxiety pill, assuming that public speaking was making him nervous.

Even now, Badr was fidgeting. This feeling of restlessness never went away. He switched on the car radio as Rashid, wearing a jazzy t-shirt, drove dangerously close to speed limits.

Egyptian singer Umm Kulthum's 'Shams El Aseel' was playing on the radio. Romantic songs stung Badr now, so he started tuning, but every station seemed determined to air the most heartbreaking song ever.

He finally punched the off button. It was a relief when the melody died, but the quiet was somehow more disquieting. Rashid glanced in Badr's direction.

"Oh, come on, man! This is only because you haven't dated properly," Rashid said, irritated by Badr's continuous mood swings.

"What are you talking about?" Badr asked.

"The same thing you're thinking about right now. Your love for little miss infidel!"

"Don't call her that! Please. Plus, it's not like I've not known any women. We used to go on those long drives during college days, remember?"

"What long drives?" Rashid asked.

"You know, when we took those Eastern European girls for Wimpy burgers near the gold souq in Deira and to Sindibad in Al Ghurair Centre in Dubai, and, and ..."

"So? Hanging out with MY female friends does not count as a date, just because our families didn't know about it!"

"Anyway, what I mean is it's not like that ... you won't understand," Badr said.

"Of course I won't! Badr, *habibi*, we're young and free! Why waste time drooling over this chick when there is so much meat in this world."

Badr gave him a look of disgust, but Rashid continued, "You're handsome enough. How can you know you really want to be with this woman only when you've never explored other possibilities."

"You mean like you do?" Badr interjected,

"Yeah, why not? What's so bad about a lifestyle where you have a brand-new woman in your arms every weekend? Most men would kill to have this privilege."

"It's not who I am. And to be honest, I don't particularly like this side of you."

"Oh, please. Anyway, this is not about me. Why are you still hung up on her?"

"There is something about her."

"What?"

"I can't describe it. Some people say, 'when you know, you know.'"

Rashid snorted in response. "No, you don't! What does that even mean?"

"You like poetry, but don't get me? I mean, when I think of her, I feel like how I feel at the beach. Happy to just be. I feel like she's the real deal."

"Badr, my dear, this relationship only exists in your head. Please stop behaving like a teenager," Rashid said, rolling his eyes. "It's 'cause she's forbidden fruit. But you're not really the rebellious kind who would write poems about her. You like being the apple of everyone's eye. I don't see you as someone who would stand up against his family, friends, and society. You care too much. You ditched thoughts of her the moment your mother told you to, you mama's boy!"

Badr shrugged and shut up. There was nothing more to say, and he didn't want them to keep bickering like an old, married couple. Instead, he turned to look at the disappearing streetlights in the rear-view mirror.

"Do you know how to swim?" Misha'al asked Badr and Rashid, after he had welcomed them to the farm with Arabic coffee and semi-translucent *khulas* dates.

"Like the winning sperm!" Rashid said, taking his clothes off and diving into the pool.

"The asshole takes every opportunity to draw attention, like he's a hero in some big Hollywood film," Badr said, laughing with Misha'al.

Tired of Rashid's theatrics, he turned to watch the football match, which was in full swing on the pitch near them.

Badr had a love-hate relationship with the sport, and only participated occasionally when his brother and cousins played a friendly match. It took him back to a mercilessly hot summer in childhood when his family had just moved into a new neighbourhood. Badr's attempts to strike up a friendship with the neighbourhood boys had gone futile as soon as he attempted to play with them at the yard close to the mosque. No one wanted to be friends with the kid who made them lose!

Badr wriggled back to the present, suddenly grateful for Rashid and the other friends he had now. Sipping on hot Arabic coffee, he looked at the guys around him.

He hadn't seen most of them since graduation. Some were lounging near the outdoor pool with fresh juices. Others were playing cards and smoking. Some kebab enthusiasts were setting up the grill. A few were up on the roof trying to find a better reception for their mobile phone signal, desperate to talk to their girlfriends and convince them they were not camping under the stars with other girls.

Badr's eyes stopped at a familiar face. It was Ahmad Al Tajir! Blue's brother! He was grilling tikkas with the other guys.

He did not resemble Blue at all, and Badr concluded that he looked like his father. No one could guess that his mother was an American Jew.

Ahmad acknowledged him with his good-natured smile, but Badr instantly looked away. The evening was pleasant, so he took a refreshing dip in the pool, before. feasting on delicious tikkas and kebabs and plummeting into card games. It was nearly 3 am when he and Rashid grabbed pillows and blankets, retiring to a corner spot of the majlis.

Some guys close to them were exchanging sweet goodnights and phone smooches with their girlfriends. One was cursing as he could not get through due to a weak signal. Rashid had put one knee over the other, and was smoking, completely ignoring the stream of 'good night darling' and 'when will we see each other again' texts from several different women.

Badr shook his head at him. He only wanted to call Blue. He wanted her to run her pretty fingers through his hair while he held her tenderly and fell asleep.

The next day, they woke up late to a breakfast of *regag*. Badr did not engage in pleasantries much and wondered if he might be an ambivert. An hour later, he joined Rashid and a few other guys at the mosque nearby for *juma'a* prayers.

Badr always went to the mosque on Fridays not only because it was compulsory for Muslim men, but also because it was his favourite part of the week. He found it spiritual to sit inside, even after the prayers had ended, not speaking to anyone, making invisible doodles on the carpet. He would think about Allah occasionally, wondering if His Creator was happy with him. But today Badr felt restless. He noticed the *imam* reading the *khutba* from a piece of paper. Apparently, it was a new law. He didn't like it. He found it boring, and the *imam* did not seem like a cleric anymore. He didn't even know how to read properly. Badr could not understand why this law had been passed. The clerics spoke the words of Allah and His Prophet! Why restrict their freedom of speech?

"Maybe they're scared of the *imams* becoming armchair extremists like Samer and some of the guys in college?" Badr wondered. "Or worse?"

He remembered reading about the Khobar Towers' bombing in Saudi in 1996, thanking Allah that he lived in a very safe place. People didn't want trouble here. They just wanted to earn big bucks and live a comfortable life.

The *imam* began the *khutba*. "In the Name of Allah, the Most Beneficent, the Most Merciful. My dear brothers and sisters, today I want to speak about a very important topic: love."

Badr was suddenly attentive, surprised the *imam* had picked such an overlooked topic.

"Why do we love someone?" the *imam* asked. "Is it because they are family, a friend, a neighbour, because they are beautiful, or they are good to us, or because they belong to our tribe?"

"Today I invite you to think about love in a different way. Allah loves you in a way you cannot even comprehend," he said. "You cannot love anyone like Allah loves you, but you can be patient with others, give them benefit of the doubt, accept apologies quickly, be reliable in times of need. If you are more religious than another, let this not become a reason for you to judge or hate him. A successful life, based on religion and spirituality, comprising good relationships, is based on love and compassion for the self and for others."

The *khutba* went on for ten more minutes until the *imam* ended it, saying, *"Aqem alsalah."*

After the prayer, Badr was still thinking about what the *imam* had said about love and tolerance. Lost in thought, he was searching for his sandals when someone lightly touched his shoulder. Badr turned around quickly and found himself face to face with Ahmad Al Tajir.

CHAPTER 10

*"We have bound every human's
destiny to their neck."*

(17:13)

A sense of immense relief washed over Badr, but he immediately suppressed it, remembering that this was a no-go zone.

"*Salam*," Ahmed Al-Tajir said in his usual friendly style. Badr had always liked him and wondered why they had never become close friends at college.

"Hey man, having fun alright?" Badr asked, trying to keep his stress levels in check.

"Yeah ... fun till now. Look, lunch is on me today, but I will need some help in bringing it here. You know Abdullah? He was supposed to help me, but he bailed on me."

"Oh, okay, no problem. Where do we need to go?" Badr asked.

"We'll go home to pick up lunch. My mother will be happy to see you. She mentioned you a few days ago," Ahmed said.

"Oh … sure … me too … I will be glad," Badr said, trying to hide his eagerness.

Soon, they were driving towards Ahmed's house. Badr was struggling to sit still as he tried to hatch a plan to impress Blue if he saw her. This couldn't be just a coincidence. It seemed like Allah was giving him a chance. As if He wanted Badr to pursue her.

"So why did your mother mention me?" he asked casually, his heart pounding.

"Oh, it was nothing really. I just told her that this gathering is for college friends, so she asked if you would be joining or not. You left a good impression on her, man."

"Really, when?"

"Oh, at the picnic in Khor Fakkan, which I sadly missed. Heard you all had a great time. Anyway, my mother thinks you're very polite. She described you as a 'good, decent guy,' to be precise."

"Oh! She doesn't know me well enough, I guess," Badr said, laughing nervously, hoping Ahmed wouldn't notice how happy he was to know that Blue's mother liked him.

"Yup … I guess she doesn't!" Ahmed joked, completely oblivious to Badr's blushing cheeks.

"Does your mother speak Arabic?" Badr asked.

"Yes, yes … almost perfectly. She learned it even before I was born. She had to memorise Qur'anic verses to pray and then she took Arabic courses. And she also taught English at a public school for girls, which is where she picked up our local accent. You had a chat with her at the picnic?"

"No … not really. I must have just greeted her. It was so crowded and noisy. I probably didn't realise she was your mother."

"Oh ... okay!"

"When did she become a Muslim?" Badr asked, hoping he did not come across as nosy.

"Two or three years after marrying my father. Maybe a year after they moved back here," he said pleasantly, as if used to this line of questioning.

"That is a story I would love to hear ... you know!" Badr said, fishing for more details.

"Yeah ... yes, it is. One of those classic Hollywood romances. I don't know about the ending, though. Well ... let her tell you one day," Ahmed replied, winking.

Ahmed's house was a thirty-minute drive from the farm, much closer than Badr's home.

The Al-Tajirs lived in a big, modern villa, the colour of a pink jasmine flower, in a brand-new area called Al Noof in Sharjah. There were only a few scattered villas around, surrounded by dunes, and a couple of camels digging into trash bins.

As Ahmed parked his Nissan Patrol in the open garage, Badr noticed a teenage girl sprinting from the kitchen towards the villa. He stepped out and followed Ahmed inside.

The kitchen was in a separate division of the house. Badr stopped a few steps behind the kitchen door so that Ahmed could announce his arrival, and the women could cover up.

A minute later, he called Badr in. The kitchen was a blend of modern convenience and traditional charm, with appliances contrasting against mosaic-tiled countertops and wooden cabinets intricately carved with arabesque patterns. Everything looked tastefully messy and smelt of *biryani*. Ahmed's mother was wrapping a salad basket with nylon wrap while two maids, one Ugandan and the other Filipino, were covering a big tray of *biryani* with foil.

"*Salam*, Badr. How are you, son?" His mother asked in perfect Arabic, smiling.

Badr remembered seeing her at the picnic, but he hadn't noticed the colour of her eyes then. Blue's eyes were bigger and brighter.

"*Wa 'alaykumus-salam,* Aunty. I am well, *Alhamdulillah.* How about you?"

"*Alhamdulillah.* It's good to see you again. How's work?"

"I'm pushing forward," Badr said, experiencing entrance-test-like-nervousness.

"He was top of the batch," Ahmed said, clapping Badr's back. He picked up a *biryani* tray that was already packed.

"*Masha Allah* ... smart and handsome. You are like the full moon ... that is the meaning of your name, isn't it?" she asked, looking at Badr with a big smile on her face.

Badr blushed and nodded a yes as he reached out to pick one of the biryani trays. It was quite large, and he needed help to open the kitchen door.

He could see two girls standing on the other side through the door's glass centre. One of them came forward and opened the door. She was tall and resembled Ahmed.

"Thank you so much," Badr said, and she smiled in response, retreating into the kitchen. The other girl was still standing outside. It was BLUE!

Badr tightened his hold on the tray as the door slammed shut behind him. His eyes locked with hers. This perk was completely worth the mental yo-yo of the past two months.

He had earned this moment with her, and it was melting all the blues away. The hollowness he had felt since he met her had disappeared. He wafted through the deep blue ocean in her eyes, wordlessly telling her about all the moments they had shared, the songs they had lived, and the kisses they had exchanged.

His eyes travelled down to her lips, but he averted them instantly. He wanted her to feel comfortable around him. With no excuse to hold her gaze for longer, he strode towards Ahmed's car outside, suddenly very conscious about how he looked in his white kandura, glad he had been working out vigorously.

"*Koi no yokan,*" he said to himself. A Japanese colleague had told him that it meant 'premonition to love.'

"Unlike '*hitomebore*' which means 'love at first sight,' *koi no yokan* is knowing that a person you've just met is the one you will fall in love with. Kind of like 'love at second sight,'" the guy had explained.

Badr had dismissed his gut feeling earlier, but this time he was pretty sure; she held the key to his heart. Placing the *biryani* tray inside a cardboard box on the back seat, he swiftly headed back to the kitchen to get the remaining items and catch another glimpse of Blue.

She was standing near the kitchen door, waiting for him with a large brown paper bag and a salad basket. Badr slowed down his pace, as if this was a slow-motion cinematic moment. Everything else faded in the background as he looked at her, covered from head to toe in black, western wear, which helped her flaunt her figure. As an engineer, he enjoyed taking things apart and fixing them up in new ways. But there was absolutely nothing he would change about her.

When he was finally close enough, she handed him a bag and the basket, her fingers brushing lightly against his. He inhaled sharply, experiencing a light electric shock.

"Badr, this is my daughter Dana," Ahmed's mother said, emerging from the kitchen and proudly patting Dana's back.

Badr was exhilarated to discover her name. It was short and pretty like her, he thought. Just two syllables he would love to roll around his tongue.

He wondered if Dana's mother saw him as a prospect for her. She was probably looking for suitors. Dana seemed old enough to be engaged, at least by Emirati standards.

"This is my elder one, Lana," she said, pointing at the tall girl. "And my youngest one, Maryam, is somewhere inside the villa."

"I am honoured to meet your family, Aunty," Badr said, nodding at Dana and Lana. They nodded back, smiling.

"I ... I must put this in the car," Badr said, clutching the brown bag and the basket. He had imagined meeting Blue a thousand different ways, but never like this, feeling so self-conscious and tongue-tied.

When he and Ahmed had finished loading the car, they turned around to find

Aunty, Lana, and Dana walking towards them.

"Thank you, Badr. Ahmed, please drive safely. You don't need to fly," Aunty said, sounding concerned.

"Badr is learning how to fly. We might soon have a pilot in the family!" Ahmed said, looking genuinely impressed.

"I ... I didn't know that you knew," Badr said, both surprised and touched by his interest.

"Everyone from college knows!" Ahmed declared.

"Oh! That is impressive!" Aunty chimed in. "I had a few classes back in the days in the US. It was a long, long time ago. What got you into it?"

"I always wanted to become a pilot, Aunty. I wanted to be a jet fighter, but *Ummi* was afraid that I would get killed. Then I almost went to the US to become a commercial pilot. But then, my *Baba* wasn't too eager about it. So, I have taken it up as a hobby right now ... I'm taking classes," he said, some old and painful sentiments resurfacing.

He was surprised at himself, as he never shared anything personal with people he had just met. He wanted to give Dana something of himself in what little time and space they had together, he reckoned.

"That's great, great that you are doing so ... these things build your personality. Never give up," Aunty said.

"Sure Aunty, I will never give up," Badr replied, giving her his best I-am-a-good-boy smile, basking in the warmth and familiarity.

"Your mother has raised a good son," she added, and Badr felt embarrassed remembering how *Ummi* had spoken about her.

"Do they have classes for girls?" Badr jumped as Dana asked. She had an unusual accent, with both Emirati and American influences. It ignited his heart, and he relished this opportunity to interact with her. She looked at him with confidence and a polite smile. He thought of the nights he had found her between his sheets.

"I ... I am not sure," he said, trying to keep his visualisation in check, afraid that everyone could see the wild fantasies zooming through his head right now.

"I only saw one girl in my class. I will ask for you if you wish," he said, making his tone formal.

"This might be your only chance! Don't lose it!" The voice in his head scolded him.

"If you don't mind, can you give me your email, perhaps? I will get them to send you some information," he added hurriedly, struggling to keep on his poker face. Exchanging emails with girls in front of their families was not common or acceptable in Emirati culture, but fortunately for Badr, Dana's folks didn't seem to think he had crossed a line. He liked their ease, the sense of freedom in their house that everyone enjoyed.

"Sure, I will just give it to you. Please give me a minute," Dana said, and hurried back inside. Badr wondered if *Ummi* would have described her as 'too liberal' if she had witnessed all this.

"Is she thinking of flying?" he asked Ahmed to avert any awkward silences.

"Not to my knowledge!" Ahmed said, looking bored. "She just likes exploring new stuff."

"You might have inspired her, Badr," Aunty said, beaming, looking like an older version of Dana.

"I'll do what I can," Badr said as Dana reappeared. He liked how she moved. So feminine! With the right mix of shyness and boldness. She handed him a small piece of paper with her email written neatly on it in capital letters.

"I will let you know soon," Badr said, waving the paper at her.

"Thank you," she said, giving him half a smile. At that moment, Badr remembered his sister Amena saying, "A woman always knows when a man is interested in her, even when he is completely out of her field of vision. She can feel his eyes on her, his interest, even if she has her back to him."

The thought that somehow Dana knew all about the conversations, the songs, the caresses and kisses he'd shared with her, was overwhelming.

As Ahmed drove out of the garage, Badr settled in the passenger seat and looked at Dana's receding figure in the rear-view mirror. He looked at the pinkness of her villa and decided he loved it. He felt the piece of paper in his hand. It was warm and smelt like jasmine. Holding it tightly in one hand, he rolled down the window with the other, breathing in the new breeze. The skies were his favourite shade of blue today and his heart was grinning again.

CHAPTER 11

*"My success comes only through
Allah. In Him I trust and to Him
I turn."*

(11:88)

Less than twenty-four hours had elapsed since Badr's reunion with Dana when he called the flying school to ask about their programme for ladies.

"Sorry, boss. We don't have any dedicated programmes. Not many women join us," the Pakistani receptionist said.

"But why?" Badr was more than a little disappointed.

"I don't know why. Girls probably get intimidated by big machines and don't want to be outside in the heat."

Badr thanked him for his weird assumptions and hung up. He was not sure if Dana's family was going to allow her to take mixed-gender classes. Most traditional Emirati families would not.

She wasn't exactly traditional, but he also didn't want his blue-eyed angel hanging around all the athletic, mostly single, not-so-bad-looking guys.

It took Badr a long time to compose an email to Dana. At first, he tried to sound formal and intelligent, but he also wanted to come across as quick-witted.

"Girls usually dig a great sense of humour," Rashid had told him.

After twenty minutes of typing and deleting his words, he finally began his email with, "This greasy, sweaty world is, unfortunately, still pretty much a man's world."

He wanted to make sure they would continue writing to each other, so he asked her a lot of questions related to her education and career aspirations.

After about an hour of perfecting the email, Badr hit 'send' and waited with bated breath. Many hours elapsed, with nothing new descending into his inbox.

Feelings of rejection started to surface. Clearly, their brief moments together had not been as important to her as they had been to him. He couldn't believe she was ignoring him while he was sending out all this loving energy into the universe. Maybe all that positive energy stuff he had been reading about lately was, in fact 'complete and utter bullshit,' as Rashid said.

The evening arrived and Badr had almost dozed off on the study table in his room when a soft sound woke him up. He looked up at the monitor and there it was! An email from her!

Taking a few deep breaths, he clicked on it, not knowing what to expect. Perhaps a short reply that would end the conversation? He let out a sign of relief as soon he read her first words. "Such a delight to receive your email ..."

She had written an even longer email than him and replied to all his questions in detail. With the biggest smile on his face, Badr replied instantly.

Soon, they were exchanging emails on a daily basis. He would check and reply to her email every morning. And that would start a round of emails exchanged every other hour until they were both home and could jump on to messenger.

He was discovering many new aspects of Dana's personality, but it didn't seem enough. She was a class topper, a biology student at Sharjah Women's College, dreaming of becoming a forensics lab scientist. Her best friend was her golden retriever Bahir and occasionally, she liked to bake. Badr loved the way she wrote, like a storyteller:

"Our Indian neighbour just visited. She has beautiful grey hair and wears starched kurtas, a gold nose ring, and silver bangles. Her name's Nafisa but she makes everyone call her Albino Aunty. I think it's cool how she's turned her lack of skin pigmentation into a superpower!"

They did not discuss why they were writing to each other. Just slipped into a silent, mutual agreement to continue. This kind of relationship was unheard of in the world they belonged to. But they continued for almost two months without saying why. Badr's mind was completely tuned in, and a luminous state had enfolded him, suffusing him with the deepest contentment.

He had never known he could feel so peaceful and yet so restless at the same time. He visualised himself living with her in their dream house. In the mornings, they would sit on hanging swing chairs on the balcony, sipping coffee. At night, he would play the piano for her after an intense session of lovemaking. And then, on weekends, she would sit next to him in the cockpit, as he took her for a trip in the clouds.

One day, she told him she needed to complete a tough assignment on statistics. Badr offered to help, finding an excuse to move their relationship to the phone. He loved hearing her amiable voice. Her tone was casual, open, even flirtatious. In the mornings, she would text him a simple *'sabah el noor'* that would keep him on cloud nine for the rest of the day.

She had both beauty and brains, and a quiet sense of humour, which showed up unexpectedly. But sometimes she would get a bit serious.

"You know, as a half-Emirati, I am not always welcome," she said one day. "Some of the girls in my class say that I look like a ghost."

"Oh, don't listen to them. They're probably jealous!" Badr said.

"And the other day, when I went to the mosque, my *shayla* was falling off my head. I was trying to adjust it, but then this middle-aged Emirati woman came up and started insulting me."

"I tried telling her that I'm Muslim and Emirati, but she wouldn't listen. She thought I was an American convert, trying to catch an Emirati husband in my net. She said, 'You Americans leave our good, pious men alone!'"

"Oh my God! But she sounds crazy. There are such people everywhere. Just ignore them, *khallas*!"

"I know, I know. I love living here. I love our culture. But I am considered an outcast, a rebel, through no fault of my own. I mean, I love my parents, and I'm inspired by their amazing love story, but it's not always easy to be their child. To never really belong to our community, no matter how much I try. I am like a cocktail prepared by my parents and served in a society where no one drinks."

"I think you're more like flavoured *laban*!" Badr said, laughing at the analogy, but she was dead serious.

"Come on. What's the difference between us? You played with Barbies and my nieces are now playing with Razanne dolls," Badr said.

"We're not that different, but we're invisible at weddings and other social events."

"Why do you even go to those events? I find them so tedious!"

"It's not only events, but sometimes our daily life is also affected. Like the other day, I parked my car outside a local's house. I had only stopped to call a friend for directions. And this local man knocked on my car's window and asked me to move, even though I wasn't blocking his gate or taking up his space."

Badr felt angry. How could anyone be cruel to his little angel?

"When we were younger, this man from the family, I think his name is Mansur …," she said.

"Mansur Uncle? You mean Fahad's dad?" Badr interrupted.

"Yes, yes, I think the same man. I don't remember properly. He would often show up at our house to talk to my dad about religion. My dad would always deal with him calmly. He enjoys dissent and he's a very tolerant person. But one day this man insisted that my dad get in his car, and they drove away."

"Really? Where did they go?"

"I don't remember, but after a few hours, when my dad returned, he seemed really rattled."

"Apparently, this Mansur person had been asking him to recite various *Surahs* and when my dad refused, because he felt he didn't need to satisfy this man as religion is between him and Allah, the man would yell *'Kafir, kafir'* and start driving dangerously."

"Oh my God! Seriously? Was he drunk?"

"He had an extremism hangover, maybe."

"Did your dad file a police report?"

"No, he didn't because he thought it would cause more trouble, especially as it was someone from the family. We already had problems because of his marriage. We thought no one would support us. For the next few months, we were quite scared this Mansur chap would do something else, and my parents even considered moving back to the US. Now my dad just ignores him at gatherings."

Badr wasn't sure how to console her. He'd always found Mansur Uncle's views rather egregious. But he had never seen him as a religious fanatic.

"Maybe he was in his younger days, the extremist with an invisible beard," Badr thought. But he was more concerned about Dana, who looked very upset.

"Okay, if he ever bothers you or your folks again, let me know! I am a pure breed; I will stand with you!" he promised. Things started to roll like a movie after that.

Badr would call her at designated times of the day, before work, after work, after gym, and before going to sleep. In between, they would text most of the time. He would expect her to answer instantly, to tell him if she was planning to go somewhere, and it pleased him when she updated him before he could even ask her.

Occasionally, she would not answer his texts or calls for a couple of hours, which drove him crazy. She didn't really explain her disappearances, but dealt with his possessiveness calmly, sweetly, reassuring him without saying much.

Badr awkwardly forayed towards romance, telling her how badly he wanted her to run her hands through the floppy mess on his head. She didn't respond at first, but then suggested they see each other. He was thrilled. They decided to meet at Wafi Mall, a high-end shopping mall in Dubai, shaped like the pyramids in Egypt.

It was not really a date as she was visiting the mall with her sisters, but they both sat down for Americano at opposite ends of Square Café and smiled at each other from time to time. He admired his white Cleopatra while shielding his gaze from her family and the other locals around. She looked like a princess, painted carefully, intricately in miniature art.

When she was about to leave with her sisters, Badr passed by their table and pretended to be surprised at running into them. They all seemed happy to see him. He handed a box of *baklava* to Dana, saying, "It's for Ahmed and the entire family."

It felt like he had a foot in the door. Their phone calls increased in frequency and would often last for hours. Badr thought she was smart, kind, and attractive in every way possible. He loved how passionate she was about everything she did. Loving her was effortless, and the more he got to know her, the more incredulous it seemed that she was still single.

"You must have a ton of proposals," Bad said to her during one of their nighttime phone calls. She was silent for a few seconds and then her melodious, infectious laughter found new arteries in his heart.

CHAPTER 12

—————•—————

"They try to hide their deception from people, but they can never hide it from Allah—in Whose presence they plot by night what is displeasing to Him. And Allah is fully Aware of what they do."

(4:108)

While love was blossoming between Badr and Dana, Rashid found himself isolated and bored with his weekend flings. He had managed to cut down his drug use, but his doctor had suggested he stay at a semi-rehab kind of facility, set up by an American expat healer in the outskirts of Dubai.

"He said I need to be more grounded," Rashid told Badr on the phone. "Seems more like they're just enticing rich kids like me to join so they can experiment with their recovery programmes, promising us better, 'sober' tomorrows. Can't believe I took time off work for this!"

"I believe the 90s were considered the 'Decade of the Brain' in the US, so it might be helpful," Badr said.

"If you say so. I'll let you know what these yankees do with my brain. Anyway, I gotta go for the poetry session."

Poetry was the only thing Rashid liked about this place. He was going to recite 'A Brief Love Letter' by Nizar Qabbani:

"You will be great only through my great love," he read and looked around at the group. His eyes briefly met with the smudged kohled eyes of a girl in her twenties.

"What would the world have been if we had not been?" he continued, looking at her curvaceous figure and her bright green dress, a smile forming on his lips.

"If your eyes had not been, what would the world have been?"

Rashid felt something he had never felt before. It bothered him, but as soon as the poetry session was over, he made his way towards the girl who was now standing next to the coffee table.

"Hi ... you, with your fathomless eyes!" Rashid said to her as a way of greeting.

She blushed in response.

"Rashid," he said, extending his hand.

"Aicha," she replied, shaking his hand awkwardly.

Aicha was surprised at his forwardness, as the Emirati men she had met so far seemed shy and aloof. They would stare at her from a distance as she jogged on Jumeirah beach every morning.

"Where are you from?" Rashid asked in his thick Emirati accent.

"I live in Dubai now."

"I mean originally?"

"Oh, I'm from Morocco."

"Oh, the Arab West!"

"*Oui*, the place with the mountains, and the beach and our famous Sahara."

"So, you must be fluent in Arabic and French as well?"

"*Oui, oui,* and you?"

"Arabic, of course. But French, I am only familiar with a few phrases."

"Such as?"

"*Voulez-vous coucher avec moi?*"

"*La shukran!*" she exclaimed, pretending to be offended, but laughing.

Within a few hours, Aicha was hooked on to Rashid, to his Kadhim al Sahir-like voice and his pierced left ear. She had never felt like this during her three-year relationship with her ex-fiancé, Daud.

"No one will ever love you," Daud had told her when she had returned her engagement ring. But a few months later, here she was, being pursued by a much smarter, richer, and educated man.

Daud had made her feel ugly, but Rashid made her feel like the most gorgeous woman in the world. The air was tense with anticipation as he pulled her into a secret, isolated corner. She felt drawn to him as he traced the butterfly tattoo on her shoulder with his finger, ran his hands through her hair, and whispered sweet compliments in Arabic.

They laughed together and talked about serious stuff. Family problems, bad relationships, friends turning into backstabbers, as he touched her painted toenails and played with her silver toe rings. Aicha wasn't sure if it was his thick dark hair that captivated her or the way he lay in her lap and recited his favourite poems.

"Your love has taught me ... how to be sad.
And I have needed, for ages
A woman to make me sad
A woman in whose arms I could weep
Like a sparrow"

(An Ode to Sadness, Nizar Qabbani)

He also sang her favourite Beatles and Fleetwood Mac songs and told her stories about cocaine cartels and psychedelics. She did not understand everything he said, but she was very impressed.

"You're so, so intelligent!" she told him.

Within a week, Aicha knew that Rashid was her soul mate. They were standing beneath an umbrella-shaped salam tree, hidden by its pale-yellow flowers and vicious thorns. She was giggling, and he was looking directly in her eyes with a mischievous look. It was a quiet, magical moment, as if they were silently exchanging an 'I love you.'

"So, do you want Rashid's palatial court?" he asked with a wide smile.

"What? Do you always speak through poems?" Aicha asked, chuckling, but she was also getting goosebumps. She had never felt so high in love and so loved before. Rashid had opened new dimensions in her brain and heart.

"I speak through poetry only in matters of the heart," Rashid said, putting his right palm on his heart and sighing loudly.

She laughed softly and then felt overwhelmed with the realisation that she wanted him to protect her from sadness. And she wanted to heal the hurt little angel inside him. They would give each other what their families hadn't.

Sometimes he would act possessive, make faces, and scold her when she was friendly with other guys. But Aicha knew he had nothing to worry about.

Rashid called their relationship 'an exciting, tandem skydive.' They made plans to visit Europe and travel to a place where they could be intimate on the beach. Buy a farmhouse in Khor Fakkan. She wanted a large bathroom with a jacuzzi and an attached walk-in closet. He said she could have everything she wanted.

Three weeks passed. On the morning of her birthday, she wore her champagne pink dress, as Rashid loved the colour on her. After an hour of perfecting her eye makeup, she wore her new silver heels and made her way to the dining area. She knew she was overdressed for the venue, but she didn't care.

As she reached the table, she was surprised to see everyone standing around the breakfast table, a cake and some snacks placed in its centre. They started singing 'Happy Birthday' as soon as they saw her. She was ecstatic. This was surely Rashid's doing. Why would anyone else care about her birthday? She blew the candle and cut the cake as they clapped. She took a piece for Rashid and looked around. But he was nowhere to be found.

CHAPTER 13

✦━━━━━━━━━━━━━✦

*"O believers! Do not betray Allah
and the Messenger, nor betray
your trusts knowingly."*

(8:27)

Badr and Rashid met after nearly a month at a restaurant near Dubai Creek. It was busy, with the Iranian merchants offloading their wares, mostly clothes and jewellery, from the wooden *dhows* and displaying them on streets swarming with tourists. Badr watched the floating *dhows* as he ordered a *falafel* wrap and a chicken mayo sandwich.

"So how was your mini vacation?" Badr asked.

"Don't ask," Rashid replied.

"What happened?"

"I met a girl."

"So? What's new about that?"

"I don't know. It felt different."

"Oh really? Is Rashid, the philanderer, in love?"

"Love? Who knows what that is?"

"So, what happened then?"

"I don't know."

"Care to elaborate?"

"Well, her name is Aicha. I was surprised to see her at the facility. She didn't look like someone who would be struggling with a fondness for coke or other such problems. Her eyes drew me. I began showering her with compliments and expensive gifts. Women really love that, and she was no different."

"I didn't think it was a big deal until one of the guys there took me aside and said, 'Brother, what are you doing? This is not allowed here. She's like our sister. We're all here to be better people. We're not allowed to get involved with the women here. Things can get ugly.' I told him to mind his own business and that no one cared since I was filling up their pockets with my dad's precious dirhams!"

"Oh no. And then?"

"So I managed to get rid of him. But the conversation kept bothering me. And I noticed something unusual. I had been discreet about my activities, but people were getting ideas because Aicha was always around me. ALL THE TIME. Except when I was sleeping or showering. She would always know which room I was in and join me uninvited. Initially, I relished the attention, her eyes watching me, following me around when I was in the same room as her. But it seemed like she had become my shadow, a piece of cloth stitched to my body."

"Her closeness started to annoy me. Her attentiveness to every word I uttered felt suffocating. One morning I noticed one of her earrings nestled in my sheets and realised she must have paid a visit to my room while I was asleep."

"That's too much, too soon!" Badr said.

"Yeah. Things were getting out of hand, and I was not having fun anymore. My initial attraction had completely disappeared, so I decided to talk to her."

"And how did she take it?"

"So, I made my way to a solitary spot in the garden and sat on one of the small wooden benches near the thick bushes. I knew she would find me, through her invisible antenna, and soon enough, I saw her making her way towards me."

"She smiled and sat next to me, but I slid away, creating as much distance as possible, hoping this would send a message."

"Yeah, you're usually pretty direct and brutal."

"Yeah, but for the first time in a long time, I felt nervous around a woman. Before I could say anything, she asked me when I would be introducing her to my parents."

Badr choked on his coffee and then burst out laughing.

"I can just imagine your reaction to that," he said.

"Yes, I thought she must be sick. I had never mentioned marriage, or even love. Hell, I'd barely only known her two to three weeks! And I know that might be enough for many traditional brown men, but I am not one of them!

"Of course not! I completely agree!" Badr said, enjoying Rashid's exaggerated retelling of his misery.

"But she didn't seem to notice my discomfort and said our wedding would be one of the happiest days of her life. That she would wear a *kaftan*, under a *takshita*, like a traditional Moroccan bride. And then asked if I wanted to dress up like an Emirati bride in a lavish white gown."

"Really? And what did you tell her?" Badr asked, laughing.

"I didn't know what to say, so I just nodded along. She kept making plans. Told me how she had attended an Emirati wedding a few years ago where they were distributing gold coins and how we could do the same. Make all her college friends jealous."

"And then? Did you print wedding invitations?" Badr asked, relishing this rare opportunity to tease Rashid.

"Of course not. She wanted to tell people at the facility, have a small party, because she didn't like the way some of the other women looked at me."

"So, you had a party?"

"Well, she must have. I told the others to throw her a party as it was her birthday."

"And?"

"Well, I didn't want a stormy separation. So, the night before, I just dumped all my stuff into my bags and left quietly."

"Rashid, you dog!" Badr said.

"It had to be done! As I drove home, I kept glancing in the rear-view mirror, afraid she might appear in the backseat or be following me in a taxi. She was just too intense."

"Won't she come for looking for you?"

"No, because I was careful. I never told her my full name, where I lived, or any other specific details. There is no way she could ever find me. At least that's what my hope is!"

Badr was about to reprimand Rashid for his cowardly behaviour, but his phone started to ring. It was his sister Amena. She wanted him to come over for tea. Badr had an inkling about what this meant, but couldn't find a way to say no. She was much older, had literally raised him, and could be very persuasive. So, he left Rashid celebrating his escape, and soon arrived at Amena's luxurious villa in Al Darrari. As he parked his car, his brother-in-law Ibrahim was manning the trees in their large, landscaped garden.

He greeted Badr with his soft smile and said, "Your new friend Samer sends his best wishes!"

"Samer?" Badr was taken aback. He had had enough of Samer and their increasingly uncomfortable conversations every weekend at the flying school. He had been relieved when Samer had told him his training was about to conclude.

"Samer from your flying school!" Ibrahim said, as they walked together towards the villa.

"How do you know Samer?" Badr asked. Now that he couldn't meet Badr at the school, he was contacting his family members.

"He comes often to the Islamic centre. As we have the same family name, he asked if we were related. He seemed very impressed with you and asked me many questions about you. I was surprised because he's generally quiet."

"Oh ... why is he so interested? I don't think I'm his type," Badr said, shrugging.

He knew these preachers quite well. They'd be self-righteous and stalk people till they gave in and converted to their hardline views. They would badmouth the 'West', as if the West was one big country, and label anything progressive as *bid'ah*. And sometimes even endorse violence. When natural disasters hit any country, they'd say it was because people had left the path of Islam.

"He likes learning about new concepts, reading, and debating. I think you guys share some common interests. Don't you?" Ibrahim asked. He seemed to like Samer, which bothered Badr.

"No, not at all," Badr replied firmly. "I didn't enjoy meeting Samer at the flying school. The only thing he really wanted to discuss was my beliefs."

"Yeah ... he is that kind of guy ... direct and confrontational."

"Also, if he has such problems with western culture, why did he study in the United States?"

"I don't know. Studies are something else, quality of education, etc. But he is a good guy, in all honesty. Spends a lot of his time at the mosque."

They had reached the door and Badr's nephews greeted him excitedly. He and Ibrahim proceeded to the lounge where Amena was sitting on a grey ottoman, like a queen, decked up in a pastel hued abaya, with makeup and jewellery. Badr kissed her forehead and sat down in front of her as an Ethiopian maid served them tea and date pudding.

He glanced at Ibrahim, pleading with his eyes that he stay, but Ibrahim smirked and retreated to the garden to romance with *neem, shereesh* and *jahanamia* trees.

Unlike Humaid and Najla, Ibrahim and Amena were a perfect ad for arranged marriages. They made it look so effortlessly blissful. They would argue sometimes, like every other couple, but their relationship was never a question mark. Badr felt close to Ibrahim and was a fan of all the articles and poetry he wrote for newspapers.

"Badr, have you thought about marriage?" Amena asked, interrupting his analysis of her wedded bliss.

Sipping her tea, she stared at him and tapped her right foot, as if expecting an immediate response. She was a teacher at a girl's high school next to her house and appeared to be very much in her role right now.

"What about it?" Badr asked, looking around at the travel souvenirs in the room with more interest than usual.

"You are good looking, educated, smart and our father is wealthy, a business tycoon, no less."

"I've just started working. And I'm still a student at the flying school. I can't afford to get married," Badr said, quickly deploying his excellent debating skills.

"That won't be a problem. Even if you don't want to take money from Baba, you know the government gives land to build a house and up to one hundred thousand dirhams in cash to Emirati men when they get married."

"What's going on? What's the hurry? Why now?" Badr asked, trying to keep his tone neutral.

"Abdullah Uncle came in yesterday to meet *Baba*."

"And?"

"He is asking whether we want Munira for you or not, as many people are interested and proposing. After all, she's grown into this attractive and elegant woman, who is religious and, from what I hear, also very skilful at managing her home."

Badr was silent. When he had seen Munira at the picnic, he hadn't been completely opposed to exploring the idea of being with her. But now the idea of marrying Munira brought a certain heaviness while imagining a life with Dana made him feel like he was made of cotton and floating in the air.

"I am not ready, ekhty. Let her marry anyone she wants," Badr said, so decisively that it took even him by surprise.

"Why?" Amena seemed astounded by his blunt refusal. "But she is so lovely. And I hear she's planning to be a homemaker. She would bring a good balance to your life, since you are so ambitious."

"I would probably like my wife to have a well-rounded personality, to be interested in stuff other than me. You know, things are changing now. Many Emirati and other Arab women are doing more than just sitting at home and waiting for arranged marriages. Some of them will become trailblazers for their societies."

"Please don't change the subject," Amena said, annoyed. "We can always find out more about Munira. I know she is studying IT at Skyline University College, unlike her older sisters, who got married right after school. Maybe her plans will change with time. You can motivate her."

"I want her to be self-motivated," Badr said, hoping this would prove to be the winning argument.

"Who knows, maybe she is. Maybe she wants to climb mountains, go to the moon, or do whatever you want her to do. We won't know until we investigate. I can go and talk to her, ask her whatever you need to know. Although, I'll tell you this: marriage is not about a person's skills or achievements. After a hard day at work, you want someone who is loving, kind, and supportive of your goals. Like I am with Ibrahim, like Ummi has been with Baba."

Badr felt frustrated as this was getting him nowhere. She was making some valid points and backing them up with real-life examples. He wanted to put an end to the conversation respectfully, but for good.

"I don't know, *ekhty*. I am just not ready. Besides, I don't like her older brother."

"What has her older brother got to do with this?" she asked, narrowing her eyes, now getting suspicious that Badr liked someone.

"I don't know. I can't explain it, but I just don't want this," Badr said, feeling exposed. He didn't want to even hint at his feelings. She'd assume it was for someone at work and give a lecture on gold digging, non-Emirati women who wore revealing clothes to entice rich and innocent Emirati boys.

"You don't have to marry her right now, you know. We can just do a small engagement to book her for you. You can marry her in two or three years, whenever you're ready to settle down."

"No. I don't want to stop her from getting married now if she wishes to. She might find a better man than me. I don't want to stand in her way."

"Is that your final answer? Don't you want to give it some thought?"

"Yes, it is, and no, I don't want to give it any more thought. Send them my best wishes," Badr replied so forcefully that Amena spilled her tea.

"Who is it?" Amena asked, as the maid mopped the floor.

"Who's who?"

"You like someone, don't you? That's why you are saying no to Munira."

"Why? Can that be the only reason? I like the idea of being a pilot. Isn't that enough?"

"If you would tell me, maybe I could help you marry this girl," she said, giving him a mischievous look, like *Ummi* sometimes did.

Badr considered this. Would Amena have the same objections that *Ummi* did? Was there harm in trying? He would have to eventually. tell them. *Ummi* and *Baba* would have to ask Dana's parents for her hand in marriage. That was the only way it worked in the Emirati community. His sisters were probably his best chance.

"Yes, I have someone in mind," Badr confessed. "She is a relative. I would only be interested in the subject of marriage if she's the one being considered."

Amena looked puzzled. She was happy to know that Badr was considering a family member, but also a little concerned with his tone. She realised he must already be in some kind of relationship with her and didn't appear to be too pleased about it as it was not a part of Emirati culture. Usually, the women of the family would find a wife for their sons and brothers.

Badr knew what Amena was thinking. A girl that had a relationship with Badr prior to engagement, prior to them selecting her, had already broken their traditions. She had no place in their family. She was already cursed. But Amena was gentle with him and just asked, "Who?"

"I know what's going on in your mind," Badr said.

"What?"

"Nothing wrong has happened. I want to do it the right way and I need you to help me," Badr said.

"It's already wrong if you've had a relationship," she said, lowering her tone. "How can you trust a girl that has betrayed her parents' trust?"

"No betrayal happened and no relationship. Just affection. We want to do it the right way. She wouldn't have it in any other way."

"So, who is she?"

"Look … it's not going to be easy. I would need your support and, most importantly, your trust."

"You are scaring me. Who is she?"

"The daughter of Sultan Al Tajir."

"The Jew's daughter?" Her face turned red.

"You are a fine teacher. Aren't you? You know she is no longer a Jew? Don't you?"

"Which one of them?" She was growing furious and ignored his statement.

"Calm down. I think I made a mistake by telling you," Badr said, standing up.

"No, no … stay, stay … let's talk about it … I am sorry."

Badr stood there for a while, thinking about his next step. He could start a war between the two families if he didn't play it right.

"If you are going to mess it for me, I better leave, and you better forget I came here, and that I spoke to you!" he said.

Amena looked at him, her fury turning into concern.

"You didn't tell me which daughter you like."

"The younger one … Dana," Badr said, as they stared at each other.

"Isn't she the one that got divorced?" Amena asked.

"What? No, she and her sisters are not married," Badr said, feeling puzzled. "You must be mistaking her for someone else!"

"No, no. I'm sure," Amena insisted.

"Do you mean the other one?" Badr asked, a sense of unease creeping over him.

"Who is the one with blue eyes?" Amena asked.

Badr took a deep breath;

"That's Dana."

CHAPTER 14

*"Do they not know that Allah fully knows
their evil thoughts and secret talks, and
that Allah is the Knower of all unseen?"*

(9:78)

As Badr grappled with his unwelcome discovery, the empty hiding places at the facility served as a stark reminder to Aicha of Rashid's vanishing act. A few days had passed, and he had left no gifts, no birthday cards, no flowers. Not even a message.

The facility's manager had told Aicha that Rashid had left at night due to some personal emergency. But they were not allowed to share anyone's contact details, so Aicha waited for Rashid to call. She could not eat or sleep. She would just sit on the floor in her room, crying, waiting, wearing her champagne pink dress, and his t-shirt over it, pretending he was hugging her.

"It's like he never existed, and no one gives a shit," she said, sobbing into the phone, when she could finally admit he was gone for good.

"What happened? Tell me everything, sweetie," her Moroccan-Yemeni best friend Aleah asked.

Aicha hadn't spoken to her since the day she had introduced Aleah to Rashid. Aleah had tried to convince Aicha that he wasn't serious about her, and Aicha had been furious with her.

"I don't know what to do. I feel so lost," Aicha told her.

"Leave that stupid place. I told you not to go there or be with him. Come and stay with me."

Aleah, independent and happily divorced, was the one who had asked Aicha to move to Dubai after her engagement had broken off and she had become a third wheel with her married friends.

"Living in a new country will heal your broken heart," Aleah had said. "You could become an artist and meet new people."

Aicha had agreed. It was the escape she had been looking for. Once in Dubai, she had started working with an artist and discovered this healing space.

Now she just wanted to move out. It didn't seem that Rashid was ever coming back for her. She returned to Aleah's villa and spent most of her time in bed, staring at the brightly wallpapered ceiling.

"Aicha, please get up. You need to move on," Aleah pleaded with her after a few days had passed with her lying in the same position.

"I can't. My life doesn't make any sense without him."

"Get a grip on yourself, sweetie! Don't waste your time on such men. You know you can have any man you want! Let the moth come to the flame," she said, painting her long nails red. She was getting ready for yet another date with yet another man.

"I don't want any man. I want Rashid!"

"What's so special about him? Is it because he's so rich?"

"No, no, it's not about money. I swear, I don't even know how rich he is, really. But he made me feel at home in this new city. He was the only one who cared for me."

"Hey, you have me!"

"Yes, yes, but life without him is like living without a heart."

"Okay, I get you sweetie. But what are you going to do about it now?"

"I don't know. I wish I knew where he is ... why he did not even call me."

"I have an idea," Aleah said, and her eyes lit up like they did whenever she had a new business idea, which would eventually flop.

"What?" Aicha was starting to feel frustrated with her friend's advice. No, she did not want to go for a walk or to a nightclub to meet other men, as Aleah kept on suggesting.

"I have a friend, Talha, a Turkish-Emirati."

"Aleah, my love, I can't imagine being with anyone ..."

"Let me finish, sweetie. He knows people."

"What people?"

"You know, CID types. I can ask him to get info on this Rashid guy, who he is. We can find him."

"He's going to help us? But why?"

"Oh, honey, it's so easy with men. You just need to flirt with them, flutter your eyelashes and they'll come crawling to you. As you know, I am more into older guys and he's younger than me plus he also told me he wants to do stuff in front of his wild pets, which is too much, even for me! So, I said no, no. But for you, I'll do anything, sweetie."

To Aicha's surprise, Aleah was right. Talha got them what they wanted in exchange for a date with Aleah. He provided Rashid's full name, address, phone number, details of where he worked, what gym he visited, who his close friends were, and so much more.

Aleah drove Aicha to the gym where Rashid spent his evenings, and soon enough, they spotted Rashid's Range Rover parked outside.

"Kabayan?" a muscly Filipino guy was talking on the phone as Aicha walked up to the reception, her heart beating loudly.

"I am here to meet someone," she said, as he put the phone down and looked at her.

"But sir … ma'am, this gym is for men," he said, while checking his hair in a round tabletop mirror.

"Oui, I don't want to join the gym! I just want to see your VIP gym member Rashid. He's here. I saw his car parked outside," Aicha snapped.

"Okay, okay, let me check," the receptionist said, sliding away. "Your name, please?"

"Just tell him it's a friend."

Aicha waited for what seemed like an eternity before Rashid and another guy walked into the reception area, accompanied by the Filipino guy. Rashid was holding a pair of boxing gloves and looking puzzled.

"Rashid!" Aicha ran up to him, with tears in her eyes.

He seemed flabbergasted, but quickly turned to the other guy and said, "Badr, I will see you later, then."

Badr nodded silently, pressing his lips, as if holding back laughter.

"Aicha … let's go outside and talk," Rashid said, moving towards the exit.

Aicha followed. Rashid opened the car door for her, and she sat on the passenger seat, hoping he would take her to the beach or to his secret apartment so that they could enjoy some time alone.

"I was so scared I would never see you again," she said, as soon as he got into the car. "Why did you leave, Rashid? Is someone sick in your family?"

He switched on the car's AC silently, looking serious. Then he threw his boxing gloves into the glove compartment. after closing it with a thud, he asked, "Aicha, what in God's name are you doing here?"

"What?"

"How did you find me, Aicha?" He sounded exasperated.

"Aren't you happy to see me, Rashid?"

"You shouldn't be here."

"But, but why? We were talking about getting married …"

"No, you were talking marriage. I was just listening to your fantasies."

"What? Why are you doing this? You're a good man."

"You don't really know anything about me."

"I know you. We belong with one another."

"Now you sound like my friend, Badr," he said, chuckling. "This is not a movie, Aicha. Wake up. I made stuff up. Just pretended to like what you liked. It's the easiest trick men like me use."

"Men like you! Trick? I don't understand. Why did you go away? Why don't you want to get married? Is it because your parents fight a lot or because I'm not local?"

"Aicha, I know a few locals married to nice Moroccan women … but I am not the marriage type."

"What is this marriage type? I'm sure we're both scared … but I know you're not like my stupid ex, Daud. You're a good, decent guy. I feel so safe when I'm with you."

He shook his head. "I am not the right guy for you. Or for anyone else."

"Why do you say that? Is it your family? Are they forcing you to get married to someone else? Some Emirati girl? You said you would leave home if that happened."

"No, it's not that. I believe marriage is just a social contract, a piece of paper. It has nothing to do with love. It has only become tied to love in recent years. Marriage has mostly been about social status and economics and reproducing kids. And I am not built for such institutional relationships."

"I really don't get what you're saying. But you should give yourself a chance. You're not a bad guy."

"Aicha, I have done sketchy stuff. And the only way I'd get married is if my parents force me, threaten to cut off the money or disown me."

"It's all about money, then? My father also has money. We could go to Morocco."

"Yeah, your dad is probably flushing all that money down a toilet in Las Vegas. And no, it's not only about money."

Aicha was stumped.

"Life is uglier than you think it is, Aicha," he said. "Please go and don't come back here."

"Wh … what?"

"Aicha, when a guy leaves you without an explanation, get the message!"

Aicha had never seen him act so cold and rude. "But, Rashid, I want to be with you. I want to marry you."

"What? Are you even listening to me, Aicha? A guy who is genuinely interested in you will never leave you in the dark or make you chase him. Remember that. It will help you a lot in life."

"No."

"What do you mean?"

"I want to marry YOU, even if it's just for a day."

"Are you crazy? Have you completely lost it?"

"What? What did you say?"

"You really belong in that loony bin."

"Please don't say that!"

"Just leave and go back to that cuckoo's nest!"

Aicha burst into tears as Rashid got down, opened her door, and loosened her seat belt. He was so close that she leant forward, wanting him to kiss her.

"Please," he begged instead, looking into her eyes. She could not see any love in them anymore.

"Can we be friends at least?" She felt desperate. She could not lose him again.

"I am sorry I led you on," he said, and turned away.

Aicha stumbled towards Aleah's car as Rashid drove away. With tears rolling down her cheeks, she repeated everything Rashid had said to her, and Aleah started cursing.

"Maybe he is not telling me something. He was too good to me. Not like Daud. I always knew Daud wasn't a good guy, but Rashid, how could I have been so wrong? It doesn't seem possible."

Aicha talked all night and kept rambling for the next two days. But she was still not sure what the truth was.

"You must think I am so stupid," Aicha said.

"No, of course not, love. You are just another woman who has fallen in love with someone who doesn't deserve her."

"Is it possible that he loves me, but cannot accept it because of problems in his past?"

"Aicha, please," Aleah scolded, losing her patience.

"Now you are being mean to me."

"No."

"I don't know what to do, Aleah. Please help me! I think I am going mad."

"I have an idea."

"What now?"

"You need to come with me, sweetie."

"But where?"

"Do you want him to come back to you? To fall in love with you again?"

"Yes, of course. I would do anything."

"Do you want to barbecue his heart?"

"What?"

"Make him suffer?"

"I don't know. I love him but I am also so angry with him."

"I will take you then."

"Take me where?"

"To a *saher.*"

"You mean like a sorcerer?"

"Yes, he can perform magic and help us, sweetie."

"You mean like with voodoo dolls?"

"No, no. That stuff is usually used in Morocco. Here it's different."

"Oh, I don't know about this, Aleah."

"I know this guy. I know people who have been to him. They go when they want to get married to someone or to break someone's relationship."

"I … I don't know about this," Aicha said, her mind whirling.

"There's no harm in trying, sweetie. It will be like an adventure! And if it works you will either make Rashid fall in love with you again or you will get your revenge. You can get whatever you want!"

CHAPTER 15

———————

"Fight in the cause of Allah only against those who wage war against you, but do not exceed the limits. Allah does not like transgressors."

(2:190)

As Rashid left the gym with Aicha, Badr retreated to the sauna. Usually, he enjoyed these solitary moments, but since the day Amena had told him Dana's secret, he had felt deeply depressed when no one was around to distract him. But the sauna was also the place where he could fight with Dana in his head and cry.

He had not confronted her yet. A part of him still did not believe it was possible. Dana, with her gentle smile and soft-spoken demeanour, had always been the epitome of innocence in his eyes. He wasn't sure what disturbed him more—that she had lied to him? That if he hadn't stumbled on to the truth, she would have delayed telling him for as long as possible? Perhaps she had not told him because she did not trust him It troubled him that she had probably shared intimate moments with someone else.

She must have kissed before. Had sex. Badr was still a virgin, and it seemed unfair to him. For the first time, he was questioning his relationship with Dana. He had always known there would be obstacles, but not internal ones. He had been so sure about her. He wondered whether she was worth the fight. Did she really love him or was he an escape from what might have happened to her in the past? Had she lied about other things as well?

Even if there was an innocent explanation behind all her secrets, this changed things drastically. Convincing his family to accept a divorced woman for their virgin son would be much harder. He knew his religion allowed him to marry divorced or widowed women, but society had made divorce such a stigma, especially for women.

Badr could almost hear *Ummi* saying, "All the unmarried Muslim girls in the family dream of you. But you've chosen a Jew's daughter who probably got divorced due to Western influences!"

Badr sat in his car and threw his gym bag on the back seat. He scrolled through his mobile, finding several calls from Dana. There was also a call from an unknown number. Badr called back and instantly recognised Samer's voice, mentally cursing himself for not saving Samer's number. He had been able to avoid meeting Samer a few times, but today he needed an excuse for not calling back Dana. During the week, he had made work an excuse to keep their conversations short.

He drove to Gérard Café, near Khalid Lake, an artificial, picturesque lagoon in Sharjah. Badr quite liked the view from the café and didn't mind waiting for Samer, who soon arrived in his white Caprice, a car all locals fondly called the 'soap.'

Samer didn't smile much, but he always seemed pleased to see Badr.

Badr had hoped he would find a girlfriend to expend his energies in another direction. But then he remembered that Samer was married. Not too blissfully perhaps, he concluded.

They ordered Americano and Samer talked about his training at the flying school, sharing some useful tips on the final flying test. Badr was no longer regretting the rendezvous when Samer proclaimed, "I am doing all of this for Allah."

The conversation had once again flown into unexpected territories.

"Doing what for Allah?" Badr asked, wondering if Samer had made a vow to make all their chats intolerable.

"We have to do everything for Allah!" Samer said.

"Yeah. Sure."

"I have set my intention, Badr. That even this piloting is for Allah. Like everything I do."

"Yeah. In what sense? How do you learn flying for Allah?"

"How would you fly for Allah, Badr?"

Badr wasn't sure how to answer that. He was a practising Muslim and considered himself sheltered by Allah. As a child, he had been taught that Allah was closer to humans than their jugular vein.

"I guess ... learning a skill makes us appreciate His creation, His *barakah* and makes us better Muslims. Hasn't our Prophet (PBUH) encouraged us to educate ourselves and even go to China for it, if we need to?" Badr asked, putting on his sunglasses to hide the disdain in his eyes.

"Sure. We should be stronger Muslims. And that is why I am doing this. But stronger in what sense, you must wonder?"

"To stand up against our enemies when needed? To be able to help our community when needed?"

"Exactly. We think alike!"

"Yes, we do, I guess," Badr said. He was in no mood to extend the conversation for longer than necessary.

"Do you believe the Muslim community needs you now? I mean, with the Jews, the Americans, and the dictators around?" Samer asked, with a sudden burst of energy.

"Sure, sure, but what can we do?" Badr asked, trying to come up with an excuse to

leave early from this extremist gibberish.
"A lot!" he said, looking excited.

"Like what?"

"There are many ways to bring them harm. To make them feel our suffering. To stop them from hindering us from becoming one again. To bring back the Caliphate. To bring back our glorious days. The days when we were the biggest empire ever. The days when they used to fear us. When we were at the heart of enlightenment. The heart of innovation. When it was a moral nation. A light in the darkness!"

"Yeah, I want the same, Samer. Don't we all? What can be done, though? Should we carry guns and kill people? Should we just cause chaos? We will just bring harm to our families. If leaders of the Muslim world call us, we will be there. We will stand tall."

"But we cannot wait for others to wage war on us! We need to be proactive!" Samer said, his voice full of emotion now.

"I am sorry, but I have to disagree," Badr said. He could not just nod to this. "I think we are prioritising progress and development. It's best to strengthen our position politically and economically. War is not the solution. There are many other ways to succeed."

"What other ways?"

"*Baba* told me how things were much harder in the past. Take this region, for instance. I think there were no paved roads or highways in many places till the late 1960s. Very few people had cars. They lived in small, wooden houses and were dependent on a few sectors, like fishing and pearl diving for their livelihood. There were also very few modern medical facilities and people relied on traditional medicines to get better. And now look, we have everything we need for a high standard of living. The Gulf countries are safe. And as Emiratis, we get so many benefits, such as free education and healthcare. Job opportunities and financial assistance. First thanks to Allah and then to our visionary leaders!"

"This is like you making *Umm Ali* and throwing good dry fruits in milk that has gone bad."

"What?" Maybe he needs something sugary to calm down, Badr thought.

"As you know, in so many other countries, the leaders are so corrupt that they live in palaces and eat seven-course meals while their people are homeless and dying of hunger," he said.

"You're naïve, Badr. Many of us are also poor, you know? We are not dying or hungry, but a false sense of security and contentment is making us lazy and dragging us down. It stops us from reaching our potential, becoming what we are destined to be. Follow the Qur'an and the *Sunnah* is what we should do," Samer said.

"So, what's on your mind? What is it that you want to do? Some of us are pursuing higher education and working hard to build a career."

Badr wasn't sure if Samer had an idea about his family's vast wealth. "Is all this a ploy to borrow money," he wondered.

"I have a plan. But I need to know what kind of man you are," Samer said.

"What kind are you looking for?" Badr asked, an unpleasant feeling settling in his gut. He wanted to ask if Samer was looking for a bag full of cash or a gullible man to recruit for one of those cults that printed pamphlets and organised large religious congregations in other Muslim countries to promote extremist views.

Samer, however, continued being vague. "I want a man who has a purpose, Badr. A man that knows Allah. A man that wants to do something good for his nation. A man who wants to do *jihad*."

"I think the biggest *jihad* is *jihad al-nafs*, striving to be a better person, a person who follows the right path and guards against evil," Badr said, feeling like a deflated balloon.

"And what is the right path? How do you guard against evil? What about holy war? How can we be happy when our brothers are still suffering in Palestine, Chechnya, Afghanistan and in so many other places?" Samer asked. The conversation seemed to be going in circles, leading nowhere.

Ibrahim had described Samer as a friendly guy and a devout Muslim. Badr wanted to tell him Samer was one of those people who talked passionately about *jihad* and

Muslim brotherhood but spent their life taking road trips through France and the Netherlands. The kind of people who chose to live in the US but continued to express anti-American sentiments while enjoying all the benefits of their adopted country.

"Look Samer, I am not sure what I want from my life right now. Give me some time to think and get back to you on this, okay?" Badr said finally, wondering how Samer would react if he knew of Badr's amorous relationship with the descendant of an American Jew and the daughter of an atheist.

Samer looked upset at the abrupt way Badr had ended the conversation. After a few seconds of absorbing his disappointment, he said, "Sure, I will wait to hear from you, *okhoy*. I hope we can meet again soon."

Badr said goodbye in his usual good-natured manner and promised himself that he would never meet Samer again.

CHAPTER 16

———•———

"There is no superiority for an Arab over a non-Arab, nor for a non-Arab over an Arab. Neither is the white superior over the black, nor is the black superior over the white — except by piety."

(Prophet Muhammad PBUH)

Badr and Dana had their first argument. It was about the Emirati singer Aidha Al Menhali, who she really liked. But Badr knew it wasn't about the singer. He was incensed, and it was hard to keep pretending that nothing was wrong. He tried to find excuses to justify her dishonesty.

"Maybe she was a victim of a forced marriage? Although her family doesn't seem to be that way. Perhaps she did not like the guy and left him," he thought.

"Badr," Dana said, sensing his distance and resentment.

"Yes?" She rarely used his name, and it felt like a balm, soothing his pain.

"Should we meet? Like properly? Not like last time at Wafi. Some place where we can talk freely?"

"I would love that!" Badr felt elated, but also feared losing his temper with her and discovering more secrets.

Once again, Badr made his way to Gérard café. *Ya Habibi Ta'ala* was playing as Badr entered the café, where a touristy couple from the Levant, were holding hands and enjoying the views of wooden *dhows* crossing the creek. A group of seagulls was resting close to the water, a few steps away from him. One of them was eyeing him intently, like someone from the Emirati community had sent him over to spy.

It was almost seven in the evening and a cool breeze was making it bearable to sit outdoors. Dana appeared, seemingly out of nowhere. If she hadn't been so gorgeous, Badr knew he would have found her sudden appearances eerie.

His body tensed as she came towards him, clad in a turquoise abaya. with a matching veil covering her face. She was looking around self-consciously, checking if any locals were in the vicinity.

"Dressing up in western clothes would have been a better cover for her," Badr thought. "Everyone would have perceived her as some American tourist."

He observed her quietly, wanting to stay calm and avoid the impulse to ask her about her divorce right away. As she sat down on the chair facing him, Badr noticed her scent. He basked in the smell of her aged Cambodian Oud that had a hint of French perfume.

"I have heard their fish is great. And they have so many options ... plenty of fish in the sea, ha-ha. Do you want to have some?" he asked, picking up the menu and turning its pages quickly..

"No. I already have a pure local one," she said, her veil still covering her face.

"Does she mean what I think she means?" Badr wondered. He loved how she could say something funny in a serious tone.

He ordered a cup of coffee while she asked for strawberry ice cream. Once the ice cream arrived, he asked her if he could taste it.

"Oh, sure."

Badr took a very small bite with her spoon.

"Take more," she insisted.

"No, I am not interested in the ice cream," he said.

"You're not?"

Badr had just wanted to be close to her. Kiss her without kissing her.

"Are you happy to see me?" she asked, with a hint of sadness in her tone.

Badr was surprised at the question, and noticed how her eyes lacked their usual vitality. He thought it was strange, given that she enjoyed many siestas, one of the excuses she would give for not responding to his messages sometimes.

"I don't think I have ever been so happy," Badr said emphatically, struggling with ambivalence.

"Do you ... do you love me?" she asked, locking eyes with him.

"God, she can be bold at times!" Badr thought. He was dumbfounded. They hadn't said the 'L' word to each other yet. Not seriously, anyway.

He inhaled and exhaled a few times. He wanted to tell her he loved her, but he felt conflicted.

"I do," he finally said. "More than anything in the world. More than you could ever imagine!"

"That is enough for me," she said, pointing her tiny pale finger towards herself.

"But that's not enough for me!" Badr said, his tone suddenly angry. He looked down at his cup of cappuccino, trying to prevent a heated confrontation.

A minute of silence went by. She extended her right hand and softly grabbed his fingers. Badr gasped. It was the first time they had touched each other.

"What's the matter?" she asked, their fingers intertwined, their hands finding solace in each other's warmth. "Is there something you want to tell me?"

"I believe you are the one keeping secrets," Badr blurted, looking directly into her eyes, his heart racing under the weight of unspoken fears. She released his hand hurriedly and uncovered her face. She had dark circles around her blue eyes. The fading light of the sun was dancing in them.

"Why didn't you tell me that you were married before?" he asked, trying to ignore his urge to hug her.

Dana looked shocked, then dismayed. She covered her face with her palms and seemed to be crying quietly. Badr instantly regretted his harsh tone and waited for her to compose herself.

"I didn't want you to go away," she said, looking down now and nervously twirling her fingers around her bowl of melted ice cream.

"Go where?" he asked in a low voice.

"Out of my life," she said.

"Why would I do that?"

"If you knew I was married. I thought you would get scared."

"Scared of what?"

"There are a lot of girls out there. I am a complicated case."

"I can handle a lot, you know. But when did you get married?" He wanted to know everything.

"We didn't get married. We only did the *nikah*."

"Oh ... ok ... so what happened?" Badr was feeling much better now. It was quite common in the Emirati world to separate at that stage, and it also meant she did not have many intimate moments with him, if any.

"He changed his mind," she said quietly.

"Good for us!" Badr said, trying to make her smile. He was no longer that interested in what had happened.

"Why do you want to be with me? I've heard many people are eager to give their daughters to you in marriage."

"Oh, come on. You're smart, beautiful, educated, kind... we make each other laugh, we can talk for hours and still not get enough of each other, and there's so much more," Badr reassured her. He wanted her to trust him completely.

She looked troubled, vulnerable, like a wounded white peacock.

"Dana, I am completely under your spell," Badr added, nodding and beaming at her. "I can't imagine what that guy was thinking when he let you go."

"You don't understand. He had a good reason," she said, not meeting his eyes.

"What is it? I promise it won't let me think any less of you."

"You won't understand."

"Try me."

Badr could see that she really wanted to confide in him. He placed his warm hand over her cold one.

"I don't want you to leave," she said.

"I won't," Badr said, as he braced himself, unsure of what was coming his way now. The past few months had been too good to be true. His mind drifted back to the day when he was about to leave for the US to become a pilot and how, within a few minutes, his dream had been snatched away from him. This time, he was sure he would just crumble.

Dana looked at him, her internal resistance melting away. Her eyes brimming with tears, she said, "Badr ..."

"Yes, Dana?" Badr leaned in, his face very close to hers now, but still appropriately distant.

"I am haunted."

CHAPTER 17

———————

*"Solomon's forces of jinn, humans,
and birds were rallied for him,
perfectly organised."*

(27:17)

The first time it happened, Dana's mother found her lying motionless under a tree in the farmhouse.

She shook Dana, whose eyes snapped open, but she was unable to speak and had no recollection of how she had ended up there. Her mother fetched her father, who carried Dana to his jeep, with her sisters in tow. The other guests looked on, their expressions a mixture of empathy and mockery.

The Al Tajirs rushed, as they knew this incident would shred their social image completely.

"People will say the Jew-atheist girl is sick. Allah is probably angry with her for not being Muslim enough," Dana's mother said, as they drove towards the hospital. "No need to give them more ammunition."

By the time they arrived at the emergency room, Dana was back to normal. The doctors concluded that she had probably had a panic attack. Dana's mother was horrified. She had grown up hearing stories of ancestors who had to be locked up due to their psychological disorders. Thus began Dana's trips to all the well-known and pricey psychiatrists and psychologists in town.

Soon, she had taken out the jewellery boxes from her side drawer and stuffed them with boxes of anti-depressants and other pills, but nothing seemed to work. The doctors kept changing her medication, but an invisible creature always returned to take her hostage.

Her mother was scared about how Dana's in-laws would react if they found out. Dana had already had a small, *milcha* ceremony with an Emirati man from another tribe, Adnan, and was legally married.

As Dana tried to come to terms with her strange illness, she looked for ways to avoid meeting Adnan, but eventually ran out of excuses. Since they had already had their *nikah*, he had become a *mahram* to her, and the families encouraged them to interact.

Dana asked her sisters to accompany her during her meetups with Adnan, who took them to Jumeirah Beach, Al Nasr Leisureland, and many other leisure spots. But Dana would feel uncomfortable throughout their outings, bracing herself for the worst outcome.

Each time they would reach their destinations and settle down, Dana would slip into a semi-trance-like state, laughing erratically at times, ignoring Adnan's attempts to engage her in conversation.

Her sisters tried their best to divert Adnan's attention and cover for her. Adnan initially dismissed her odd behaviour as mere shyness or nervousness. But by their fifth outing together, his concerns had grown. He sensed something more serious was at play and was determined to find out what it was.

An opportunity presented itself when Dana's sisters left them alone briefly to buy snacks from a food stall nearby.

Adnan looked at Dana closely as she stood barefoot on the shore, laughing like a child, playfully dodging the waves, trying to kiss her feet. He moved a step closer to her and looked into her eyes, which were full of happiness and mischief.

Then, in an unexpected blur of motion, Dana whirled around, her small frame moving with surprising grace and strength. Before Adnan could react, she had closed the distance between them, her laughter turning into a triumphant shout. With a swift, friendly shove, she knocked him off balance, sending him sprawling onto the sand.

Adnan was completely caught off guard by the strength hidden beneath her delicate exterior. Dana's face hovered above him, her eyes sparkling with delight. She seemed pleased with her impromptu victory. Meanwhile, her sisters, who had returned with Safari chips and Vimto, looked horrified at what they had just witnessed.

After an awkward silence, Adnan got back on his feet and said, "Let's go home!"

He did not say a word the rest of the way. Dana's sisters were too embarrassed to say anything, and by the time they reached home, they all had an inkling of what was about to happen.

A week later, Dana's mother-in-law called her mother and, after some small talk, made an excuse to call off the wedding. She sounded apologetic, and never asked about Dana's behaviour.

Despite a sense of relief, Dana's self-esteem tanked along with her social life. She felt vulnerable, scared someone would find out the real reason behind her divorce. She continued to feel a presence within her, with no explanation or cure in sight, until one day, when their favourite neighbour, Albino Aunty, showed up at the house, clutching a large jute bag in her hands.

"What is this, Aunty?" the girls asked, excited as Albino Aunty—who had no daughters of her own—always brought back interesting gifts and souvenirs for them from her travels to India.

"Oh, these are pure pashmina shawls, made with the finest Himalayan cashmere wool," she said, taking out a black one, tracing the intricate embroidery patterns on its borders with her finger.

"Do you like it?" she asked. "These are some of the best ones you can find in Kashmir."

She reached into her bag to reveal more shawls, and Dana selected a captivating pink one, admiring its intricate *tilla dozi* embroidery, made of metallic threads, dipped in gold.

"How do I look?" she asked, as she draped the shawl around herself. But before anyone could respond, the shawl flew off her shoulders and fluttered away.

Dana woke up from a dreamless, deep sleep, and found herself lying on the sofa. Across from her, Albino Aunty, her mother, and her sister Lana were speaking in hushed tones.

Albino Aunty looked uncharacteristically serious. Dana realised she must have had another episode. She could not bring herself to meet anyone's gaze, her cheeks flushing a deep pink.

"Oh no. This doesn't seem like a mental illness," Albino Aunty said. "She wouldn't be laughing like that during a panic attack, believe me."

"Then, what is it?" her mother asked, her voice anxious.

"I am not completely sure," Albino Aunty replied. "But when I was young and living in India, I once visited the mausoleum of a Muslim saint, Makhdoom Shah Daulat, with my cousin-brother. It was near the Ganges, in a village called Maner, and was once considered one of the finest Mughal monuments in the state of Bihar."

"I usually don't go to mausoleums, but I'm fond of history and old architecture. So, I paid a visit and as I was walking around, a horde of poor people gathered outside the building. They sat on the stairs near a frail, bearded man, probably some kind of faith healer, who was lightly hitting this girl with the remains of a broom made of grass and reciting some verses."

"The girl's hair was long and open, covering her face. Her hands were fluttering, and her body was shaking, seemingly involuntarily. When I think of Dana's behaviour today, I remember that incident. Some of Dana's movements were similar, but she doesn't seem to be in pain unlike that poor girl in Maner."

"Oh, we don't believe in that kind of thing," Dana's mother said hurriedly.

"No, no, I am not recommending you take that approach."

"What was wrong with the girl?"

"I think someone had either practised black magic or she had been possessed by a jinn."

"What?" Dana's mother shrieked, as Dana sat up and started laughing along with Lana.

Dana believed in jinns, but being possessed had never even crossed her mind. She couldn't believe something like that could happen to her. It all seemed so removed from her reality, stuff she had only seen in movies. But when Albino Aunty looked solemnly at her, she stopped giggling.

"Sorry," she said, feeling embarrassed now.

"You know, even our beloved Prophet (PBUH) was bewitched. According to narrations, a spell was cast by tying strands of his hair into eleven knots. These were wrapped around a date palm frond which, along with a comb, was thrown into a well named Zhi Arwan," Albino Aunty said.

"We will surely investigate this further," Dana's mother replied. As she left, Albino Aunty promised not to say a word about this to anyone.

From then on, Dana's family could not stop talking about jinns, magic and faith healers. Lana designed a wall-hanging with *Ayat ul Kursi* to protect the family from malevolent glares.

Albino Aunty would visit them every week with a new remedy to treat Dana. Her mother also confided in Aunt Sofie, one of her sisters in the US, who, in turn, scared her further by sharing some Jewish beliefs and stories about magic.

Dana saw her mother getting sick with worry and then finally embrace the World Wide Web to search for medical-magical manuscripts in Hebrew, forbidden books of Jewish magic, *pulsa dinura* or 'death curse' and *Ets ha-Da'at* (The Tree of Knowledge), a book from sixteenth-century Italy with one hundred and twenty-five magic spells.

Dana was afraid that her mother would soon either ship her off to some remote village in India or to meet some Jewish mystics with her aunt for *r'fuah sh'leimah*. But fortunately, her dad, always the calm one in any situation, put his foot down and encouraged Dana to continue with her medicines and talk therapy.

"Telling you all this has been very hard for me," Dana said, teary-eyed, as she finished narrating her story. "I quite liked you even when I first saw you. Then, when you visited us at our home with Ahmed, I was already divorced. I wasn't really interested in flying, but I wanted to speak to you."

"I am glad you did," said Badr, who had been silent during Dana's narration. It was difficult for him to grasp all that she had shared.

"Initially, I dismissed my interest in you as a diversion from my ailment, especially on the days I was almost bedridden. I thought there was no way you could be serious about me."

"And why is that?" Badr asked gently, looking at her very affectionately, the magnetic pull she held over him stronger than ever before.

"I thought you would probably marry someone who did not hail from an American-Jewish-atheist background. But at some point, I don't know when, with your texts, emails, and calls, I became hopeful. I liked how you had lodged yourself into my life."

"I had read about how people got butterflies when in love, but I felt very safe and peaceful whenever we interacted. It was like my sickness would disappear completely," she said, her eyes lighting up.

"You don't need to worry about it now," Badr said in a comforting voice. "We will find a way to heal you."

CHAPTER 18

———————•———————

"From the evil of whatever He has created, and from the evil of the night when it grows dark, and from the evil of those witches casting spells by blowing onto knots, and from the evil of an envier when they envy."

(113:2-5)

While Badr was still grappling with the shock waves Dana's revelation had sent through him, Aicha sat twiddling her thumbs, unsure if she wanted to follow Aleah's plan. It sounded crazy, but she could not forget Rashid.

"It's totally out-of-the-question. He is always, always on my mind. Even when I'm running on the treadmill or getting my arms waxed or trying to paint. Our long talks are running through my head, all day long, like I'm watching a TV soap," Aicha thought.

"My love for Rashid is stronger than any drug I've ever had. And I don't know how everything could have been a lie," she would say to Aleah, recalling how smitten he had been with her.

That morning, as Aleah drove her towards the smaller and less-developed emirate of Ajman, Aicha looked out of the car window, searching for Rashid and his Range Rover. There was nothing out there but dusty roads and neighbourhoods with small, Arabic- style homes.

She gazed at the palm and nabch trees on the way, offering shade in small courtyards, and reminisced about the promises Rashid had made while they sat under trees at the facility: the grand wedding, the home they would build, the new car he would gift her.

As they crossed Ajman's expansive sixteen-kilometre-long silvery beach, Aicha wistfully drifted back to her daydream of strolling hand in hand with Rashid on beaches in Mauritius.

After they had passed by the popular, retro locality of Al Bustan, the roads became narrower and brought Aicha back to her surroundings. She watched children playing, barefoot and unsupervised, with livestock wandering in the small pens attached to the houses. She was feeling very agitated when they finally stopped in a mysterious, unnamed street.

Aicha stepped out of the car and was surrounded by vast expanses of land, a few leafless trees, and a colossal, grey villa with crows flying above it.

"It's like one of those haunted house movies I can't watch by myself," Aicha remarked, feeling an increasing urge to flee as she stared at the house.

"Why is there no bell here?" Aleah exclaimed, knocking loudly on the black iron door. She made a fist and banged on it until a tall Tunisian man, a servant or possibly a protégé, opened it. He was very skinny and expressionless and had a cleft lip.

They followed him through a garden sprawling with thorny bushes and cacti. There were narrow spaces to walk through, and it was hard not to get scratches.

"Clearly the wrong day to wear short sleeves and high heels," Aicha thought. Her feet were already hurting, and she feared twisting her ankle.
"I don't know if I really want to go inside this lonely villa," she whispered to Aleah,

looking at the large windows covered with black curtains.

"It reminds me of death and other bad things," Aicha said, but Aleah insisted they keep following the skinny man down a dark passage. Soft light emanated from eye-shaped fixtures on the ceiling, their small, round bulbs resembling irises.

Aicha noticed line drawings of weapons, celestial symbols, moths, witch-like hands, and dolls etched into the stone walls. Various inscriptions in different languages were also present, though they were difficult to decipher.

"This place is like a dark art gallery," Aicha said, gasping for breath as they crossed a short, plump, beast-like, one-eyed man with a weird smile.

"It's just a sculpture," Aleah said.

Aicha looked at its big forehead, with the Arabic letters k-f-r written on them. His neck was wide, and he was wearing a crown, with an army of *shaytan* figurines standing behind him.

"I think he's ugly, but so lifelike," Aicha said shuddering.

Their host glanced at her, looking offended, as if he had sculpted this masterpiece.

"My love for Rashid is the only reason I am tolerating him and the creepiness around us," Aicha whispered, but Aleah shushed her.

Their host finally stopped and opened a door on the left. They entered a chamber, with a small reception area in front of a makeshift lab. The two women covered their mouth and nose, a foul, cooked-lizard-kind-of smell making them dizzy and nauseous. But their host seemed to be nose blind as he marked their attendance in a register and then opened a small wooden door in the corner.

They bent down to walk through the door and entered another room, a big one with no furniture and just two large bulbs, hanging from the ceiling and flickering. It had scented candles and incense sticks lit in the corners, helping cover the smell that had followed them.

The air conditioning suspiciously seemed more than perfect. Aicha shivered and wished she'd brought a jacket.

A man, probably in his fifties, was sitting cross-legged on a rectangular, raised platform in the middle of the room. The *saher*. Aicha thought he looked like a giant black bear, wearing a black *kandura*, made from moonlight fabric. His head was covered with a black cloth, a rather funny fusion of a *ghutra* and a turban.

Aicha sat beside Aleah on a hard, cold mat placed in front of him. He was looking down at hundreds of small palm-leaf manuscripts of what appeared to be occult mantras and magic spells in Arabic, handwritten in black and red ink.

Aicha spotted a rare Persian horned viper hissing and moving around in a glass box behind the *saher*. She had seen a few in Morocco before and was not a fan of the hornlike structure over its eyes.

"Is this venomous snake also part of the service?" she asked.

"Shh. Remember why you are here," Aleah whispered as Aicha shifted uneasily on the mat, questioning why she had agreed to do this.

Just then the *saher* looked up at them, his eyes hard and lined with black kohl.

"Welcome," he bellowed, with a grand sweep of his enormous hands, as if performing on stage.

"Before we get into the matter, for which you are here, I would like to tell you that I am *Baba* Abdul Dhahir and I've been using *sihr* for over thirty years, shaping the course of people's lives," he said.

"I don't know which city of India I come from, but as an infant I was found on the doorstep of a mosque in the city of joy and magic, Calcutta. I was adopted and trained by a brilliant guru, who also sent me to the jungles of Assam and a small Indian village there, Mayong, known as 'The Land of Black Magic,' to gain my *ilm al-sihr*."

"I have travelled to many countries in search of knowledge and lived in Kyoto for two years, where I trained with local shamans. I've helped many Japanese women get love from their chosen partners or put a curse on people they don't like. And I have also gained knowledge of subjects like astrology, numerology, and palm-reading. I've learnt to overpower jinns, demons and spirits of the planets. They accept my spiritual superiority," he continued.

Aicha tried not to roll her eyes.

"So, tell me, my dears, what are your names and what is it that you want?" he asked. "Do you want to learn about the future? Find a lost item? Or eat away your pain? Cure a disease? Or make someone fall in love with you? Get married? Or conceive? Or take revenge?"

"I'm Aleah. This is my friend Aicha. She was betrayed by a local man called Rashid. But she still wants to be with him."

Aicha couldn't believe how Aleah had summed up her misery in two short sentences.

"So, you want to make him fall in love with your friend again?" *Baba* Abdul asked, smiling, revealing a gold molar.

"Yes, I want him to come back," Aicha said. "I know he really loves me, but something or someone is keeping him far away, blocking our marriage. But we belong together. He and I, we are meant to be."

"Okay, I understand, dears. Now listen to me carefully. I will need to perform several spells and invoke a jinni who will help us make a mark on his heart and soul and bring him back to you."

"Okay." Aicha was unconvinced, and he seemed to notice.

"I would have you know that because of my huge magical prowess, one of my Arab clients, a VIP who I reunited with his beloved, brought me here. He helped me gain more knowledge of Islamic occult sciences. I have even read all the volumes of Ahmad al-Buni's *'Shams al-Ma'arif al-Kubra',* which has many chapters on the magical use of numbers, squares, and alphabets to communicate with jinns and spirits," he said, switching to near-perfect Arabic and speaking in the Al Khaleeji accent.

"Now people, including many Arabs, and even some westerners, travel to see me from all corners of the Middle East, and even North Africa ... because of my intercessory powers," he added.

"Okay. But I want to know how you will do this?" Aicha asked. She knew nothing about dark magic, and Aleah seemed to be doing this for the thrill. Her friend liked new experiences, even if they were weird.

"First, we must settle the funds," *Baba* Abdul said.

"What?" Aicha asked, baffled by his business-like tone. "Isn't he going to show us his work first?" she wondered.

"Badees," he called out and the Tunisian man appeared with a cash box.

Aicha did not want to pay him just yet, but Aleah insisted they hand over the hefty deposit. Aicha had arranged it by selling some of her favourite jewellery pieces, her Berber necklace, antique headbands, and even family heirlooms.

She could not ask her stingy mum and her gambler-dad for money. They had already paid a lot for her stay at the facility, although they'd said it was a waste of time and money, 'just a place to hang out with other elite kids.' And then Aicha had left the place without any explanation. Now she was afraid of asking for more money and getting hit by a million questions.

She reluctantly handed all the cash she had to Badees as *Baba* Abdul cleared his throat.

"I will need some things from you," he said.

"Yes?" Aicha asked, still eyeing the money Badees was carrying away from them.

"Write down his full name here and his mother's name as well," he instructed, giving her a blank sheet of paper and a fountain pen with red ink.

The possibility that this red ink may, in fact, be blood, made her squeamish. She took out the paper Talha had given her with Rashid's information, including the names of his family members.

"Do you have anything of his? A personal item?" *Baba* asked, once she was done writing.

"*Oui*, I have his t-shirt. I haven't washed it. It has some strands of his hair stuck to it. And his scent."

"Perfect."

She gave him the t-shirt and the paper, after which he opened what appeared to be a copy of the Qur'an. He started reciting some verses, but something didn't sound right. The words and phrases seemed all jumbled up and didn't make any sense.

"He's reading it in reverse," Aleah explained.

Aicha was not very religious, but she knew this was forbidden. Kufr. An unforgiveable sin. As was black magic. She was nervous about crossing lines from which there would be no turning back.

"This is the price of love," Aleah whispered. "Doing things that you never thought you would do."

"Even going against your faith?" Aicha asked. But then she remembered Rashid, his love, his hugs. She would do anything to get him back. If only he knew of the sacrifices she was willing to make for him.

Baba Abdul closed the Qur'an and Badees showed up with a bowl of water, a black hen, and a sharp knife.

"What is he going to do?" Aicha asked Aleah, experiencing a sudden shortness of breath. Aleah was quiet and did not look at her.

It wasn't the first time Aicha was going to watch a bird's sacrifice, but today it seemed totally unnecessary.

"Do we really need to do this?" she asked, feeling desperate.

Baba Abdul looked surprised by her question, and his expression softened. "Yes, my dear, we must make great sacrifices to get our heart's desire," he said.

Aicha held her breath and closed her eyes, covering her ears with her palms. The clucking soon stopped and some minutes later, Aleah nudged her.

"It's done," she said. She seemed to have enjoyed it.

To Aicha's relief, Badees had already cleared the mess. *Baba* Abdul was now writing something with a handmade wooden pen and what seemed like the hen's blood. Aicha felt nauseated.

"Here we write what we intend to do with him," Baba Abdul explained, as he scribbled some phrases next to Rashid's name. Muttering under his breath, he blew on the paper, folded it, and handed it to Aicha.

"Place this paper, somewhere close to him. Perhaps in his home or bedroom or somewhere in his surroundings."

"His bedroom?" Aicha asked.

"I will ask Talha to take care of it. Perhaps place it in his car," Aleah murmured.

Aicha was aghast at how Aleah always had a solution, and a man ready to do her bidding. She was not the prettiest of women, but she had every other man in every room flirting with her. She had some kind of hidden power over them, which Aicha wished she had had over Rashid.

Baba Abdul held up Rashid's t-shirt and soaked it in a bowl of water, which had turned blood-red. Once the t-shirt was completely drenched, he passed it to Aicha and said, "Bury the t-shirt in his garden or somewhere near his home. Soon, he will weep real tears. Nightmares will disturb his sleep, and he will come running back to you."

Badees cleaned Baba Abdul's hands with a towel and gave him a bottle of water along with another small, unlabelled bottle, like the ones used for herbal medicines. *Baba* added several drops of the mixture to the water, shook the bottle and then gave it to Aicha.

"Do I need to drink it?" she asked.

"No, Rashid does. Preferably on the eve of the full moon."

Aicha wondered if Talha would be up for all these challenges. Aleah would probably have to do more unspeakable things to convince him. She watched Badees place a dark brown leather-bound notebook on *Baba* Abdul's palms. He rose from his platform, his large head not far from the ceiling.

"I will now summon the jinni by using one of the most powerful invocations there is. Listen and feel its power!"

Badees served them a mixed-herbs tea while *Baba* Abdul flipped through the notebook.

He began reading, his eyes blazing. "From the perceptible world, *alam al-shahāda*, the hidden world, *alam al-ghayb*, and the world of the imagination, *alam al-takhayyul wa 'l-barzakh*. I call on to Aicha, whose place is in the east, in the fire …"

He described the jinni's location in detail. Sometimes he spoke in other languages, expressing their intention to have power over Rashid. He ended the ritual by invoking the names of several jinns for *tawassul*.

"We have succeeded," he announced proudly. "She will completely possess him, and it will be very difficult for anyone to cure him till you get him back."

Aicha didn't like *Baba* Abdul much, but a sudden wave of gratitude washed over her. She was sad but hopeful once again as Aleah called Talha and made plans for completing their feat.

CHAPTER 19

*"And say: "Truth has (now) arrived and Falsehood perished:
for Falsehood is (by its nature) bound to perish.
We send down (stage by stage) in the Qur'an that which is
a healing and a mercy to those who believe: to the unjust it
causes nothing but loss after loss."*

(17:81–82)

B adr spent many nights, pouring over books and articles on black magic and jinn possession. He was determined to help release Dana from her demon's captivity and then figure out how to get married to her.

There was a lot of information available, and Badr was exhausted trying to determine which route to take. He drove towards Al Mulla Plaza, on Al Wahda Street, where many of his expat Arab friends lived. He was going to meet an old friend, Naji, a skinny Lebanese with a great sense of humour.

They had met after a long time and spent some time talking about their old memories of Al Mulla Plaza, when it used to be the main plaza in the city. But soon the conversation drifted towards magic and jinns. Badr lied about helping a possessed male relative. He was not proud of his dishonesty, but he needed to protect Dana and her secret.

"My sister's behaviour became a bit abnormal last year," Naji told him. "After a lot of effort and research, we found that her mother-in-law was practising magic on her, with the help of a *saher*."

"What did you do?" Badr asked, glad to have finally met someone who had first-hand experience with a loved one's possession.

"We went to a *motawa*."

"The religious scholars who lead prayers, deliver Friday sermons, and settle disputes?" Badr asked.

"Yes, and they also help people suffering from the evil eye, black magic, or jinn possession."

He took out his cell phone and scribbled a name and number on a piece of paper.

"Here you go," he said, handing it to Badr. "This is Sheikh Ali's number. He is originally from Iran and quite well-known as an Islamic alternative healer."

Naji assured Badr of Sheikh Ali's credibility. Soon, Badr set up a meeting and asked Dana to make an excuse to her family so that they could go and meet him together.

Sheikh Ali's humble brown house, with large windows, was connected to a big mosque. As they stood outside and rang the doorbell, they could hear kids playing.

"*As-salamu alaykum*, I am Sheikh Ali," said a short, fifty-something, bearded man, opening the door.

"*Wa'alaykumu s-salam* Sheikh, I'm Badr, and this is my sister, Dana. I called you a few days ago. We need to discuss a personal matter with you."

"Of course. I remember. Please follow me."

They crossed an open courtyard, where four children of different ages and sizes were playing carrom, a popular tabletop game, in which the players flicked discs trying to knock them to the corners of a carrom board. Two toddlers were running around. Badr smiled at them as Sheikh Ali took them inside a compact, sparsely furnished *majlis*, where they settled down on worn-out floor cushions.

The walls were decorated with a few blue lanterns and a frame with the ninety-nine names of Allah written with a Khamish pen in a beautiful, calligraphic script *Kufic*.

"A gift from some affluent and happy client," Badr guessed, then began explaining Dana's condition. Sheikh Ali nodded, as if he understood.

"So, will you be able to help us?" Badr asked, scared of getting his hopes up too high, too soon.

"Well, first, we must determine what the problem is ... whether it's a psychological disturbance or magic or someone's given her the evil eye. But please understand that certain things cannot be cured quickly," Sheikh Ali said. "People come to me expecting miracles. But only Allah is the healer. I am just carrying out what He has asked us to do in such scenarios."

"I understand. But how will you find out what the problem is?" Badr asked.

"I will perform *ruqyah*. As you might know, it's an alternative healing method based on the Quran and Hadith. We use it to treat people suffering from the evil eye, magic, jinn possession and even physical ailments."

"Some people misunderstand the concept and think *ruqyah* is for communicating with evil spirits, but it's not."

"How does it work?" Badr asked, feeling a little positive now.

"Well, the method is based on practices carried out by the Prophet (PBUH) for self-treatment or to help his companions and others."

Sheikh Ali raised his hands for *du'a'* and started reciting *Surah Al-Falaq* (The Daybreak) and *Surah An-Nas* (Mankind).

Dana's face was partly obscured by a light-pink veil. She extended her left hand towards Badr, silently inviting him to hold it. But he remained still, hesitant to touch her in front of Sheikh Ali or distract him from performing *ruqyah*.

She withdrew her hand, picked up a tissue from a box placed near her, and methodically began to tear it into small pieces.

Sheikh Ali continued reciting Quranic verses while observing her closely. He paused occasionally to ask questions, to which Dana responded with her characteristic calm. Aside from her serene demeanour, the only notable change was her eventual grip on Badr's hand despite his resistance. She clung to it tightly, as if seeking reassurance.

"Look, my children," Sheikh Ali finally said. "I must be honest with you. I don't completely understand what's happened to her. Usually, people yawn, struggle to stay awake, feel itchy or are unable to hold their hands or legs up or straight. It can feel as though they're burdened with a heavy weight in their hands. They may also shed tears quietly or begin speaking in a different tone. But Dana has not displayed any of these signs today. I do sense something, but she doesn't behave as though she has been influenced by the evil eye or possessed by a jinn."

"Okay," Badr said, feeling confused and disappointed.

"Have you already tried to heal yourself in the Islamic way?" Sheikh Ali asked Dana. She nodded.

"Have you done the daily prayers? Used the holy water and the herbal mixes?" he asked.

"Yes," she said. "My mother did some research on it with a neighbour's help, and we have been following all the Islamic rituals for healing."

"I asked my parents about *ruqyah* as well," Badr said. "They recommended that the affected person recite *Surah Al-Baqarah* (The Cow), *Duaa Al Tahseen* for protection, and *Azkar Al Sabah Wal Massa* for the remembrance of Allah."

"Yes, she just needs to keep saying her prayers and practising the daily rituals," Sheikh Ali emphasised.

"But what else should we do?" Badr asked, now pacing back and forth. The *majlis* suddenly felt very constricted.

"Don't overthink or overdo it," Sheikh Ali said, standing up and leading them out. "I can't help beyond this."

Badr felt dejected. It seemed so anti-climactic.

"Isn't there any other way you can help her?" he asked, feeling desperate, as they crossed the courtyard and walked towards the gate.

"She is doing what she is supposed to do. I'm sorry. I don't know any other way to assess her," Sheikh Ali replied, pressing his lips and looking deeply apologetic as he held the gate open for them to leave.

He did not ask for money, but Badr dropped a few hundred dirhams in a box near the gate, as was customary. He stood with Dana in silence, trying to understand how they had reached this dead-end. Perfectly shielded by a *ghaf* tree, they watched worshippers arriving at the mosque for *asar* prayers.

Badr's shoulder brushed against Dana's. She did not move away, but she also avoided making eye contact. To divert her, Badr pointed at blue-spotted Arab butterflies flying near the tree. Dana smiled in response, but her eyes were sad and serious. Badr really wanted to hug her, but he couldn't risk it in such a public place.

He drove towards Dana's home quietly, as she stared out the window, stopping his Nissan Patrol a few streets before her neighbourhood. She had to walk the rest of the way, as they couldn't be seen together.

"I don't know why I didn't have any of the symptoms I usually do, though they are not exactly how Sheikh Ali said they are supposed to be," Dana said as she prepared to get down. "Maybe because I was so scared that I would act crazy in front of you. I don't want you to see me that way, ever!"

"Believe mee, there is nothing that can make me think less of you," Badr reassured her.

"Thank you."

"You don't need to thank me, *habibti*."

She smiled, then opened her handbag and took out a small, transparent perfume bottle.

"What is this?" Badr asked, as she handed it to him.

"You can spray some on your hand at night or when I'm unreachable," she said. It was the Oud perfume she always wore.

"What are you thinking?" he asked her, cradling the perfume bottle in his hands, as she gave him an exhausted, half-smile.

"That I'll be okay. Because I've got you and a whole army of loved ones and well-wishers protecting me," she said, as she got down from the car.

Badr watched her walk away. slowly and forlornly. until she reached the end of the street and vanished.

CHAPTER 20

"...whoever takes a life—unless as a punishment for murder or mischief in the land—it will be as if they killed all of humanity; and whoever saves a life, it will be as if they saved all of humanity."

(5:32)

Badr was sitting in the reception area of his office, going through his pink book, when he looked up at the television screen and froze. Big plumes of dark grey smoke were forming around the top of a familiar, tower-like building and then his favourite white bird flew into a tower next to it.

"The World Trade Centre in New York," the newscaster said, as everyone gathered around to watch.

Badr frantically called Dana. She was also stunned.

"I can't talk much right now," she said.

He spent the rest of the day in a chaotic blur. Upon arriving home, he found his house crowded with neighbours and relatives discussing the attack on the twin towers. Rashid also dropped in to chat.

"God, this is all so crazy," he said, looking uncharacteristically shocked. "I really need to get away somewhere."

Badr was all too familiar with Rashid's sudden, occasional need to disappear, and encouraged him to take a holiday. He was worried about Dana and called her again as soon as he woke up the next morning.

"I am going with my mother to New York," she announced.

"What? Why? When? Is it safe to go right now?" Badr asked, taken aback.

"We just heard that my mother's cousin was also a victim of the terrorist attack on the trade towers," she said. "She wants to spend time with her family and support them, and no one else can join her now. Plus, she can't leave me alone with my problem."

"But for how long?" Badr asked, feeling panicky. He didn't want Dana to leave.

"I don't really know, Badr. Maybe a few weeks. A month maybe."

He was silent.

"The change of atmosphere might actually help me," she said.

"I don't want you to go," Badr said.

"But I can't say no. I have no reason to."

"Why not? Do it for me. Don't leave me. My flying test is coming up. I can't do it without your support."

"Badr, please try to understand. I can't stay. But I will write to you every day as soon as I get my hands on a computer."

"What if your mother marries you off to someone over there?"

"No, of course not. Not after our last experience. Plus, I wouldn't agree this time."

Badr knew he was being unreasonable, but an angry storm was brewing inside him. That day, he could not control his anger. After a heated argument, he hung up on her, unwilling to be rational and accommodating.

A day passed without any communication with Dana. It was unusual for them not to talk or text each other throughout the day.

The next day, Badr woke up with a dull ache of regrets, guilt clinging to him like a shroud. He had never lashed out at Dana before. The argument replayed in his mind, a tangled mess of hurtful words and emotions. He tried to call her, but her phone was switched off.

A week passed and there was no sign of her. Every notification on his computer felt like a potential email. Badr felt furious again, but kept following the news to see how things were unfolding in New York. He was repeatedly hearing Osama Bin Laden's name; he was an important fighter in the Afghan-Soviet war, who had allegedly been supported by the US before going rogue, entering the world of militancy and creating a terrorist group.

Some still regarded him as a freedom fighter, a *jihadist* in Afghanistan. Others spoke of him as a terrorist, who had organised the hijacking of commercial flights in the US and ordered horrible attacks in the name of Allah and Islam.

People trying to understand the situation in light of the Qur'an were circulating various verses over text messages.

"He is the One Who has revealed to you O Prophet the Book, of which some verses are precise—they are the foundation of the Book—while others are elusive. Those with deviant hearts follow the elusive verses seeking to spread doubt through their false interpretations—but none grasps their full meaning except Allah. As for those well-grounded in knowledge, they say, 'We believe in this Qur'an—it is all from our Lord.' But none will be mindful of this except people of reason." (3:7)

Some people were ashamed, others felt he had avenged what had happened in Palestine and Iraq. Like many others, Badr did not want any part of it. He had been diverting himself and calling the flying school for the past few days, but no one was answering his calls.

It was strange because the school was usually open seven days a week. He searched for an alternate number online and found one for the management's office.

The phone kept ringing for a while and Badr was about to hang up when someone answered.

"Who is this?" the man asked in a serious but low tone. Badr could barely hear him.

"Hello, this is Badr. I am a student at the school, and I was wondering when ..."

"Don't ever call here again," the man said, and hung up, leaving Badr doubtful about what he had heard. A nagging feeling told him that something had gone terribly wrong. His coffee cup untouched, he hurriedly left for work, trying to clear his head.

As he stepped into the office building and signalled a 'Hi' to the receptionists, he glanced at the TV screen on the wall. A number of pictures appeared. 9/11 suspects apparently. All brown men.

They zoomed into one photograph. Flashing on the screen was the photo of a man with a modern beard.

CHAPTER 21

"Fight in the cause of Allah only against tho██who wage war against you, but do not exceed the limits. Allah does not like transgressors."

(2:190)

Samer was suspected of being one of the hijackers on Flight 175.

"Twenty-three-year-old Samer Alfatwa is allegedly the pilot who flew the plane into the south tower of the World Trade Centre," the news anchor read.

Badr tried to wrap his head around the terrifying reality emerging on the screen. His mind was screaming what he had buried in his subconscious—the knowledge that something was very wrong about Samer. But his entire focus had been on maintaining his distance from this spokesperson for extremists. Of course, he could have never imagined anything of this magnitude. Nobody could.

Badr nearly spilled his coffee when the news anchor said that Samer may have received training directly from Osama bin Laden.

"That's why they had to close the flying school," Badr said. In a moment of stark realisation, the precariousness of his situation became immediately clear. The room felt chilly as he thought of government and intelligence officials looking through the profiles of students, searching for those who had been in frequent touch with Samer, and met him outside the school.

Badr had ignored the last couple of calls Samer had made to him before leaving for the US, but he knew he could still be in the limelight as a friend or worse, a protégé of the terrorist and a potential extremist.

"This can't be good," Badr said, and left work quickly without notifying anyone. Upon reaching home, he almost ran into *Baba and Ummi's* bedroom, panting as he explained the situation.

"Slow down, Badr. Please don't worry." *Baba* said, looking worried himself. "Keep a low profile and let me see what we can do to protect you."

Feeling jittery, he spent the afternoon with Rashid, who had no idea of his friend's situation or mental state. As they watched an action movie, Rashid again talked about how he needed to get away.

"I might go to the Empty Quarter to clear my head," Rashid said, opening a packet of chips, but Badr barely heard him. Later that evening, Badr saw *Baba* again.

"I'm afraid you can't stay here Badr," he said, with a stricken face. "They might suspect you too, since you knew him for a while, met him several times. We can't take that risk."

"Okay, but where should I go, *Baba*? Should I leave the country?"

"Yes, but we would need some time to sort that out. It might not be safe to travel with your name. For now, you should find a place where you can stay for some time without being noticed. And no cell phones! I am sure all of us will be under surveillance very soon if we aren't already. They've already closed your flying school."

"When will they reopen it?"

"I am not sure. It's hard to say anything right now … we don't know what's going to happen next."

Badr realised he hadn't even had the time to absorb the shock of what all this meant to him personally. It wasn't only that he was now linked to a terrorist, who would probably be plastered on every TV screen for a very long time, but also that his dream to fly had crashed once again.

He decided to go out and think about his next steps. As he was moving through the aisles of a grocery store, he received a text message. It was from *Baba*.

"Don't come home and please switch off your phone," it said without further explanation.

Badr's pounding heart made himfeel dizzy, sick, and feverish. He left the store quickly and vomited near his car before getting in. Breathing heavily and loudly, he ignited the engine and quickly drove out of Sharjah, in the direction of the northern emirates.

He wanted to get as far away as possible from home and took the road leading to Ras Al Khaimah, with no specific plan in mind.

"What could they want from me? I only happened to be at the same flying school with Samer. How do they know we talked? Will they torture me? Do they have the right to torture someone who has done nothing wrong?"

Badr asked himself all kinds of questions. The sun was setting, and he had not figured out where to spend that night. It seemed that the only option was to sleep in his car.

He knew his friend Omran lived in Ras Al Khaimah. But what could he say to him? How would he explain the situation to him? Omran could get into trouble because of him. Badr did not want Samer's legacy to cause any further damage.

As he looked towards his left, Badr realised he was driving close to the Red Island.

With his mind shutting down, he veered towards the old part of the island and drove on until he reached the beach. That night, he preferred the island's unknown horrors over the terrors of the real-world.

Switching off the car lights and the engine, he locked the doors. Every sound and movement around him brought about a new wave of sweating, trembling, and dizziness, until he plunged into an abyss of exhaustion.

CHAPTER 22

*"Miserable indeed was the price
for which they sold their souls, if
only they knew!"*

(2:102)

"So, where's your dad?" Kunal asked.

"He's dead," Rashid replied, drowning his melancholy in *karak* tea.

Unaware of Badr's plight, he was on his way to Rub' al Khali. A wretched little cafeteria with neon lights had caught his eye and soon he had found himself talking to this strange Indian guy. He didn't know when and how the conversation had landed on his dad. It was easier to end the discussion than explain how his old dude was rarely around and seemed to barely know him.

Before leaving, he'd told his dad he was off to the Empty Quarter for meditation.

"He believed me. Shows just how close we are. He doesn't know me at all, does he? Doesn't know when I'm lying, and when I'm telling the truth," Rashid thought as he clutched his warm terracotta cup.

Meanwhile, Kunal had already moved on. He was telling Rashid how he had come face-to-face with an Indian rattlesnake while travelling through a remote village in Odisha, India.

"Did it try to poison you? How did you get away? Did you end up killing it?" Rashid asked eagerly, as he loved hearing gripping true stories. Occasionally, he would recount these tales to impress others, pretending they were his own experiences.

"Yes! I cut its head off and ate it."

Rashid choked on his tea. "That's the craziest story I've heard in a while, dude," he said.

"It's true. But I have loads of these stories."

"Such as?"

"Well … a few years ago, when I was in high school, *Dadda* and *Ma* put each other in jail in Dubai for some extramarital shit they'd both done."

"What? Your parents did that?"

"Oh yeah. They had trained our moustached servants to be Hercule Poirot and collect evidence on each other's hanky-panky. I tell you; no one knows your family like servants and babies. We assume they're not paying attention because they don't say much, but they know everything."

"But what happened in jail?"

"Oh, nothing memorable, as they both got out the next day … the benefit of having high-profile connections. My younger sister, Nidhi, stopped growing after that."

"What do you mean?"

"I mean, she was so stressed she got stuck at four feet eleven inches, although everyone in my family is so tall."

"Gosh, no one's normal and everyone's screwed!" Rashid thought. His mind drifted to Badr. People also liked to confide in him because he had some kind of saviour complex, and he actually gave a damn!

Rashid knew that, unlike Badr, he was a sarcastic asshole, but they were still best friends, because they'd always been together, dragged each other through school, college, driving tests and so much more. Those kinds of friendships stuck for life, it seemed. But Rashid was also annoyed with Badr. He seemed to have mentally checked out since Dana entered his life, and more so since she left for New York.

"Did you know white people like her stole algebra from the Arabs? Do you prefer *kosher* over *halal* meat now?" Rashid had teased him. He now chuckled at the memory of Badr's pink-with-fury face.

He left the cafeteria, telling Kunal how he wanted to become 'a grain of sand in the majestic desert.' He didn't find Rub' al Khali daunting and inhospitable, as some people described it.

It was just hot. Not the best time of the year to visit. But he had to get away, with the hope that modern wheels and the air-conditioned comfort of his 4-by-4 would protect him during the day.

He set up camp near an orange-yellow Oshkosh water tanker, which had been abandoned in the middle of the Bu Hasa desert. No one really knew how it ended up there, but it had become a picnic site for off-roaders.

Rashid sat near the tanker and waited for the pristine sunset. He wanted to lie under the stars at night and dwell on what Badr had told me about the Hubble telescope.

"You might even witness a meteor shower if you're lucky," Badr had said.

Lucky. Rashid laughed at that word. It wasn't that he considered himself unlucky. When people asked him how rich he was, he'd say he was the 'private jet type' who rolled on cash in bed. He slept most nights on a waterbed in a multi-storeyed villa, the kind most people could not even envision. He called it a "museum of the freaky rich" where his mum splurged on silk-and-velvet curtains and classic Turkish furniture.

Rashid didn't really like his house, though. He gazed at the vast emptiness around him. His hands stabbed the dune as he listened to the hiss of sand grains. The sun was about to set, so he started a small fire and lay down with his old Sony Walkman, listening to Amr Diab sing *'Habibi, ya nour el ein.'*

His mind drifted to all the women he had been with over the past few months. Nothing had lasted for more than a few weeks. It was exciting in the beginning, this playboy-ish lifestyle, but now Rashid was feeling the burnout of being fake-charming, of these ephemeral relationships.

He reflected on the fleeting moments when he had felt like he was in love. It had felt both remarkable and baffling. His mind drifted towards melancholic, hooded eyes, with mascara-lifted lashes. But he didn't want to think about her.

"Oh, Aicha, you turned out to be such a disappointment. Couldn't make those feelings stay," he said to the navy-blue sky, shimmering with stars and a yellowish moon. He switched off the Walkman and was glad of the calm quiet of the dunes. Wafting towards a state that almost resembled peace, he heard someone pushing their way through the monstrous dunes.

"It's probably just some off-roaders or Bedouins passing by," he thought. He was in no mood for small talk and covered his face with a blanket, pretending to be asleep.

"Rashid," a woman called out, and he almost jumped. His eyes opened and darted around to find who his unwanted guest was. Before he realised what was happening, she was very close to him.

"Aicha," he whispered, unable to breathe properly, wanting to push her away. His nails sank into the sand as she choked him without even touching him. His body contracted as he pleaded with the incognito presence for mercy and release, but an energy of intense rage had begun to feast upon him.

THE PRESENT
CHAPTER 23

*"And there are other gains which are
beyond your reach that Allah is keeping
in store for you. For Allah is Most
Capable of everything."*

(48:21)

A few days had elapsed since Abdulaziz had revealed himself as the gatekeeper. After the initial shock was over, Badr had strangely felt more comfortable around Abdulaziz, as if he now knew the man. It had prompted Badr to pour out his life's story.

A weight lifted from him as he divulged every detail without reservation. He couldn't fathom why he was confiding in Abdulaziz with such candour. Perhaps because he knew Abdulaziz was a distant relative of Sultan Al Tajir, Dana's dad.

Abdulaziz listened attentively, his demeanour quiet and thoughtful. When Badr finished his narrative, he gently probed, "So why aren't you with Dana now?"

"I just told you everything that happened. It's all so complicated."

"Excuses," Abdulaziz remarked, sipping his Suleimani *chai*.

"Maybe ... I thought I was doing my best," Badr replied, wondering if he could have done anything differently.

"So, you think she is haunted?" Abdulaziz asked.

"Yes ... that's what she told me. Although I've never witnessed anything unusual when I'm with her. But I believe her."

"But why didn't you marry her?"

"I would have married her," Badr said, feeling judged. "But my parents would strongly oppose our match. You know how it is in our community. They are set in their ways. They still see her mother as Jewish and dad as an atheist. Adding to that, there's now this whole issue of Dana's divorce and, on top of everything else, she is haunted. Not sure if her family would want her to endure another humiliation."

"Excuses ... excuses!" Abdulaziz exclaimed, casting a disappointed look at Badr.

"What would you have done?" Badr asked, going red with fury. He did not like the implication that he had somehow failed Dana.

"I would have married her anyway," Abdulaziz declared firmly.

"I really want to, believe me," Badr insisted. "I just didn't get enough time before my life turned upside down. But this phase I am in, I believe it's just a hurdle I need to overcome. And then I will find a way to take away her distress and be with her."

"Okay," Abdulaziz replied, not sounding convinced. "But given how Sheikh Ali wasn't able to help you, how do you plan to find a cure, or even understand what's happening to her?"

"I don't know, Abdulaziz," Badr replied, feeling tired. "Do you think that ... maybe the jinns could help me?"

As soon as the words left his mouth, Badr felt his request was so absurd. Asking the jinns for assistance seemed like a stretch.

"The jinns?" Abdulaziz also seemed taken aback by the suggestion. The two exchanged quiet glances as they turned the idea around in their heads.

"Well, it might be worth trying," Abdulaziz conceded after a brief pause. "I will ask for their permission. But you will need to earn their trust before asking for any favours."

Badr nodded, unsure about what to expect. A few days later, they were finishing a frugal lunch of *daal* fry with *kuboos,* when Abdulaziz announced, "I have some good news for you."

Badr was walking towards the kitchenette, which Abdulaziz claimed to have built all by himself. He stopped in his tracks.

"Really? What?" he asked, a feeling of dread rising from the pit of his stomach, colliding with excitement and optimism.

"The first tribe of jinns, the *Mashaikh,* has agreed to meet you tonight," Abdulaziz said, almost smiling, clasping his hands together.

"*Mashaikh?* Like religious scholars?" Badr asked, taking a deep breath, telling himself there was nothing to fear. He wanted to do this.

"Yes, they are religious scholars," Abdulaziz replied, as he brushed his teeth with *miswak.*

"Will you be doing the same ritual that you did that day ... open and close the gate?" Badr asked, still trying to wrap his head around what was happening.

"Yes, of course. I am the gatekeeper."

"But do I need to see it again?" Badr asked, remembering beast-Abdulaziz.

"Not necessarily," Abdulaziz replied. "Just wear some musk and come to their gathering directly."

"Their gathering?"

"Yes, it's kind of like the *majlis* you Emiratis have."

"You mean we Emiratis have?"

"I am an outcast, remember? The black sheep of the local community."

"You're a beast sometimes."

"We all are."

Badr smiled and asked, "Do I need to know a summoning incantation? We didn't really study mythological and supernatural occultism in school, you know."

"No, we are not practising magic here. They will reveal themselves to you. I have already told them about you."

"Shared my CV with them, did you?" Badr couldn't believe he was chatting so casually about meeting jinns, like they were his new neighbours.

As the evening arrived, he put on a clean *kandura*, said his *maghrib* prayers, and embarked on his mission.

The sky was a nice pink-orange, and the sun was setting as he followed the directions Abdulaziz had drawn for him on a piece of paper. They were difficult to understand, but Badr managed to make his way via the narrow alleyways to the abandoned mosque, close to the market area and the sea.

A deep sense of apprehension settled over him as he faced the bizarre encounter ahead, uncertain of what to expect. He had always prided himself on taking calculated risks, but lately life seemed to be yanking him out of his comfort zone a little too often, with no elderly wisdom or compass to guide him.

He looked at the rust-coloured, chipped coating of the mosque's ancient walls and its conical minaret. He had seen it before on the internet, on a British map of this mosque from the 1820s. It had twenty domes, which had survived the war and all the upheaval this town had seen.

He reached the mosque's entrance and opened the door, slowly, soundlessly, striding into a dark space with a dim light flickering in the distance. Taking deep breaths and small steps, he moved towards the light. He felt some resistance. His feet rubbed against an incredibly soft object. He retrieved the small torch Abdulaziz had asked him to carry and switched it on.

A pair of deep blue eyes were staring at him. They reminded Badr of Dana. The resemblance was uncanny, but these eyes were not human. The most beautiful sand cat Badr had ever seen, with light grey and white fur, was brushing against his legs, probably the equivalent of a hug in the cat world. They sized each other up for a bit. Then Badr picked him up, and he settled in his arms instantly, as if they belonged together.

Badr fancied keeping a pet cat as Prophet Mohammad (PBUH) was very fond of these feline creatures. As a child, he had been told a story about Prophet Muhammad's beloved cat, Muezza, who had fallen asleep on his robe. When it was time for the Prophet to pray, he chose to cut off a portion of his sleeve rather than disturb Muezza.

Reflecting on this story now, Badr found solace as he gently stroked the cat. For a few minutes, it eased his apprehension about the impending encounter with the jinns. But his furry companion soon leapt down and darted away, vanishing into the shadows.

Badr stepped forward, and the space expanded. It seemed much cleaner than the rest of the island. Like it had been mopped rigorously with some disinfectant and sprayed with sandalwood *attar*. The walls were dark brown and had thin, golden floral and geometric motifs painted on them. Traditional Arabic lamps and lanterns had been hung above the motifs, with small balls of fire burning inside them, without any wicks or wax.

Badr reached what appeared to be the main chamber, covered by a thick, golden curtain. He could hear soft murmurs in Arabic.

Taking a deep breath, he slowly moved the curtain from the right side and peeked inside. It was quite a large room, illuminated in the middle with moon- shaped lights, with the corners shrouded in darkness.

Men and women, clad in simple, colourful robes, were sitting on red-and-gold velvety low-level couches, laid out on a raised platform. The men were all seated on one side, the women on the other. A green curtain, made of tissue-like fabric, hung protectively around them as they listened to a bespectacled and dwarfish man speak. It seemed like an exclusive social club.

"We have many beautiful examples in Islam about how to sustain good relationships. When the Prophet Muhammad (PBUH) received the first revelation, he fled to his home in the middle of the night. He was trembling and saying, 'Cover me up!' So his wife Khadija, *Ameerat-Quraysh*, quickly wrapped a blanket around his shoulders and helped him calm down. She was also the first person and woman to follow Islam."

Badr spotted Abdulaziz, sitting next to a tall, slim, and bearded man. Their eyes met and Abdulaziz interrupted the speaker, addressing the room, "Let's welcome Badr!"

Everyone went quiet and turned to look at him. Badr felt like an intruder. Avoiding eye contact with anyone, he sat down next to Abdulaziz and glanced sideways at the man sitting next to him, who was neither very old nor very young.

"This is Aabid, the chief of *Mashaikh*," Abdulaziz said.

Badr's mouth fell open. "Is Abdulaziz trying to tell me this man is a jinn?"; he wondered.

Abdulaziz relayed the bad news gently. "You know, Badr, we're the only humans in this cave."

Badr stared at him in disbelief. He looked at the men around him. Their faces were glowing and, unlike human skin, were not impacted by light, age, pigmentation issues, and infections. They had a *zebiba* on their foreheads, the devout sign which appeared sometimes when someone laid down their head in *sujood* regularly.

"Welcome to *Majlis al Mashaikh*, Badr," Aabid said. "We generally don't allow visitors at Al Jazirah Al Hamra to see us, but you are Abdulaziz's guest, and he has spoken highly of you, so we've made an exception."

Badr wondered what Abdulaziz had been telling them. They barely knew each other, but he was glad to know that Abdulaziz had a soft spot for him.

"I am glad to be here," he said, scared of offending the jinns in any way, his heart racing.

He looked at the table in front of them, where several glass bottles of olive oil were resting, and a handful of green and black olives lay arranged in an Islamic geometric pattern on a plate.

"Feel free to put some olive oil on your hands if you wish or eat the olives. They are fresh, soft, and tangy, and come from a holy tree and cure around seventy diseases," Aabid said, and recited:

"Also, a tree springing out of Mount Sinai
which produces oil and relish for those who use it for food." (23:20)

A jinn with a pitcher and basin appeared to help Badr wash his hands. He obliged and then ate a green olive. Surprisingly, it was not bitter at all.

"So, what are you seeking, Badr?" Aabid asked, as Badr savoured the olive's mild sweetness, rolling it over his tongue.

"Nothing," Badr replied.

"Your friend is not very honest, Abdulaziz," Aabid said, frowning.

Badr was not sure what to tell him. Abdulaziz had asked him to win their trust before asking for help.

"Is there something that is bothering you?" Aabid asked again.

"*La, la,* I am just here for a few weeks. Then I'll go back."

"Do you want any answers from us?"

Badr felt he was drowning under Aabid's silent stare. After an uncomfortable pause, he managed to say, "My life has been in turbulence lately. So I am seeking answers. But I am not sure if you can help me."

"All I can say is Allah has given us powers that humans do not possess. And Allah wants you to use your intellect and ask questions."

"O believers! Do not ask about any matter which, if made clear to you,
may disturb you. But if you inquire about what is being revealed in the Quran,
it will be made clear to you. Allah has forgiven what was done in the past.
And Allah is All-Forgiving, Most Forbearing." (5:101)

Badr was not sure where to begin, what to tell him and how much. It might be best to be evasive and keep it vague until he knew more about these jinns. He was still pinching himself to check if this was a dream.

"I ... I want to help someone," said Badr while eyeing Abdulaziz for guidance.

"We thought you are the one in need of help?"

"Yes ... yes, I am. But this someone is more important," Badr said, feeling a sudden surge of affection as he thought about Dana.

"More important than you? Explain please!" Aabid said.

"She is someone I love," Badr replied, feeling more confident than he had since landing on the Red Island.

"Love? What an interesting concept. I don't fully understand it from a human perspective. I hear it is the most beautiful feeling but can also be an agonising obsession. The more you try to understand it, the less you will understand."

"What do you mean?" Badr asked.

"There is no single way to describe or experience love. Each person will tell you a different story of a different type of love or loves in their lives and the moments that symbolise them."

"But there must be a way to define what love is," Badr said.

"Why do you need to define it when you can just feel it?"

Badr looked dissatisfied with his answer, so Aabid continued, "Love is the devotion Prophet Ibrahim (AS) exhibited as he journeyed to Mount Arafat and blindfolded himself to slaughter his son, Prophet Ismail (AS), as instructed by Allah through a series of dreams. It's the love Allah had for Prophet Ibrahim, when He intervened and substituted a ram for the sacrifice, sparing Prophet Ismail."

"It's what motivated Prophet Ibrahim's wife, Hajar, to run in the desert, between the hills of Safa and Marwa, seven times, searching for water for her thirsty son, which led to the opening of a well in Makkah, Bi'ru Zamzam."

"It's what Maryam bint Imran felt as a virgin, single mother, ready to face all trials and challenges that came with giving birth to Prophet Isa (AS)."

Badr nodded, encouraging him to continue.

"I can tell you more about divine love. Allah is *Al-Wadud* (the Loving One). His love can also be seen in His kindness as He is also *Al-Ra-uuf* (The Kind); in His protection as He is *Al-Wali* (The Protecting Friend), in His gentleness as He is *Al-Lateef* (The Gentle), in His forgiveness as He is *Al-Ghafur* (The Forgiving) and in many of His other attributes."

"But can you love another as much as you love Allah?" Badr asked.

> *'Yet there are men who take (for worship) others besides Allah,*
> *as equal (with Allah): They love them as they should love Allah.*
> *But those of Faith are overflowing in their love for Allah.*
> *If only the unrighteous could see, behold, they would see the penalty:*
> *that to Allah belongs all power, and Allah will*
> *strongly enforce the penalty.' (2:165)*

"Does this mean you cannot truly love other people?"

"No. In fact, the Prophet said, 'You will not enter Paradise until you believe, and you will not believe until you love one another.' But only Allah's love can bring you real peace and happiness."

"But what about the love between a man and a woman?"

Aabid recited:

> *"O humanity! Be mindful of your Lord Who created you from a single soul,*
> *and from it He created its mate, and through both He spread*
> *countless men and women." (4:1)*

"But what if you love someone who is different from you?" Badr asked.

"Different?" Aabid asked, looking confused.

"It's forbidden for humans and jinns to fall in love," the dwarfish, bespectacled jinn, Malik, interjected.

"Really?"

"Yes."

"Okay, but what if you're different in other ways."

"You just heard me speak about our Prophet (PBUH) and his first wife Khadija, known to us as *'Umm al mu'minin'* or 'Mother of Believers.' As we all know, she was fifteen years older than our Prophet, had been widowed twice before she married him, had children from her previous marriages, and had a higher social status and more wealth than him. She ran a successful business and employed him prior to the marriage," Malik said.

"Yes, yes, I know all this. It's remarkable, though sadly much less acceptable in the society we live in today. But what if two people have different beliefs?" Badr asked, wishing he could bear it all, but it seemed too soon, too risky.

Malik recited:

> *"This day are (all) things good and pure made lawful unto you. The food of the People of the Book is lawful unto you and yours is lawful unto them. (Lawful unto you in marriage) are (not only) chaste women who are believers but chaste women among the People of the Book revealed before your time when ye give them their due dowers and desire chastity, not lewdness, nor secret intrigues." (5:5)*

"And what if love disappears between two people?" asked Badr, thinking of Humaid and Najla.

"Have you read the story of Barīrah and Mughīth in *Sahih al-Bukhari*?" Malik asked.

"I am not sure," Badr replied.

"Barīrah wanted to separate from Mughīth, even though her husband loved her deeply," Malik said. "The Prophet (PBUH) asked Barīrah, 'Will you take him back? For he is the father of your child?' So Barīrah asked, 'Are you commanding me to do so, O Messenger of Allah?' And he replied, 'I am merely interceding on his behalf,' to which she said, 'I have no need of him.'"

"So, you see, love is a matter of the heart and cannot be forced. If you don't love someone, you will not be able to do justice to the relationship," Malik added.

"And how do you know if a relationship is good for you?" Badr asked.

"Your relationships should bring you closer to Allah," Malik said. "It should encourage you to do good deeds for the sake of spiritual recompense."

Badr nodded as a jinni moved closer to them. She seemed interested in their conversation. Aabid, the leader, nodded at her, as if giving her permission to join them. She had a sweet face that seemed to have forgotten how to smile.

"Asiya will tell you how she has paid the price of ignoring divine love. A bad jinn placed her under a spell," Aabid said.

Badr looked at Asiya's downcast eyes, the dark circles beneath them. She placed her right hand on top of her left one, lowered her gaze, and started speaking in a soft voice. "I was young, but as soon as I met him, I knew he was from amongst the bad jinns, the Zār."

"What did he do?" Badr asked, trying to be gentle. She seemed very fragile, like she'd disperse into the air if he blew on her.

"He committed many sins," she said. "He was like the merciless, tyrannical *Firaun*, the ruler of ancient Egypt during Prophet Musa's (A.S.) time. He would say, 'Treat me like a god and don't question my actions.'"

"He wanted me to earn his love through complete obedience. He would fly into a murderous rage if I disobeyed, hitting, starving, and humiliating me. My life felt like a quicksand. I wondered if taking my life would be a faster way to end the pain I was feeling."

She was about to cry so Badr tried to divert her. "Asiya ... how did you escape?"

She took a deep breath, as if it was getting hard for her to continue the conversation.

"One day, I was going through excruciating pain," she said. "And I tried to end my life, but a glimmer of hope or faith—faith that this wasn't it and that life could be different—stopped me. I remembered how the Qur'an says:

'Nor kill (or destroy) yourselves: for verily
Allah hath been to you Most Merciful.'" (4:29)

"I started praying to Allah to release me from my suffering:

'O my Lord! Build for me in nearness to
Thee a mansion in the Garden and save me from
Pharaoh and his doings and save me from
those that do wrong.'" (66:11)

"And then?"

"Then, by the grace of Allah, I met some good jinns and jinnis. I found love unexpectedly in the form of their friendship. We would sit together in circles, my friends and I, and they asked me to speak my truth."

"I began sharing my story. A few moments of courage and the love of my friends changed my life. They were the voice of God. They showed me the reality of my tormentor and reminded me of divine love, which is unlimited, pure, and perfect."

"Then what happened?"

"When I reconnected with the divine, I felt the power of the spell break. I recognised that what was keeping me captive was not love, but dark magic."

"And what do you think love is?" Badr asked.

"I don't know what love is. I know what it is not. Anything that takes you away from Allah, from doing good deeds, is not love."

Badr was quiet as he reflected on this.

"I feel that your experience of love has been quite different from mine," she said, her mood suddenly lighter, as if telling her story again had freed her once more from the burdens of her past.

"I don't know about that," Badr said, feeling awkward as all eyes were on him again. "It also feels like a spell is keeping me captive, but I don't want to break out of it ... I don't want to forget the most enchanting and incredible years of my life."

The meeting ended abruptly as it was time for the jinns to depart and the gate to close. Although Badr had not managed to get to his main question, he felt almost hopeful. There seemed to be a purpose behind the twists and turns of fate, a reason why the Red Island had drawn him in. It was here that he could find a way to cure Dana. An unseen force tugged at his gut, whispering that something momentous was about to unfold.

CHAPTER 24

* ———————— *

*"Now let man but think from
what he is created!"*

(86:5)

As he stood at the entrance of a dark and narrow corridor, a wave of crimson washed over Badr's vision.

His hands and feet tightly bound, with snakeskin cords biting into his wrists and ankles, all he could do was fix his gaze on the corridor ahead, which faded into a swirling vortex of smoke, the red tinge dissolving into a pale grey emptiness ahead.

An unsettling feeling gnawed at him; his intuition picking up on a silent cry from a distressed loved one. But he was chained, powerless to reach them and intervene.

He looked ahead, unable to blink, as the smoke swirls morphed into a dense, charcoal cloud, dominating his line of vision.

Raw anxiety clawed at his insides as Badr watched the cloud form the silhouette of a towering woman, her flowing black *abaya* swallowing her form. A veil obscured most of her face, except for her mouth, which was open, a scream trying to escape her lips.

"Khash yah la, maq tif mar," a voice, like the hiss of a serpent, slithered into his ears.

Badr could not understand the words even though they sounded Arabic. His mind strained to decipher her cryptic chant.

"Sif har bas daf tah zah rah qab nis jah dal fik lam waj shin qal mar asa dah zar qib bak ram tah," the woman chanted, her voice rising in pitch until it scraped against his sanity, like a relentless fire alarm echoing through a confined space.

Badr desperately wanted to cover his ears, but his hands could not break free. He listened until he couldn't listen anymore. His eardrums exploded.

As he awoke with a jolt, Badr's eyes locked onto ants traversing the mud-brick ceiling. It was afternoon and another random nap had done him more harm than good. It wasn't the first time he'd had this vivid nightmare. But today it had assaulted his senses.

Drenched in sweat, he put his hand on his palpitating heart. Unable to find solace in his surroundings, he decided to venture to the human side of the island.

There, amidst the bustle of daily life, he sat down to eat, hoping to find some respite in proximity to other humans. But they offered no comfort. He overheard snippets of conversations about a war in Afghanistan and Samer.

"He is a friend's cousin. Very polite. I don't believe he's a terrorist," a man whispered.

"I heard someone stole his passport," another said. "I think he was one of the victims."

Badr listened as he continued to eat a *shawarma* quietly in the corner. He knew Samer was guilty, no matter how unbelievable it seemed to others. The man's words still echoed in his memory. He had said he was 'flying for Allah.' He had clearly pledged his life to misguided martyrdom.

Controlling his impulse to jump into the conversation, Badr devoured his meal and escaped to an internet café nearby, his only lifeline to home.

He had devised a way to send messages to his family anonymously. Using a new email address, he had enlisted his friend Sultan as a covert messenger since Rashid had been maintaining radio silence.

Sultan had written back, reassuring Badr of his family's wellbeing. But a nagging suspicion lingered in Badr's mind. Something felt amiss. Sultan appeared online on messenger and started to chat right away.

"Is there anything else I should know?" Badr asked, after exchanging greetings.

"Well, I didn't want to trouble you with it," Sultan wrote.

"What is it? Please tell me," Badr wrote back, alarm bells going off in his mind. Did it have something to do with Dana?

"Rashid has disappeared," Sultan wrote.

"Rashid? Why? What happened?" Badr asked, shocked. He had met Rashid the same day he had to make a run for the Red Island.

"Was he experiencing withdrawal symptoms?" Badr typed, recalling how Rashid had said he'd stopped using altogether.

"I don't know. He went away to Rub' al Khali," Sultan wrote. "To meditate, apparently."

"The Empty Quarter?" Badr vaguely remembered Rashid mentioning it, but the meditation part didn't sound right. Rashid was always making fun of western yogis who went to Indian ashrams to turn over a new leaf and lost their fashion sense to 'freakish, colourful clothes and beady jewellery.' He'd say the attire had some sort of placebo effort, hoodwinking people into believing they had achieved nirvana.

"He probably used that as an excuse to go away and not tell his family anything. They don't seem to care that much anyway," Badr said.

"Perhaps," Sultan said seriously. "We don't really know what happened, Badr. But no one has been able to get in touch with him since he left."

Flashbacks flooded Badr's mind as he headed back to the grocery store in Alhumriya. Memories surfaced of countless college nights he'd spent at the police station, tirelessly leveraging his connections to pull Rashid out of his self-inflicted chaos.

Those experiences had etched a truth into Badr's soul: it was possible for a person to not like someone or their behaviour, but still love them like a brother.

He felt a strong urge to call Rashid, but was nervous about switching on his mobile phone, worried the CID might be trying to trace his location, even though he'd heard it was a long-winded process.

He walked towards the landline phone at the grocery store, contemplating his next move. Before he could make up his mind, a shrill ring pierced the air. He was startled, as was the store owner behind the counter.

"Hello, you want to give grocery order?" the store owner answered. After a few quiet seconds, he handed the receiver to Badr, looking even more confused.

"It's for you."

"Me?" Badr wondered if the CID had tracked him through the internet café, even though he had been so careful.

"Hello?" he answered, faking a British accent.

There was silence at the other end except for an occasional, distant sound of someone breathing heavily.

"Rashid?" Badr whispered, his mind flashing with memories of their trips to Indian restaurants, the tasty paratha sandwiches and the appropriately brown, overly sweet *karak* tea they used to order.

"... *ah, gh...,* " said a woman, jerking him back to the present. It was the same hypnotic, hair-raising voice from his nightmares.

Hissing sounds followed, making his skin crawl, as they metamorphosed into words, incoherent and disturbing.

"Who ... is ... this?" Badr asked, a graphic image of bleeding vocal cords appearing in his mind.

"... a woman to gather my pieces like shards of broken crystal," the feminine voice recited in Arabic. Loud and clear.

Rashid was a fan of Syrian poet Nizar Qabbani, but Badr knew this couldn't be him. He would never sound like that, even if he was playing a prank or had gone insane.

Badr's throat dried up as he felt her getting closer, even though they were only connected by phone. Afraid that she would somehow devour him, he hung up, breathing rapidly. The store owner was nowhere to be seen.

The phone rang again, and he instinctively moved away, but the relentless ringing persisted. Trembling, Badr weighed his options before ultimately deciding to leave. As he hurried toward Abdulaziz's house, the insistent ringing faded into the distance, replaced by a barrage of questions flooding his mind.

"Who is this woman? What did her strange words mean? What language was she speaking in? Did I have a nightmare earlier or was that real, too?"

It all seemed to have an undeniable connection to Rashid and Badr couldn't stay put. He nervously tapped his fingers on the cold floor, the only sound breaking the incessant hum of insects. With his thoughts entangled, his frustration grew. After a futile attempt to etch a plan, a single, stark truth slowly settled in his gut: finding Rashid was the only way forward. And there was only one way he could find Rashid.

CHAPTER 25

*"Your Lord has proclaimed, 'Call upon Me,
I will respond to you.'"*

(40:60)

Abdulaziz had received an invitation for Badr from the *Ulema*, the group of jinns that included scientists, doctors, architects, engineers, psychologists, writers, poets, and other intellectuals.

"They heard of your interesting rendezvous with the *Mashaikh* and want to see you to gain a better understanding of humans," Abdulaziz said.

"But you're still human, right?" Badr asked, pretending to be scared.

"I think they now see me as one of them," Abdulaziz said. "After al, l I know not much of what is happening in the outside world except for the gossip I overhear on the other side of the island.

"I would be happy to be the subject of their research," Badr said.

That evening he made his way through the dusty streets to an abandoned school building, feeling bolder than he had prior to meeting the *Mashaikh.*

Following Abdulaziz's instructions, he walked up a large flight of stairs towards the library on the upper floor.

On the wall next to the library's door was handwritten the first revelation of the Quran, encouraging people to learn:

"Proclaim! (or read!) in the name of thy Lord and
Cherisher Who created
Created man out of a (mere) clot of congealed blood:
Proclaim! And thy Lord is Most Bountiful
He Who taught (the use of) the Pen
Taught man that which he knew not." (96:1-5)

As Badr finished reading the verses, the wooden sliding door panels opened crosswise, revealing a short old jinn, with glasses sitting crooked on his nose.

"Badr, welcome to *Majlis-e-Ulema.* We've been waiting for you," he said, his voice much bigger than him.

"Thank you," said Badr, following him inside. The library was much more spacious than he had anticipated. Wooden bookshelves with thousands of books were lining the walls and kissing the ceiling. In the middle of the room, there was a very large copy of the Qur'an placed on a grand, carved wooden *rehal*, with verses written in golden ink.

As Badr moved forward, awestruck, a group of jinns and jinnis sat on large floor cushions behind a long, low-rise wooden table. Lamps shaped like ancient Arabic scrolls lined the centre of the table, illuminating their faces. Badr could only make out their facial features once he was close to their gathering.

He spotted Abdulaziz, perched against a cushion made of camel fur, and took a seat next to him. Some of his hosts were eyeing him with tight smiles and hushed conversations. They reminded Badr of the snooty people with double PhDs and bankers with fat wallets that he met socially at clubs like Sharjah Wanderers and Costain.

A midget-jinn, Qazam, was sitting nearby and seemed ready to take notes on his computer. Badr was impressed by how they had managed to get a machine in there. He wondered if they had internet as well.

Badr tried to make eye contact with Qazam, hoping to ask him about the internet, but the midget-jinn looked away.

"He's introverted, but an expert scribe and will be making notes for research purposes as the jinns don't often have humans in their midst, socialising with them like this," Abdulaziz whispered.

Badr looked around at the jinns and jinnis immersed in reading and one-on-one discussions. Akil, the jinn who had welcomed him, appeared to be friendlier than the rest. He was the leader of the *Ulema.*

"I ... I have a question, if you don't mind," Badr asked, wanting to strike up a conversation with him.

"Yes, please, feel free to ask," Akil said.

"What can you tell me about love?" Badr asked. This strategy had worked well with the *Mashaikh.* It had made Badr realise that jinns, much like humans, enjoyed talking about love.

Akil beamed at Badr, looking pleased with the question.

"Why do you want to know?" he asked.

"I am in love with someone ... but ... certain events have made me doubt ... its future," Badr said, feeling awkward.

Akil nodded, and to Badr's relief, didn't press for more details.

"The question really is, my dear, whether two people can experience or define love in the same way? But we, the *Ulema*, believe all such questions and topics are worth exploring," Akil said.

Then, addressing the group, he said, "Our human friend here is questioning love."

Badr turned pink with self-consciousness as Akil told the group, "You may take turns and share your thoughts."

The jinn sitting at the head of the table, on Badr's right, introduced himself. "Hi, I am Aalim, I'm a scientist."

"Wow. So, what does science say about love?" Badr asked. He was always fascinated with science and using it as a tool to unravel the mechanics of everything.

"Love is certain regions of your brain lighting up," Aalim said. "When you're attracted to someone, your brain releases high levels of dopamine and norepinephrine, the chemicals that make you giddy and euphoric, and the ones that can also make you lose your sleep or appetite."

"Oh." Badr could completely relate to the euphoria and the sleeplessness. The frequent highs and lows, the mood swings, all of it.

"Love is a disease. It makes you lovesick," interjected Tabiba, a stern-looking doctor-jinni. "It can raise cortisol levels."

"Don't I know that? My stress levels have been shooting up ever since I met Dana. All the tossing and turning, worrying, and waiting, guarding against anyone and anything that could split us up. Someone should have warned me before I fell in love, not that a warning would have prevented it," Badr thought, feeling amused.

"The main control centre of love in the brain is the hypothalamus," said Al'aesab, a neuroscientist. "It collects the various stimuli felt by the body, such as sounds, smells, and touches, and produces oxytocin, the love hormone, and creates the physical response to emotions linked with those stimuli."

"And to add to that, love is in the details," the architect–jinn, Bani said. "It's about visual pleasure as well as functionality, what people refer to as compatibility. It gives you the superpower of admitting that you're wrong in a situation. Romantic love is finding someone you want to build a home with."

Badr envisioned the quaint, artistic villa he had envisioned designing with Dana.

"Love is a gravitational force pulling you towards someone," Muhandis, the engineer-jinn said.

"So, you can't help it?" Badr asked. "Even if circumstances are not favourable?"

"Well, it survives only when it's structured, when problems are fixed with logic and rationality," Muhandis replied.

Muhasib, an accountant, snorted and said dryly, "Love, like everything else, is a transaction. Give and take. Nothing is free in this world, not even love."

Badr wondered if that was true and asked, "Can love ever be unconditional as people say it should be?"

"Well, there is another way to look at it," Tajir, an entrepreneur-jinn said. "The more you invest, whether it is time, emotions or money, the more the love grows."

"But things don't always add up," Abdul Haseib, the mathematician, asserted.

"What do you mean?" Badr asked, intrigued and overwhelmed by this bombardment of definitions and theories on love.

"It means there is no fixed deal. Things can go up and down, change any day," Tajir explained.

Badr thought of Dana's secrets. He didn't like the direction this conversation was taking now. He was a realist, but also an optimist.

"Love is a form of the sacred, which appears in various social conditions, and can blossom or fade depending on many factors," Akil said encouragingly.

Lughawi, the linguist, read from a scroll. "In Arabic language, there are eight stages of love. *Al Hawa* (interest), *Al-Sabwah* (desire), *Al-'Alaqah* (attachment), *Al-Kalaf* (infatuation), *Al-'Ishq* (all-consuming love), *Al-Najwa* (heartache), *Al-Wodd* (pure love and friendship), and *Alhuyam* (insanity or complete freedom in loving another)."

"And can these overlap with one another?" Badr asked.

"Of course," he said. "There are also many ways to express love in Arabic. For example, in the Levant, you will find many say *'to'borny,'* which means that you want your beloved to outlive you. But it's used more as a jest, a casual way of talking about love, rather than a serious declaration."

"Oh." Badr shrugged. He had no time for casual and turned to the biologist, Alimu al'ahya'i, who was next in line.

"Romantic love, deep attachments, sex drive and reproduction are all systems in the brain, which can operate in any combination," he said seriously, seeming dismissive of all the other definitions. "It's all about reproduction, survival, and the continuity of a species."

"This overinflated concept of love is an imaginary one ... look at all the other creatures. Is it love that they share with one another?" he questioned forcefully.

"It ... it should be love. What else?" Badr replied, his mind juggling the question.

"I am afraid that is not the case," Aalim interrupted. "There are other feelings that come to play across in most creatures. Their instincts, feelings of peace and hope. A certain mix of what we call 'love.'"

"Can you elaborate?" Badr asked.

"In order for creatures to live and survive, they need to be hopeful of the prospect of a future. They need to feel the day is worth living. And living in peace and not under threat is crucial to go on with daily activities like mating."

He then asked Badr, "Have you noticed how once you fell in love, you felt very hopeful about future prospects, but not so peaceful due to the fear of it not being real or not achievable?"

"Yes. This how I feel now!" Badr said, sounding depressed.

"Well. You need to have a balance of both. Hope and peace to keep you alive, Badr," he concluded.

Badr thought about his relationship with Dana, how nerve-racking it had been at times. But he realised he had savoured every bit of loving her and being loved by her until all the secrets came up and she departed to New York without even a proper goodbye. But this wasn't the time to drift there. This was the right time to solicit support, the main reason Badr had wanted to meet the *Ulema*.

CHAPTER 26

*"His Seat encompasses the heavens
and the earth, and the preservation of
both does not tire Him."*

(2:255)

As silence settled upon the room, Badr cleared his throat, the sound echoing through the library like the rasp of a desert wind.

"There's something urgent i want to talk about," he began, his voice low.

Akil, his beard flecked with silver, met Badr's gaze with an ageless wisdom.

"Speak freely," he said.

Despite Akil's comforting presence, a tremor ran through Badr. He felt intimidated, although he knew he could scoop Akil up with one hand.

"It's about my friend Rashid," he said. "He dabbled in recreational drugs, but when I last saw him, he had left it all. But recently, more darkness has crept into my dreams. I see visions of a woman. I am not sure if she is human. But I dismissed it as a nightmare ... until today."

"What made you change your mind?" Akil asked.

"I spoke to a friend who said Rashid had disappeared," Badr replied, a note of urgency creeping into his voice. "Then, I got a call. It was the same woman, her voice slithering through the receiver, whispering Rashid's favourite poem in a way that chilled me to the bone!"

Badr looked at Akil and other members of *Ulema*, his eyes pleading for their empathy.

"What did you do then?" Akil asked.

"To be honest ... I chickened out," Badr blurted, feeling embarrassed. "I just hung up."

"You get scared easily?" Akil asked, looking dead serious. Badr was annoyed.

"How can he ask me that? Here I am, socialising with you fiery beings, aren't I?" he thought.

"No ... that's not the point," he replied in a clipped tone. "I believe ... I don't know ... he might be ... possessed maybe?"

Since discovering Dana's secret, Badr had spent hours devouring books and articles on jinn possession and black magic. He could consider this as a plausible explanation for the eerie events of the day.

"Was he dwelling in an isolated spot?" Akil asked.

"I was told he went off into the desert by himself ... I think to Rub' al Khali, the Empty Quarter."

"Is he spiritual?"

"No, no, quite the opposite," Badr said, chuckling slightly. "More of a … trying-to-turn-over-a-new-leaf kind of thing."

"Was he going through a period of darkness and disengagement from his faith?" Akil asked.

Badr knew Rashid wasn't particularly religious or spiritual, but he had never thought of him as depressed. They had mostly had good times together. An image of him, Rashid and Sultan doing handstands flashed through his mind.

"I don't think so," Badr said. "Why do you ask?"

"Sometimes jinns and jinnis target people who have lost their way. They are easier to possess, especially if they are spiritually dead."

Badr didn't like the judgement in his tone, but did not want to argue.

"He did sometimes speak about feeling alone when he was a child. His parents weren't around a lot and a Filipino nanny looked after him. But she was also sent away when he turned nine or ten. His older brother lived abroad while he was growing up, so he felt like an only child," Badr said. "But he lives like a king."

"Abu al-Ala al-Ma'arri said that kings are sad creatures," said a cute jinni, Ani, who wore owl-like glasses. Badr smiled at her, and she blushed.

"Are you very close to this friend?" Akil asked.

"Yes, yes. We've known each other since childhood. We're best friends. No, more like brothers."

This was the first time Badr had thought so deeply about Rashid. It struck him as odd how someone so close to him was still a bit of a mystery. They had built a bond on the surface pleasures of lifelong shared experiences, but the tapestry of Rashid's life had remained unseen.

"So, can you help me find out what's happened to him?" Badr asked, feeling he had let Rashid down somehow, always trying to fix him without asking why he needed to be fixed in the first place.

"Well, we could try," Akil said. "Since it is for a good cause. But where was Rashid last seen?"

"Not sure, but he said he was going to the Empty Quarter, to the red sand dunes," Badr replied.

"A desolate place," Akil mused.

"Can you send someone there to look for him?" Badr ventured cautiously.

"Yes ... you!" Akil declared.

"But I can't leave Al Jazirah right now!" Badr protested.

"Why not?"

Before Badr could respond, Abdulaziz cut in. "Perhaps we should confirm Rashid's presence first. It's the second largest desert in the world ... Badr cannot possibly find him there on his own. He wouldn't stand a chance."

Akil considered this, then nodded in agreement. He conferred with the other jinns for a while before selecting the youngest and strongest jinns, Hakim and Talib, to accompany Badr on his mission.

"Describe your friend," they requested.

"Describe him?" Badr asked. "Well, he has typical Arab features ... he's about five-foot-nine, lean. He has long, black hair, which he often wears in a short ponytail. Usually, clean shaven. Sometimes he has stubble because he said some women like it. A local who doesn't always wear *kandura*. Tries to speak English with an American accent. Smokes a lot and then chews gum."

"And what is his mother's name?"

"His mother's name?" Badr was bewildered.

"Yes, we can use it to trace humans."

"I believe it's ... it's Kalthoom al-Mansouri," Badr said, surprised he remembered it given how infrequently Rashid talked about her.

"If you find him, bring him here, to Al Jazirah Al Hamra," Akil instructed.

"What if he is possessed? Why do you think some jinns possess humans?" Badr asked.

"It depends. If you intentionally or unintentionally hurt them. Or they may be sent by other humans practising black magic. Or, in a few rare instances, if they fall in love with you."

It seemed hard to determine the cause of Rashid's plight, if he was, in fact, possessed. He had always been popular with women, but as far as Badr knew, things had never gotten serious.

"Has he managed to sweep some wicked jinni off her feet, only to leave her hanging?" Badr wondered.

"Badr?" Abdulaziz said in his usual reprimanding tone.

"Yes?" Badr asked.

"It's time to leave."

CHAPTER 27

"Victory comes only from Allah."

(8:10)

Hakim and Talib were all geared up for the mission and had even repaired Badr's broken car window. Badr jumped into the driver's seat, placing his backpack on the passenger seat.

He surveyed Hakim and Talib, wondering if they would make the journey easier by summoning a magic carpet. But to his annoyance, they were sitting in the back seat, behaving like teenage boys. Both were smitten with the same jinni, and tangled in an intense debate on who would conquer her heart.

"My soul burns for her, brighter than a flame!" Hakim declared.

Badr rolled his eyes at their adolescent bickering, but the gesture was lost on the two impassioned jinns.

Talib, the more eloquent of the two, countered Hakim by quoting the dreamer-poet Ibn Arabi:

> *"My heart can take on any form:*
> *A meadow for gazelle,*
> *A cloister for monks,*
> *For the idols, sacred ground,*
> *Ka'ba for the circling pilgrim,*
> *The tables of the Torah,*
> *The scrolls of the Qur'an.*
> *My creed is Love; Wherever its caravan turns along the way,*
> *That is my belief, my faith."*

Badr sighed softly, resigning to the prospect of a long, arduous journey. Some three hours later, Hakim observed how the familiar cityscape, the buildings, the power wires, and the streets had all but disappeared. In front of them was a landscape that seemed untouched by humans, straight out of a science fiction movie.

Badr had visited Rub' al Khali before, but only during winter months and in the company of 4-by-4 enthusiasts, not with two emotionally immature jinns. He dodged the *sabkhas,* the gigantic dunes threatening his Nissan Patrol, realising the rest of the journey needed to be made on foot.

After parking his car, they rested on gravel plains surrounded by towering sand dunes. Badr felt afraid of disturbing the large, hostile red sands. He was also scared of finding Rashid there. He had never seen his friend break down or cry or even be sick, except when he had measles in the fourth grade or suffered injuries while boxing.

Soon, they resumed their journey, Badr's feet sinking in the sand and stumbling on what felt like bones, possibly of animals or humans who had gotten lost way in the unforgiving desert. It was still quite hot, so there were no tourists around.

Badr could see some Bedouins, the desert nomads, riding camels in the distance. He waved to them.

"Who are they?" Talib asked.

"The *Bedu,* desert dwellers," Badr said. "I admire them. They've been around for thousands of years, much before any western or other explorers came to the Empty Quarter. I think they might be able to help us."

"How?" Hakim asked, snorting. He seemed to look down on humans.

"They survive by eating dates and bread, hunting, riding around on camels and drinking water from waterholes," Badr explained. "They're known for their resilience, living a life that is difficult every day."

"Every rooster crows on its own dunghill," Hakim said.

Irritated by Hakim's condescension, Badr fell silent and observed as three Bedouins—two older men and one who appeared to be his age—approached. They were wearing their typical, loose-fitted white tunics and head cloths, their animal skin-shoes protecting them from the hot desert sand.

They had two Salukis, the indigenous breed of dogs known for their speed, intelligence, and loyalty. They had been the guards and favourite hunting companions of the desert people for thousands of years and Rub' al Khali was known to be a special breeding and hunting ground for them.

The *Bedu* could not see Hakim and Talib, but the Salukis barked, sensing their presence. Badr moved forward and explained to the *Bedu* how he was looking for a friend who had lost his way in the desert. They didn't show much emotion but agreed to help Badr locate Rashid in this fearsome, unpredictable environment. Badr climbed atop the camel of the younger guy. His name was Saleh. He held on tightly as Saleh raised the camel abruptly to an upright position.

Soon they were crossing dune after dune, up then down. Badr felt queasy, gazing at the large sandbox they had immersed themselves in. He didn't know if he was experiencing motion sickness or stress.

"It feels like I am going from one *ma'ashara* to another, searching for my friend's body, and at the same time afraid I will die of heat and isolation, or be killed by warring tribes, if they still exist," Badr told Saleh, who just nodded.

After about thirty minutes of riding with nothing but sand in sight, came upon a water tanker. Lying near it was a black Sony Walkman and a pair of Ray Bans.

"These are Rashid's," Badr exclaimed, pointing at them.

"That means he is here somewhere," Talib whispered, patting his back.

"It's nearly buried in dust. Must have been here for some time. I just hope he's alive," Badr said, getting worked up.

"Don't give up hope," the old *Bedu* next to him said in a surprisingly comforting voice, reminding Badr of *Baba*, his life, family, bed. Dana. Driving around with the windows rolled down during winter, singing along with the radio.

Holding tears back, Badr picked up Rashid's stuff. They continued to ride around the desert looking for Rashid until the evening arrived. The *Bedu* invited Badr to their tent, and he agreed.

"The tent's made from black goat hair that keeps the tent cool during the day and warm during the night, although it's open from the sides," Saleh said while Badr helped him light a campfire. "It's the authentic version, not the rigged stretch tents that many Bedouins use nowadays. The fibres can even block out water when it rains."

They said their *isha* prayers under a million stars, then had *regag* bread with cheese, honey, and eggs for dinner. They also drank laban, made by churning milk in a bag made of animal skin.

"Clearly these people are not the hungry, thirsty Bedouins that British explorer Wilfred Thesiger talked about," Badr thought.

He lay down, his back sore after the long camel ride, admiring the moonlit dunes through a gap in the tent. The night was melancholic, yet peaceful.

Saleh lay down next to him. Badr was in awe of his human GPS skills that had helped them navigate the desert, although they still hadn't found Rashid.

Staring at the tent's ceiling, Saleh said, "The evil eye can bring a man to his grave and a camel to the cooking pot."

"What?" Badr asked, surprised.

"It's a common saying among the Bedouins. Some people ascribe it to Prophet Mohammad (PBUH). I just wanted to warn you ... don't think about going for a walk during the night, even if you can't sleep. Evil spirits and jinns are usually prowling around."

Badr raised his head a little to look at Talib, who was far away, but still directly in his line of vision. He winked at Badr conspiratorially. Badr wondered how his *Bedu* friends would react if they knew they were sleeping with the jinns, albeit innocent ones.

"Have you seen anything? Like an evil spirit or a jinn?" Badr asked Saleh.

"Yes. Last winter, on a cloudless night, I saw a blaze break out in the middle of sand and rock."

"Oh. Can't that happen in the desert?"

"It can, under the scorching heat, but not at night. Especially not during winter. There was an awful cackling echo within the green flames."

"Green?"

"Yeah, they were dancing diagonally before going out as abruptly as they had appeared, and that's not all. I saw a pale woman in rags."

"A woman?"

"Yes, she was standing on top of a tree just before the blaze."

"What did you do?"

"Luckily, she vanished when the blaze appeared," he said, shuddering.

Badr wondered if it could be the same woman who had called him. He did not want the night to end on this unpleasant story and to dream of women with long arms hanging from the branches of old trees. He asked, "What do you think about love, Saleh?"

Saleh looked perplexed.

"Maybe I need to stop throwing this question at people and jinns," Badr thought.

Saleh blinked, dispelling the emotion that had briefly appeared in his eyes.

"There's a story there," Badr realised. "I guess everyone has a story. Some tale of love, loss, hurt or betrayal."

"Why do you want to know?" Saleh asked.

"Think of me as a scientist researching on love."

"Aren't you a pilot?" Talib interrupted.

"Yeah, Abdulaziz told us," Hakim added in an accusatory tone.

Badr ignored them completely and went on, "So, tell me, Saleh, what do the Bedouins believe about love?"

"We write incredible poetry. A lot of it is about love."

"From the desert I come to thee,
On a stallion shod with fire;
And the winds are left behind
In the speed of my desire.
Under thy window I stand,
And the midnight hears my cry:
I love thee, I love but thee!
With a love that shall not die
Till the sun grows cold,
And the stars are old,
And the leaves of the Judgment Book unfold!"

"That's beautiful," Badr said.

"Yes, it is a Bedouin love song, but ..."

"But what?"

"I believe the poor have no right to love. Especially if their beloved is from a rich tribe."

"So, her parents married her off to someone rich?" Badr asked. It was a typical tragedy of their culture.

"No. It was simpler."

"How so?"

 She said love and marriage are two different things."

"And then?"

"Then she married someone rich."

Badr didn't want to appear insensitive by asking more questions, and Saleh had already turned away from him, closing his eyes.

The next morning, they said their *fajr* prayers and watched an incredible sun rising above the gold and red sands.

Saleh seemed to be in high spirits and was eager to teach Badr how to make traditional Bedouin coffee.

It was Badr's first time making any kind of coffee. He knew he would have probably learnt to do all kinds of household stuff had he moved to the US alone, without the family, the house help, and the cooks taking care of everything.

"Put these coffee beans in the pan and roast them over the fire. Meanwhile, I'll boil water in this pot," Saleh said.

Badr complied. This was a skill he could use to make life in Al Jazirah more interesting.

"Grind the roasted beans with *mehbash*, please. I will grind these cardamom pods," his mentor instructed.

They put the coffee and cardamom together in a pot and Saleh poured boiling water over them. The coffee was ready!

Badr felt a sense of accomplishment after a very long time as he drank the coffee from a small cup with no handles. Its intense aroma and taste drove away all the sleep and mental fog his brain had been harbouring. He was ready to resume their journey with much more optimism than the previous day, although Badr knew his impulsive friend could be anywhere. He could have even crossed the border to live it up in Oman.

They mounted the camel and rode in the same continuous motion as the previous day. However, Hakim and Talib seemed restless. They were zooming around, looking for Rashid at supersonic speed. Soon, they disappeared, and Badr started to feel agitated again. There was not a single person or building in sight. Just the desert and its overpowering silence.

Saleh glanced at Badr with understanding.

"I am probably not the first visitor to have this reaction to the solitude and magnificence of this sea of sand," Badr said, and Saleh nodded.

Since they were too far from any mosque and there was no water available for *wudu*, they stopped in the middle of the dunes to perform *tayammum*, cleansing their hands and faces with grains of sand. Then, they said their *juma'a* prayers, with one of the older *Bedus* leading them.

Badr was in *sujood* and praying fervently for Rashid's welfare, when he heard voices, distant and echoing.

"We found Rashid, we found him!"

Badr completed the *rakat* and looked up. Hakim and Talib were gliding towards him. But Rashid was not with them.

"Where is he? Is he okay?" Badr asked, standing up.

"We don't know," Hakim said.

"Is he ... dead?" Badr asked, dreading the answer.

"No, he is breathing," Talib replied.

"But where is he?" Badr asked, relieved to know that Rashid was alive.

"He's on Tel Moreeb," Talib said.

"What's that?"

Saleh had completed his prayers and was walking towards Badr, looking puzzled.

"What's what?" he asked.

"Tel Moreeb?" Badr asked, remembering that Saleh could not see or hear his jinn companions.

"The Terrifying Mountain, near Liwa Oasis? It's the world's tallest sand dune."

"Tallest?"

"Yes, around sixteen hundred metres long and three hundred

"That's where Rashid is."

"Sorry, what?"

"Yes, I ... I sensed that he's around there."

"*Okhoy*, that's nearly a one-and-a-half-hour camel ride from here," Saleh said, looking confused.

"Rashid used to talk about visiting Tel Moreeb ... plus I am quite intuitive," Badr said, not making eye contact. He could not think of any other believable explanation.

"Okay, we can try going there," Saleh said, not convinced. "But if we don't find him there, we need to part ways."

"Why? Do you have other plans?"

"Yes, we do. Just because we are nomads doesn't mean ..."

"We should get going soon," Badr interrupted, afraid that he might have offended Saleh. "I don't know what state he is in. If he needs any medical help."

Saleh and the others galloped towards Tel Moreeb, while the Salukis transformed into desert demons, running at around twenty-five kilometres per hour or more. Badr held on to Saleh and the camel's hump, his legs pressing into the animal's sides. He'd only seen camel races, never actually ridden a racing camel.

"We are getting closer to Tel Moreeb now," Saleh said as Badr looked ahead, shielding his eyes from the harsh sun with his left hand.

The dune was huge! As they got closer, he could see something blue on top, but his vision was affected by their speed. Once they were very close, he realised it was a thick blue blanket covering what appeared to be a corpse.

Rashid's most annoying habits—his excessive smoking, sarcastic comments, and pain-in-the-ass stubbornness—flashed before Badr's eyes. He wanted to be subjected to them all over again.

As they reached the top of the dune and unmounted, Badr ran as fast as he could towards the mummified human. Hakim and Talib were already circling the lump.

Badr hesitated as he came close to the blue form, not sure if he wanted to remove the blanket and discover what had happened. Sitting beside the blue figure, he touched what appeared to be the head, as a solitary tear rolled down his check.

Saleh also crouched down. Together, they carefully removed the blanket. It was Rashid!

Badr gasped as he looked at Rashid's mouth, fingernails and toes, which had turned blue and ash grey. He looked like an anorexic, in the advanced stages of his illness, his waist nearly imperceptible, his hand veins prominently visible, his odour that of spoiled food.

"He's breathing," Saleh said.

They quickly took Rashid to a green-blue sporadic lake in the desert, a small trace of what used to be a fresh lake thousands of years ago. Badr stood looking at the sand swirling into the lakes and into some green, camel pastures nearby.

"I want to wash him. The stench is unbearable," Saleh explained, as he dragged Rashid into the lake. The smell diffused, but Rashid showed no signs of waking up.

"Maybe he's in a coma. Should we take him to a hospital?" Badr asked.

"You probably should," Saleh advised.

"Let's go back to Al Jazirah. We have doctors there," Hakim suggested.

Badr looked at him doubtfully, wondering which medical school the jinns had attended.

"I am pretty sure his ailment is not physical," Talib whispered, trying to reassure Badr.

Saleh and his companions dropped Badr to his car's parking spot. He thanked them profusely and tried to hand them a few hundred dirhams, but they refused to take it.

Many hours later, they reached Al Jazirah, where the doctor-jinns circled Rashid and took him away, leaving Badr alone.

Exhaustion overcame him, so he curled up in a secluded corner. The cat with wise blue eyes appeared. He had become Badr's feline companion on the island. Abdulaziz had told Badr the cat was a jinn named Maftoon, but Badr had his doubts. He looked into Maftoon's deeply expressive eyes as his furry friend snuggled against him with a comforting purr.

"He can sense when I need warmth, just like Dana did when she soothed me," Badr mused. She would say things that worked like a band-aid whenever he was feeling low.

Badr gently stroked Maftoon's fur, gratitude welling within him. His plan to seek help from the jinns and rescue Rashid had worked out well. He could sleep peacefully for a while, at least till the sun returned, and he had to strategise his next move.

CHAPTER 28

"Is not He Who responds to the distressed one, when he calls Him, and Who removes the evil."

(27:62)

The next morning, the jinns still did not have a diagnosis for Rashid.

"We can only know what Allah chooses to reveal to us," Aabid, the leader of *Mashaikh* said. "But we are hopeful that Maftoon will be able to tell us. He has a good sense about these things."

"Maftoon? The cat?" Badr asked, perplexed.

"Yes. He's one of the best when it comes to these investigations."

Badr did not find this very reassuring. Had his own situation not been so precarious, he would have taken Rashid to a hospital straight away. Now he was having a hard time imagining the cat coming up with answers, but desperation clung to him like desert sand. He wanted to believe them. After all, he couldn't have found Rashid without their support.

As he sat alone near the shore, listening to the waves, his mind travelled to Dana and the Oud perfume she had given him. It was still in his car's glove compartment.

As he played around with the memory of Dana's gift, a new idea to help Rashid appeared. Badr stood up and dusted the sand off his jeans. He needed to take a risk again and make yet another a call. Three cold fingers gently touched his collarbone, making him jump.

It was Rashid.

Badr was stunned to see Rashid lurking behind him, not sure whether this was good news or bad news. If he had to choose one word to describe Rashid in this moment, it would simply be 'normal-ish.' Although something seemed different about his friend. He couldn't quite grasp what it was.

"Rashid, you're awake? I can't believe it!" he exclaimed.

"Yes," Rashid said. He was wearing a white, hastily stitched, creased shirt with a weird design in the colour of Emirati Sidr honey.

"Can't trust those jinns with their fashion sense!" Badr thought. But it was good to see someone had given Rashid a sponge bath.

"What happened to you, man?" he asked, noticing some cuts on Rashid's arms. There were like angry-red grill marks.

When Rashid did not respond, Badr said, "It's good to have you around, though."

"Come, let's go for a drive and I'll tell you everything," Rashid said.

"Where will we drive to, Rashid?" Badr asked, taken aback by Rashid's suggestion. "We just found you, half-dead, in the middle of nowhere!"

"I want to grab something to eat. I'm starving!" Rashid said, a hint of his old swagger returning.

"Yeah, but we can walk to the other side."

"I'd rather drive. I haven't eaten for days. Don't have the strength to walk much."

"Oh ... okay."

Badr led him towards his Nissan Patrol silently. He wanted to ask Abdulaziz for advice or to accompany them, but the island was deserted and quieter than usual. The jinns would be returning at night. Rashid must have woken up and left his room as there was no one was guarding him, Badr concluded. Perhaps they had cured him?

As he was about to get into the car, Rashid snatched the keys from his hands and got into the driver's seat.

"Hey!"

"*Yalla*, come on."

"Rashid, I really don't think you should drive right now."

"I am okay, dude. You know me. I can do this even while I'm sleeping."

"An exaggeration. Typical Rashid," Badr thought. "Maybe he is just pretending to be crazy. But why was he in a coma-like state for so long? Drugs?"

Getting into the passenger seat reluctantly, he put his seatbelt on while Rashid started driving through the wilderness, until they reached the almost-built road. Rashid braked.

"What happened?" asked Badr.

He started accelerating in response.

"Let's keep the car slow man. Lots of freckled rocks here. It's bumpy and I don't want a puncture."

Rashid ignored Badr. It was starting to feel like a bad idea. Badr was not sure what to expect as he scanned the road ahead for obstacles.

"Careful, please!" He was not a nervous passenger, but he didn't like the way Rashid was dodging the rocks.

"Why did you bring me here?" A familiar voice made him jump. Badr snapped his head around to stare at Rashid. He was looking straight ahead. He checked the rear-view mirror. There was no woman in the back seat or anywhere in the vicinity.

"Stop the car!"

"You shouldn't have brought me here," he said, his voice taking on the same high-pitched tone that made Badr's skin crawl, like nails scraping against a chalkboard.

"It was a mistake! You should have left us alone!"

Badr couldn't believe his eyes as he watched Rashid mouth the words and stomp on the accelerator. He glanced in Badr's direction, his eyes icy-cold, like his heart had been chewed up and spat out by the devil. Badr knew it would be no use begging Rashid to spare him. Dana's sorrowful blue eyes flashed in his mind. He couldn't just give up.

"Rashid!" Badr said, pouncing on him, trying to take control of the steering wheel. But Rashid pushed him away with such force that he went flying to the window. A wrong angle there and he would have crushed his skull.

Badr winced in pain, rubbing his head, trying to heal the blow. He was sure Rashid was going to collide with one of the trees or a camel any minute now.

"Watch out!" Badr yelled, as Rashid almost ran over a cat.

"It might be Maftoon," Badr thought, though he couldn't be sure, as the car raced forward at a manic speed, rivalling a Japanese bullet train.

Badr knew if he tried to jump, he would probably die or become disabled. A peculiar nauseous feeling, which he reserved for very rare, nerve-wracking situations, came up. There was only one thing he could do now. Pray *Ayat-e-Karima*, which Prophet Yunus (AS) had recited when he was trapped in the belly of a whale:

"There is no god but Thou: Glory to Thee: I was indeed wrong!" (21:87)

He kept repeating the prayer loudly, and Rashid slowed down in response, as if his arms and feet were freezing, and he could not drive anymore. They had almost reached the island's exit when the car stopped of its own accord, as if it had gotten stuck in debris. Badr watched a dust storm emerge and circle around them. Like a tornado taking over everything. Rashid looked stricken; his mouth clamped shut. He was completely motionless now; his hands no longer clutching the steering wheel.

Badr's head was spinning, and the mud and sand outside made it hard to see anything. But he could hear voices in the distance. Someone was chanting. He squinted and noticed something strange. The sandstorm was churning out sculptures. A group of brown silhouettes had emerged. They morphed into faceless men wrapped in cloths of sand. Seeing them march towards the car, Badr wondered if someone had alerted the jinns and they'd come to rescue him. He pulled the lock and tried to open the door. But it wouldn't budge. As he struggled with it, a very cold arm found its way around his neck.

Rashid's hold was so strong that Badr couldn't move at all and any attempt to escape seemed futile.

"You will break my neck!" he cried, but Rashid wouldn't let go of him. As heavy breathing caressed the hair on his neck, Badr felt his internal organs curl up into a foetal position.

"You can't take him away from me," she whispered in his ear.

"Who are you?"

The brown men were getting closer, and Rashid's grip loosened as they recited *'Astaghfar'* to ward off evil. When they had surrounded the car completely, Rashid let go of Badr completely, looking repulsed. Covering his ears, he squirmed in his seat, his skin turning a cancerous yellow.

As the entire area thronged with muscular, brown men, some of them opened the car doors, pulling Rashid out from one side and Badr more gently from the other.

Badr felt ensnared by the crowd of hundreds and was afraid of being hurt, but he soon realised they didn't have a physical form. He couldn't touch or feel them, but his body was moving forward, as if these intangible creatures were carrying him. They transported him to the abandoned school of the *Ulema*.

Badr stood on the school's steps, shaking, sweating, shivering. He watched the brown creatures disappear one after another, melting into the ground, with dust clouds spinning and swirling. Soon, there was nothing left apart from small mounds of sand and clay all around him.

Coughing and covering his nose, Badr stumbled inside and entered an old and empty classroom. It was lit by torches, hung on the walls, fires glowing inside them. There were signs that a blackboard once occupied one of the walls, where white geckos were now crawling up and down.

Badr was not a fan of reptiles, apart from turtles, and shuddered as the geckos moved. He was relieved to see Abdulaziz, Akil and Aabid standing at the other end of the room, talking to a man he did not recognise. They also seemed relieved to see him.

Rashid was sitting on the floor near them, his face bent down, his hands and feet in chains, with bugs trying to crawl up his body.

It reminded Badr of his days in junior school, when Rashid had been frequently punished for his cruel practical jokes. He would sit outside the classroom in the same way, doing his silent time, thinking over what he had done. But Badr always knew he had no regrets and was only coming up with more tricks. Later in life, he had fortunately replaced his tricks with sarcasm. But Badr couldn't believe Rashid had nearly killed him today. Rage was rising somewhere inside him. He couldn't die and leave Dana and his family alone with grief. He wanted to slap the devilish female out of Rashid. She was the one who had taken them on the group suicide mission.

"I am very blessed to see you, Sheikh Badr."

Badr's rage dissolved as the unknown man walked up to him, extending his hand. He looked into the man's deep blue eyes.

"You bring me joy and happiness," he said.

"Maftoon?" Badr asked. He was stunned to see quite a hunky jinn, probably a heartthrob amongst the jinnis.

"Yes, I'm Maftoon, Sheikh Badr. Can I serve you anything?" he asked, illuminating the surrounding space with his smile.

"No ... no thanks. I am ... I don't need anything ... and I am not a sheikh!"

"Ooh ... so humble of you ... this a sign of being blessed ... Allah must love you so much, Sheikh."

"Thank you. But what do we do now? About Rashid?"

"Maftoon can help us," Aabid said, joining them. "That's why we have called him. He is the one who sent the *Aljaysh* to help."

"Aljaysh?"

"Yes. The third tribe. They're an army. We summon them usually when there is a big crisis, some kind of physical altercation like this one. They're our muscle jinn-brothers."

He then asked everyone to sit down in a circle around Rashid, leaving enough distance to ward off any more murderous attacks. Rashid drew his legs up close against his stomach, bowing his face down, as if all the manic energy had left his body and he could barely sit up.

Aabid, Akil and Maftoon started reciting Quranic verses for protection from evil:

> *"Soon shall We settle your affairs, O both ye worlds!*
> *Then which of the favours of your Lord will ye deny?*
> *O ye assembly of Jinns and men! If it be ye can pass beyond the zones of the heavens*
> *and the earth, pass ye! Not without authority shall ye be able to pass!" (31:33)*

Abdulaziz and Badr joined them, noticing how Rashid's body was reacting. He moved his head up while his eyeballs travelled down to the ground. He convulsed and tried to gnaw at the chains. But they were too strong for him. He muttered monosyllabic exclamations, as if speaking to the air¬¬¬—just as Dana had described some of her possession episodes. But unlike her, Rashid was loud and aggressive."

"No! Stop!" His voice quivered with emotions.

Finally, when nothing worked, he stopped resisting. His eyes closed and his head drooped down.

Maftoon and the others had been watching his moves closely. They exchanged notes amongst themselves. Abdulaziz was quiet and looking at Badr.

"So can we expect a happy ending?" Badr asked.

Abdulaziz laughed, but it was not a happy laugh.

"There are no 'happy' endings. The words contradict each other," he said.

"Why doesn't he ever give me a straight answer?" Badr wondered, feeling extremely tired. He had been hoping this was it. That they would recite a few verses and the *sahera* possessing Rashid would depart. But he knew he should have known it wasn't so simple, given how they had been unable to find a cure for Dana. It all felt like a pointless charade. A prelude to more barbarity.

Maftoon cleared his throat and looked at Badr, like a doctor presenting a grave diagnosis.

"We believe your friend has been possessed by a jinni."

"Okay. I thought so," Badr replied, very unhappily.

"We don't know who she is, but she is not from Al Jazirah Al Hamra. Not from our tribes. Her possession seems to be motivated, not by love, but by a burning desire for vindication and vengeance. She's fierce and even slashed the ropes which a jinn, one of the *Aljaysh*, had tied Rashid with before leaving him alone on the island."

"Okay … so what does that mean? What would a jinni have against Rashid?"

"Her power over him is intact. Maybe he hurt her in some way or someone else has sent her to avenge rejection," Akil said.

Badr was well aware that Rashid was a reckless flirt. It was possible that he had broken more hearts, and a woman scorned wanted to get back at him.

"But what am I supposed to do now?" he asked.

"We can only tell you this much. What Allah has chosen to reveal to us. He is All-Knowing," Aabid said. "Allah is All-Powerful. He can even make mountains go up like carded wool."

Badr realised he would have to find a way to rescue Rashid. Even it meant taking a detour from planning his escape from his own mess and reuniting with Dana. But a flicker of hope ignited within him. Perhaps aiding Rashid wasn't a roadblock, but the path that would ultimately lead him to his own freedom and Dana's healing.

CHAPTER 29

"(God) said: 'what prevented thee from bowing down when I commanded thee?' He said: 'I am better than he: thou didst create me from fire and him from clay.'"

(27:62)

"Allahu Akbar, Allahu Akbar."

The call to prayer rose from several minarets as Badr drove through the curving Hajar mountains and stopped near a compact, ancient mosque. He was on his way to Fujairah, to Sheikh Omar's home. A Kenyan, with roots in Yemen, Sheikh Omar was a highly revered *motawa,* recommended by Sultan's friends.

As Badr got down from the car, Hakim, Talib and Maftoon stood outside it to say their prayers whilst guarding Rashid. They had tied him neatly, wrapped him up in a soft blanket and given him a special tea that had induced a sleep-like state, but his eyes were wide open.

Badr tried to shake the image of Rashid's fixed stare and walked inside the prayer hall. It smelt of an aged carpet and the *bokhour* of oud.

By the time the *Imam* started his sermon, the hall was packed with worshippers, and some had to line up outside to pray. Sun-baked, but devoted!

The *Imam* started talking about the importance of prayer, which struck Badr as funny because he was preaching to people who were already praying. He then jumped on to the suffering of Muslim brothers in Afghanistan and Palestine, and the importance of *jihad*, reminding Badr of Samer. The killer of dreams. He tried to stifle his anger and divert himself by praying for Rashid and Dana.

"That's the most important thing right now," he told himself.

When he resumed his journey, he watched families heading towards Fujairah's sandy beaches.

They reached Sheikh Omar's house early evening after driving around the same mountain for a very long time. Nestled among the rugged mountains and thick, green trees, it was an ancient villa built with brick and mud, prior to the 1971 union of the UAE. But it looked like the building's sandy-coloured exterior had been refreshed recently. Three-storey tall, the villa lay next to a large mosque.

Badr wondered how many people drove all the way there to pray, as there were not many houses nearby.

"We'll leave you here," Hakim said as they walked to the main gate slowly, arms around Rashid, pulling him forward gently.

"What do you mean?"

"You can go in with Rashid. We'll be around in case you need any help."

"But how will I contact you?"

"Maftoon can go in with you. Tell them you couldn't leave your cat alone or something. So, if you need us, just send him to look for us."

"Okay," Badr said, and rang the bell as Hakim and Talib disappeared. A bald and bulky Sudanese man, dressed in what looked like a long, white maxi, answered the door. He took one look at Rashid hanging on Badr's arm, and helped take him inside.

A few families were sitting in the open courtyard in groups, whispering amongst themselves. An Irani teenage girl was throwing tantrums in one group while an Emirati boy, probably in his twenties, was rolling on the floor in another. They were all there to seek Sheikh Omar's help, given his strong reputation in the magic and jinn possession market.

The villa was spacious and well-furnished, unlike Sheikh Ali's home. They were assigned a room on the third storey. Badr was glad he had called ahead and had a chat with the Sheikh about Rashid's situation. The Sheikh had suggested they stay with him for a while as it sounded 'complicated and dangerous' for all involved.

The Sudanese man put Rashid on a king-size bed that was covered with a printed bedsheet, with big rose-pink flowers and hunter-green leaves, the kind almost everyone in the UAE had. Badr was about to sit on the edge of the bed but turned around as he heard footsteps.

A woman, with reddish-brown hair, a freckled face, and a mysterious air, had entered the room. She smelled funny, like clothes that had been sitting in a box for a very long time.

"*Ana* Aminah. Lunch?" she said in a Syrian accent, clearly not bothered about greetings and salutations. She tapped her foot and frowned at Maftoon.

"Hi Aminah. Nice to meet you. What about my friend?" Badr asked, pointing at Rashid.

"Hamza will take care of him," she replied, nodding at the Sudanese man.

"He can be dangerous."

"Dear, this is not our first time dealing with the possessed!"

"Okay," Badr said, a little intimidated by her tone. She led him to a dining room plus lounge area. A fusion of the casual and the luxurious. Badr sat down on an opal sofa against big, white cushions, adorned with vibrant *talli* embroidery.

He admired the beautiful patterns created with cotton and synthetic metallic threads.

"Sir?" A sweet-looking, young Indian boy had appeared with a bowl of water and lemon. Badr rinsed his hands, and the boy helped him wipe them on a small towel. The place felt more like an inn and a museum of artistic things than a religious leader's home.

On the walls, black and gold frames held Arabic and Islamic calligraphy,. mostly verses from the Qur'an. Some were modern, created with synthetic paint and markers. Others were more traditional, designed on handmade paper with a *qalam*.

It seemed that Sheikh Omar had seen more prosperity than the humble Sheikh Ali and didn't mind splurging.

As if she could read Badr's mind, Aminah said, "He wants to provide a good environment to those who are suffering. Most of the things you see here have been donated. We get VIPs here, you know."

"I see." Badr wasn't sure why she was still around. "Is she going to watch me eat?" he wondered.

"Food is served," the young Indian guy announced just then.

Badr was ravenous and gobbled his lunch, not really noticing what he was having.

"Sheikh Omar has summoned you," Aminah said as soon as he was done.

He followed her to a large *majlis* where a large, burly man sat, wearing a white *kandura* and a chequered red and white headdress. Badr shook hands with Sheikh Omar, but oddly, he couldn't really feel his hands. He seemed very calm and centred, and Badr hoped some of his energy would rub off on him, take all his anguish away.

"What is distressing you?" he asked, his voice powerful but kind.

"Me?"

"Yes, you told me about your friend. But how are you doing?

Well ...," Badr tried to gather his thoughts to answer this unexpected question. "I ... I feel like ... for the first time in my life, I feel like I have no control over any aspect of my life."

"All control is an illusion. Only Allah is *Al-Muhaymin*, the Preserver of Safety, and *Al-Aziz*, the Mighty One."

"Yes, but I can't understand why He does certain things."

"That's why we need to surrender to His will. Allah never promised that this life would be a bed of roses."

"Yes, but my life was so perfect."

"Sometimes we get so used to the status quo that we think everything is perfect and we ignore things that might need to be addressed."

"No, seriously, my life was perfect. I had the education, the career, the family, friendships, love. I really don't understand this phase of my life."

"Things happen."

"But I feel like someone has cursed me. I don't understand why Allah helped me climb the peak, only to hurtle me down the mountain."

"You know, this is the human condition. Even the Prophet (PBUH) experienced such emotions and depression. There was a point in his life when he did not receive any revelation for several months and he questioned if Allah still loved him; why he had been abandoned; if he had done something wrong and was no longer deserving of being an apostle."

"So how did he overcome this?"

"Allah revealed a Surah to uplift him:

Your Lord O Prophet has not abandoned you, nor has He become hateful of you. And the next life is certainly far better for you than this one. And surely your Lord will give so much to you that you will be pleased. Did He not find you as an orphan then sheltered you? Did He not find you unguided then guided you? And did He not find you needy then satisfied your needs?" (93:3-8)

They were both quiet. Badr wanted to tell him about the recent incidents in his life and seek his advice, but this was about Rashid.

"So, what can we do for Rashid?" Badr asked.

The door opened, as if in response to his question. Hamza brought Rashid in on a wheelchair. His eyes were droopy, his stare fixed on the floor now. He was still tied up, although the blanket was off. He looked like an old man in a hospice, Badr thought.

"I fed him some soup," Hamza told Sheikh Omar.

Sheikh Omar stood up and walked towards Rashid, circling around the wheelchair, waving his hands in the air, as if trying to catch a butterfly.

He then untied Rashid's hands and extended his own, but Rashid was still unable to hold them. His fingers were shaking, struggling, as if some force was stopping him from placing his hands on Sheikh's palms.

Placing his hands on Rashid's head, Sheikh Omar closed his eyes, muttering. Rashid's hands fell in his lap. His body was contorting, but his reaction was milder than usual, probably because of the special tea.

Badr pressed his back into a cushion, wishing Dana's soft fingers were caressing him.

"Who are you?" Sheikh Omar bellowed. Rashid did not answer.

"Who are you?" he asked again.

Rashid's lips were moving, but he seemed to be having difficulty speaking. After five minutes of struggle, he was finally able to whisper one word: "Aicha."

Badr's bones shivered at hearing the same female voice again.

"Good to know it has a name," he thought and then suddenly remembered Aicha from the gym and what Rashid had told him about her. She had seemed like a person, not a jinni.

"What do you want?" Sheikh Omar asked Rashid.

"Him."

"Who?"

"Rashid."

"Why?"

Sheikh Omar bent down and moved his face close to Rashid's, who whispered something in his ear. It all seemed unreal to Badr.

"You were right," Sheikh announced, turning towards Badr. "It seems your friend is completely under the control of a jinni. He hurt someone and now she's on a mission to destroy him by possessing him through the dark arts."

"Okay. So, can you make her forgive him?"

"No, I don't think so. Only Allah can bring any healing and freedom for your friend. She seems to be under the influence of *Satan*. She's angry and believes that because she's made of fire, she can outsmart a human made of clay."

"Then, what do we do now?"

"Hamza will need to get some things."

"What things?"

He lifted a piece of paper from a grand wooden writing desk and handed it to Hamza.

"You need to get all this," he instructed Hamza.

"You can rest tonight, and we'll begin tomorrow once Hamza has brought us what we need," he told Badr.

Badr thanked him profusely and retired to his room. He watched Hamza lock up Rashid in a cell-inspired room attached to this own.

"It's sad that we need to treat you like a criminal," Badr said, sitting down next to the door and knocking on it.

"How are you, my friend?"

There was no answer.

"I miss you."

Badr wondered if Rashid could hear him.

"Tell me what happened to you." But Rashid did not respond. And neither did the jinni, much to Badr's relief.

"Get well soon," Badr said, retreating to his bed in the pitch-black room. It was very quiet, and he could almost hear his despair when a woman started wailing.

CHAPTER 30

*"One's devilish associate will say, 'Our Lord!
I did not make them transgress. Rather, they
were far astray on their own.'"*

(50:27)

The following morning, Badr was summoned to Sheikh Omar's chamber after Hamza delivered the items the Sheikh had requested. Rashid was already there, a frail figure slumped in an armchair, his bones protruding as he fought off sleep. His hands and feet were bound, and Hamza observed him closely, like a hawk watching its prey.

"I see you've brought enough to fill up a wooden chest," Sheikh Omar said to Hamza.

"Sorry, I wasn't sure how much would be needed," replied Hamza.

"That's okay. It will benefit the other people here … if you're fine with that," he said, looking at Badr, who had paid for the items.

"Yes, of course," Badr said, taking a seat opposite Rashid.

Sheikh Omar started reciting some verses from memory:

"And say: 'Truth has (now) arrived and Falsehood perished:
for Falsehood is (by its nature) bound to perish.

We send down (stage by stage) in the Qur'an that
which is a healing and a mercy to those who believe:
to the unjust it causes nothing but loss after loss.'" (17:81–82)

"I will be performing *ruqyah* now," he said. "As you know, it's the practice of treating illnesses through *Ayat* and invocations as prescribed by the Messenger of Allah, peace be upon him."

He performed *wudu* in the attached bathroom and offered two *rakat*. "Let's start." He vocalised his intentions. "I ask Allah to remove all evil from Rashid's life with these words of the Qur'an. I pray Allah provides solace to Rashid, both spiritually and physically."

Opening a copy of the Qur'an, he started reading *Surah Al-Baqarah* loudly. He blew over Rashid's head, who squirmed in his seat, now wide awake, but mute.

"The four *Quls*, the last four Surahs of the Qur'an, including *Surah Al-Ikhlas* (Monotheism), *Surah Al-Kafirun* (The Unbeliever), *Surah Al-Falaq* (The Daybreak), and *Surah An-Nas* (Mankind), are extremely effective in protecting people from the evil eye," Sheikh said, and recited them.

"As Rashid cannot recite these prayers right now, you will need to read them three times in the morning and evening, three times before going to sleep and once after every salah," he told Badr.

He handed Badr a bottle of olive oil and extended his palms. Badr poured a generous amount onto his hands.

"Use olive oil in eating and for applying (on the body), for it is from a blessed tree," the Sheikh quoted a Hadith from *Jami` at-Tirmidhi*, rubbing his palms together.

Placing them on Rashid's shoulder, neck, and arms, he recited *Ayat ul Kursi* to invoke Allah's protection.

Rashid's eyes revealed agony. His body tensed up, and he seemed to be in intense pain. Badr found it hard to watch as the scene unfolded and sank back into a cushion.

Sheikh Omar recited the last three *Surahs* of the Quran again, this time keeping his mouth close to a bottle of water, repeatedly blowing over it.

"This is *Zamzam*," he said. "I brought it from Makkah when I went there for *Umrah* last month. According to Sunan Ibn Majah, the Messenger of Allah (PBUH) said, 'The water of *Zamzam* is for whatever it is drunk for.' Make sure he drinks it during the day," he said, handing the bottle to Hamza.

"We can also do some saltwater treatment to expel dark energies from the body. In *Sunan Ibn Majah*, our Prophet (PBUH) is quoted as saying, *'Salt is the master of your food. Allah sent down four blessings from the sky fire, water, iron, and salt.'* Because of its healing properties, he also used it to treat poisoning. He rubbed salt water on the place where a scorpion had stung him, while reciting the four *Quls*," Sheikh said.

"Grind these and soak them in Rashid's ice-cold bath water daily, for seven days," he said, picking up the green *Sidr* leaves. "As recorded in *Sahih al-Bukhari*, Prophet Muhammed (PBUH) recommended treating oneself with cupping and sea incense."

"Burn the *al-Qust al-Hindī*, the Indian incense, and *al-Qust al-Bahrī*, sea incense, in his room so he can sniff it."

> *"Then to eat of all the produce (of the earth) and find with skill the*
> *spacious paths of its Lord: there issues from within their bodies a drink*
> *of varying colours wherein is healing for men: verily in this is a*
> *Sign for those who give thought." (16:69)*

"Make sure he has honey every day with his breakfast or mixed with lukewarm water," Sheikh said.

"What about the dates?" Badr asked.

"Give him seven. In *Sahih Bukhari*, Allah's Messenger is reported have said that if a person eats seven *Ajwa* dates in the morning, *'neither magic nor poison will hurt him that day.'*"

"Okay. And the barley?"

"The Messenger of Allah (PBUH) asked for barley broth when a family member was unwell. He would say, *'Indeed it mends the heart of the sorrowful and relieves the heart of the sick, just as one of you removes dirt from his face with water.'* So, ask the cook here to make *Talbina*, using ground barley with husks. Make Rashid drink it like a soup. It's thin and raw and will be good for him."

After a pause, Sheikh Omar looked at Badr and said, "Take Hamza's help. Also, make sure Rashid is in a state of *wudu* throughout the day and before he falls asleep at night. Take him to the window close to the mosque so he can hear the *adhan* five times a day. And recite these *Surahs* and blow over him during the day."

Badr nodded, grateful to be able to do something that would make a difference rather than just watching as a helpless spectator.

"You can also wrap some sea salt in a tissue, rotate it clockwise while reciting *Surah An-Nas* seven times, then discard the salt in a sink. And sometimes, when he is bathing, add a handful of coarse sea salt to his bath. You can also add rose water to the bath water, so he has a pleasant experience."

Badr tried to make a mental note of all the instructions. "How many days do we need to follow these rituals?" he asked.

"Until he improves. Intention, conviction, patience, and consistency will give us results," Sheikh said. "Make sincere *dua*, especially in *tahajjud*. It will *Insha Allah* bring great reprieve and assistance from Allah."

Badr expressed his gratitude to the Sheikh, then helped Hamza take Rashid back to their room. On the way, the wailing woman peeped at them through a window, as if curious about Rashid's ailment. His eyes met hers, but she retreated quickly, closing the drapes.

CHAPTER 31

◆————————◆————————◆

"Remember when He caused drowsiness to overcome you, giving you serenity. And He sent down rain from the sky to purify you, free you from Satan's whispers, strengthen your hearts, and make your steps firm."

(8:11)

"The government orders banks to freeze the assets of over sixty individuals and organisations suspected by the United States of funding terrorism," Badr read out from that morning's Gulf News.

"They didn't freeze my assets, so stop freezing my brain," Rashid yelled, as he took a shower, the bathroom door half-open.

It had been one gruelling month. Badr had kept himself busy by following current affairs, drafting emails to Dana but never sending them, and focusing on Rashid's recovery. He had followed Sheikh Omar's instructions to a T. At first, he had felt disappointed because there wasn't any noticeable change in Rashid's behaviour. But after a week, the rituals seemed to have anesthetised the jinni.

As her influence dampened, the raging inferno within Rashid also dulled. He would still get triggered and recoil from Quranic recitations or the adhan, as if the jinni was repulsed and tormented by them. But after two weeks, he became more subdued, as if they had successfully gagged and bound his captor.

Badr could see the bad energy slowly withdrawing from Rashid's being, the bruise-like patches on his body disappearing. He was able to eat more than just soup and regained some of his lost weight. He even managed morsels of conversation though Badr wasn't always sure whether he was present or still living in the apocalyptic world inside him.

Each day, Badr would diligently lead him through the daily recitation of Surahs, his own voice thick with emotion as Rashid struggled to repeat the sacred verses.

Finally, the day arrived when they felt confident that Rashid's violent urges had been quelled. Hamza untied Rashid's hands and feet, and Badr chopped off the messy, long hair framing his friend's face.

That day Rashid appeared to be free of all discomfort. His expression was no longer haunted, and he had managed to shower on his own.

This was a double victory, Badr thought. A turning point. Not only had he managed to find a way to heal Rashid, but now he could find a way to bring Dana to Sheikh Omar. The path ahead, though still uncertain, held the promise of answers.

As Badr mentally strategised Dana's rescue and recovery, Rashid sat down next to him and helped himself to *shakshuka* for breakfast.

"So, *habibi*, why did you save me?" Rashid asked, managing a half-smile. "Why did you delve into darkness and pull me back?"

"*Enta 'umri*! How could I let you plunder the Arabian desert and taste the meat of our endangered, talismanic oryx?" Badr asked, a playful glint in his eyes. The tables had turned, and it was Badr's chance to tease Rashid.

"I am in no mood for jokes, Badr," Rashid said, remaining stoic.

"But how could I have let you die all alone in that desert?" Badr asked, pouring coffee for Rashid.

"Maybe I deserved it. Whatever happened to me."

"No, of course not. Nobody deserves this. And this is coming from me, a guy whose leg you've been pulling all your life."

"You don't know me anymore."

"What do you mean?" Badr pressed. "Me, you, and Sultan, we're like brothers. Always have been."

"Yeah, but you know only one side of me. Can anyone know anyone else completely?" Rashid asked, his voice tinged with a newfound weariness.

"It seems the jinni has turned you into a philosopher," Badr teased, a hint of lightness in his voice.

"Hardly," Rashid muttered, dark shadows creeping back across his face. "I pervert beautiful things like love. Defile them. I have become the kind of man people warn their daughters about."

"Allah is 'Oft-Forgiving, Most-Merciful.' Maybe this incident is the wakeup call you needed," Badr said.

"Maybe. It's not so simple," Rashid said, sighing. "And I have a confession to make."

"Confession?" Badr asked, finding it hard to accept this new Rashid, without his penchant for dark humour.

"Yes," Rashid replied, his voice laden with regret. "The reason I always teased you so much, especially about Dana, was because, even though I love you like a brother, I envied you."

"Envied me? Why?" Badr did not like this unwelcome intrusion into his world, which was already a *nidaal*, jinn-stricken and generally falling apart.

"You have the perfect life," Rashid said.

Badr laughed silently, thinking about how little Rashid knew about the recent mishaps in his life.

"Rashid, no one has a perfect life," he said. "Some of us just hide the imperfections well."

"No, no, listen to me. You have dreams. You are passionate about your career. And most importantly, your family deeply cares about you. The reason I stopped visiting your place was because it was kind of debilitating for me to see your family being so warm and nice to you while my home had no friggin' concept of love. I am kind of a loser now, envious of his own brother."

"Don't say that. You're going through a tough phase. You need to find a way to escape it."

"Badr, there is no oasis in this damned desert," Rashid said, his laughter a harsh, hollow sound.

"What do you mean?" Badr asked, frowning.

"There is no escape for people like me."

"Why not?"

"For me, trying to escape is like running from a burning fire, only to plummet off a cliff. The pain and restlessness, they never stop. It's like I am always blindfolded and can't see any beauty in the world."

"Rashid, it's been a harrowing few months," Badr said gently. "It's taken a toll..."

"No, you don't understand!" Rashid exclaimed, stamping his foot.

Badr fell silent, deciding it was best to let his friend vent.

"You can be normal," Rashid said, banging the table with his fist. "You don't fantasise about going to sleep and never waking up. You can love someone with

your whole heart and be loved back, unlike me."
"Many people love you. Even if some love you in a more twisted way, like Aicha."

"Aicha?" The name seemed to send a jolt through Rashid. His face drained of colour, then flushed a deep crimson with rage.

"Aicha? Did she have something to do with all this?" he asked.

"You don't remember anything?" Badr asked, torn between being honest and causing consternation.

"I remember driving to Rub' al Khali. A shadow taking hold, hijacking my body. I was thinking about Aicha at the time, but then I thought it was an evil spirit. And since then, I have been drifting on and off, as you know."

"How did you feel?" Badr asked, treading cautiously.

"I don't remember much of it. I get flashes of feeling like my soul had left my body. And then feeling excruciating pain. The thoughts in my head have been galloping around like untamed horses. I don't know any more what was real and what was a nightmare."

Badr filled him in on what had transpired since they had recovered him from Rub' al Khali and landed in Fujairah.

"Oh my God. It all makes sense now. It must be Aicha. She is behind all this misery. I am going to thrash her! How dare she?"

"Is she the one you told me about? The one who followed you to the gym?"

"Yes," Rashid growled. "She's a stalker! Came after me, found my whereabouts."

"Anyway, it's all over now, *khallas*!" Badr said.

"Easy for you to say! You didn't just battle demons and death, and all because a pythoness is obsessed with you!"

"Rashid, calm down. I am on your side," Badr pleaded, wishing they could just go back to enjoying familial intimacy.

Rashid face remained a mask of thunder, the veins in his forehead running around with murderous thoughts. He had always had mood swings, but possession seemed to have amplified them.

"Sheikh Omar wants to see you both in his chamber," Hamza announced, entering the room suddenly, his voice breaking through the charged atmosphere.

"A lecture on religion and piety is the last thing I need right now," Rashid grumbled, banging his coffee mug on the table.

"Rashid, this guy saved your life. Look, I know your anger might be justified..."

"Might be?" Rashid scoffed.

"I mean..."

"Okay. You go ahead."

"Please don't do this here," Badr pleaded.

"I will join you after smoking," Rashid said, his voice thick with defiance.

"You have cigarettes?" Badr was aghast.

"Yes. I borrowed them from one of the men in this mad house," Rashid replied, a sly smile playing on his lips.

Badr stared at him, feeling embarrassed, hoping Hamza had not heard the words 'mad house.'

"I'll see you in a bit," Rashid said, dismissing Badr, who proceeded to Sheikh's chamber alone.

"Words cannot express my gratitude," Badr said as soon as he saw Sheikh Omar.

"You don't need to thank me," Sheikh replied. He recited:

> *"If Allah touch thee with affliction none can remove it but He;*
> *if He touch thee with happiness, He hath power over all things." (6:17)*

"But Rashid should continue praying and ask for Allah's forgiveness. He should stay here a bit longer so that we can observe him and ensure that he has recovered completely, and the jinni has left him alone for good," Sheikh Omar said.

Badr readily agreed, and a silence descended on the room as they waited for Rashid to make an entrance. He found himself drawn to the new Persian Qashqai Tiger Rug, a gift from one of Sheikh's clients. He understood the sentiment behind them. This man's services were priceless. No gift or cash could compensate for what he had done for Rashid.

A sliver of movement caught Badr's eye. He looked at the door to the chamber, which was slightly ajar, and revealed a glimpse of Maftoon. Badr was surprised to see Maftoon had finally scurried out from his hiding place under their bed. He looked at Badr with anxious blue eyes.

"Excuse me, please," Badr said to the Sheikh, his heart hammering. He quickly followed Maftoon, who sprinted towards the bedroom. A torrent of thoughts and fears raced through Badr's mind.

"Is she back? Where is Rashid? I hate how impulsive he is. Maybe I shouldn't have left him alone?"

As he entered the room, Badr noticed a silver Arabic bowl lying on the terrace. He rushed towards it only to find it overflowing with cigarette butts. The only other occupant of the terrace was Hamza's adopted pigeon, walking around, bobbing its head, its broken wing on the mend.

"It's probably easier to heal wounded animals than broken humans," Badr muttered, a wave of despair washing over him. He peered over the edge, half-expecting to see Rashid sprawled on the gravel path below. But there was no sign of him.

An hour bled into another as Badr combed the room and then the entire villa. A chilling realisation finally settled upon him: Rashid had left, taking with him nothing but his pain.

CHAPTER 32

———————————

"And We have destined For them intimate companions (Of like nature), who made Alluring to them what was Before them and behind them; And the sentence among The previous generations of Jinns And men, who have passed away, Is proved against them; For they are utterly lost."

(41:25)

"Aicha?"

"Rashid?"

"Can we meet Aicha?"

"What?"

"*Wahashtini*. I hope you can forgive me."

"Oh."

"I was afraid. I didn't realise how deeply I loved you, so I asked you to go away."

"I ... I can't believe this. I had almost given up hope...."

It had been easy for Rashid to get Aicha's phone number from the facility manager. He'd promised *wasta*, the local system of having clout, to get the man's brother-in-law out of jail. But first, he wanted to put an end to Aicha's wickedness, once and for all.

After recovering his car from Rub' al Khali, he had asked Aicha to meet him at one of his dad's hotels in Dubai, located near what residents fondly called Chicago Beach.

As Rashid entered his dad's private lounge at the hotel, his blood pressure shot up. The lounge was uncomfortably familiar, with its palette of warm colours, Arabian lantern lights, crystal chandeliers, Turkish vintage rugs, and spotless white sofas. He knew by the scent of stale cigarette smoke that his dad had been spending time there.

It had been many years since Rashid had visited the lounge. He vividly remembered playing there, all alone, sometimes with a marble chessboard, while his dad would be in the master suite next door. The man would sit on his rattan teak wood armchair, briefly afterwards, crushing his cigarette in a crystal ashtray, looking smug.

"Don't checkmate me!" he'd say, and Rashid knew this was a warning; he was not to tell anyone about his father's guests. Women, clad in black *abayas*, who would arrive with a short, thin African man, their faces painted with pink blush and red lipstick.

A soft knock on the door jolted Rashid out of his reverie. He opened it to find Aicha, in a crimson-red *kaftan*, standing next to an old Indian security guard.

"Rashid...," Aicha said, breathing heavily, her disbelieving eyes lighting up.

"Please come in," Rashid said, with exaggerated politeness, holding the door open for her as she strode in slowly, nervously.

"Sir, the master suite next door is empty," the security guard said, giving Rashid a look that said, 'the apple doesn't fall far from the tree.'

Rashid scowled in response and closed the door with a slight thud. He turned to Aicha, who had kicked off her shoes, as if she was planning to stay a long time.

"Aicha," he said, moving closer, with a tight smile on his face. Her jasmine perfume reminded him of both his initial attraction to her and the intense hatred he now felt.

"Rashid, I … I was very surprised you called …," she began.

"How are you, Aicha? All okay?" Rashid asked.

"*Oui*, but I thought I'd never see you again. I was losing hope," she said, oblivious to his mocking tone, tilting her face up towards him, as if she expected him to lean down and kiss her.

"Let's not waste time," he said sternly, moving back slightly, his fists now clenched. It had been a while since he had given anyone a piece of his mind. Usually, a lousy driver on Sheikh Zayed Road would be at the receiving end of his relentless stream of jabs.

"Stop pretending to be so innocent!" he said, ready to unleash his darkest side.

"What do you mean, Rashid?" Aicha asked, her eyes widening.

"I know what you did!" he replied.

"What? What are you talking about?" she asked, rubbing her temples.

"Don't pretend like you don't know anything, Aicha. Don't act like you didn't just try to kill me!" Rashid said, his voice carrying across the room.

"Kill you? I … I love you!" she replied, her hands trembling slightly, as she tried to put them on his cheeks.

"You think this is love?" he asked, pushing her hands away.

"I ... I just wanted you to fall in love with me again," she said, her eyes welling up with tears.

"Are you delusional?" he asked, his loudness causing slight tremors, making the chandeliers sway.

It ... it was my friend's idea," Aicha said, retreating.

"What friend? You mean Aleah?"

"Yes, my best friend. You met her."

"That obnoxious woman sent me suggestive texts the same evening you introduced me to her!" Rashid said, feeling exhilarated by the slap-in-the-face he had just delivered.

"What?" Aicha looked appalled.

"Was she helping you or getting back at me for rejecting her seductive moves? Some friend she is."

"I can't believe it!" Aicha exclaimed, as an unwelcome realisation struck her.

"Aicha! Listen to me. I was never in love with you! I told you when you showed up at the gym. Why couldn't you just leave me alone?"

"I ... I was miserable," she said, closing her eyes momentarily, as if relieving the disappointment and betrayal she had experienced. "I couldn't believe that our relationship was over. I have always been involved with men who won't marry me, but don't leave me alone either. You left. Good guys leave me."

"Is this some new stupid theory you have concocted along with crystal meth and your dark magic potions?" Rashid asked.

"*Non, non*, it's what my life was like till you came along. Rashid," she said. "Please believe me, my intentions were pure. I have been going so mad, waiting for you to come back to me. I have always wanted to be with a nice guy like you, someone who would take care of me."

"Are you high? I am not a nice guy as far as women are concerned. My appetite shifts. But you wanted to own me, you stubborn, precious princess, didn't you? I am not some Arabic plush toy that your gambler-Dad can just buy for you! You never loved me!"

"That ... that's not true."

"And why would I love you? Tell me, what's so special about you?"

"I ... I ..."

"You know I'm surrounded by women who look like Russian and French models?"

"But you made me feel beautiful. You said you loved the way I looked."

"That's what I say to ALL women. It's like a tape playing on repeat, because it works on every dumb woman like you, every single time!"

Aicha was sobbing loudly now, but nothing could stop Rashid's diatribe.

"You really want to know what I think about you? I think you're ugly, your hair is thin like a straw, your skin is so rough like it's covered with scales," he said.

"Please, please don't speak like that," Aicha pleaded.

"It's true. I don't like your curves. I like women with hourglass figures. You don't have it. I only paid attention to you because you were the only thing in that effing place I could classify as a girl ... well, almost."

Rashid knew this was below the belt, even by his own standards, but his fury had escalated to a dangerously high level.

"You're just saying these things to hurt me because I hurt you. Can we just forget everything, Rashid, and start fresh? Patch things up?"

"Do you think performing magic on someone is a joke? It's unforgivable!"

"And betraying someone isn't? I told you everything about myself, all the bad things that happened to me...," she said, sobbing loudly.

A wave of guilt washed over Rashid. He noticed a small tattoo of his name near her left elbow, but dark, insidious voices invaded his thoughts, reminding him of how she had tried to ruin him.

"So, this is more about vengeance than love? Finally, you admit that!" he said, vague images of his possession, of being tied and led around like an invalid, flashing through his eyes.

"*Non, non*, it's, it's *compliqué*," Aicha said.

"No, *ma cherie*, it's not *compliqué*! I will make you leave my country forever! How dare you mess with a local! You have no idea about the kind of people I know and the things I can do!"

"I ... I'm sorry."

"Sorry is a sorry word. It doesn't mean anything," Rashid quipped.

"Things can be good again, between us," Aicha said, her eyes sparkling with tears and some remaining shreds of hopefulness. "We could get married."

"And we'll sleep on feather pillows and feather beds," Rashid replied, rolling his eyes. "Aicha, are you so dense? I sleep with a new woman every other week."

"You are joking, right? That can't be true. Tell me the truth."

"The truth? The truth is, I love you as much as my dad's *khaizaran*!"

Aicha started to weep like a wounded poodle, her kohl liner spreading down her cheeks.

"Enough with the dramatics!" Rashid snapped. "Are these crocodile tears meant to manipulate me?"

"Tell me the truth, Rashid," she said. "Or I swear, I'll do something drastic."

"Emotional blackmail will get you nowhere," he shouted.

"Do you want me to die?" she asked, a chilling desperation flickering in her eyes.

"I would set my German Shepherd on you, if I had the chance," he spat, thinking she looked like a grotesque caricature of her former self.

"I did all this only because the *saher* told me I could get you back."

"Aicha, I was with a hot Asian chick a day after I drove away from you. There is nothing you can do to get me back. You never had me. I was never the person you thought I was."

"But you must feel ... something?"

"Feel what? I am going to meet a fiery Brazilian, after our little tête-à-tête."

"No." Her voice was low now.

"And then I will unwind in a Turkish hammam, indulge in some desert rose rituals. Maybe I'll ask her to join me!" he added, smirking.

"You've turned my fairy tale into a horror story!" she spat out, her tone suddenly hostile.

"Oh, did you really think we were in a mysterious kingdom of unmatched beauty and untold wealth? Tell me, are we living in the *1001 Nights*?"

Aicha's lips quivered. Her gaze drifted towards the raindrops tracing erratic paths down a glass window. Suddenly, she seemed unfocused and whispered something, as if talking to herself.

Rashid felt a gratifying sense of accomplishment as he watched Aicha's silent distress overtake her. His phone rang and as he retrieved it from his pocket, he decided it was time to move on.

CHAPTER 33

*"Every soul will taste death.
And We test you O humanity with good
and evil as a trial, then to Us you will
all be returned."*

(21:35)

Abdulaziz opened his eyes, taking deep and steady breaths, as the evening sun gently caressed him. He was not yet ready to leave his meditative state and watched the waves reach the shore and shift the sands.

He tried to hold on to serenity, an occasional visitor, but a subtle movement towards his right intruded upon his awareness, prompting him to turn his gaze.

A solitary figure was trudging towards him. Abdulaziz wondered if a curious tourist had made the unfortunate decision to meet the ghosts of this town. After squinting for several minutes, he realised it was Badr, looking much shorter and unrecognisable as he huddled under a light grey blanket, shivering, even though the weather was not chilly.

"Badr," Abdulaziz called out, rising from his large resting rock by the shore, confusion clouding his brow.

Badr's shoulders were slumped, his pace painfully slow, as if he was dragging a boulder. Abdulaziz quickly closed the distance between them, and Badr halted, but he would not make eye contact, his face white and etched with the kind of despair Abdulaziz had only seen in paintings depicting the horrors of war.

"Are you hurt?" Abdulaziz asked, noting the complete absence of Badr's innate, unshakeable positivity, which he'd maintained even during his toughest days on the island. Today his face was like a dark and overcast sky.

"What is this?" Abdulaziz asked, motioning towards the rolled-up newspaper he was crushing with his right hand.

"I ... I was at the grocery store," Badr said, his voice barely audible.

"What's the news?" Abdulaziz asked, taking the newspaper from his hands and unrolling it.

"So ... as I ... I told you before," Badr mumbled, struggling to string his words together.

Abdulaziz flipped through the newspaper, not sure which section he was supposed to read, until Badr laid his index finger on one of the inside pages.

There was a black-and-white photo of a young Emirati man with a mischievous grin plastered on his face. He was doing a handstand against a blurry backdrop of a college campus.

"Rashid," Badr said, looking down at the photo, a wave of grief surging up.

"What?" Abdulaziz exclaimed as his eyes finally landed on the headline, 'Dubai billionaire's son passes away.'

He quickly scanned the news story, which said that Rashid had passed away in his father's hotel and that condolence meetings were being organised at this family home. The cause of death was not mentioned.

Abdulaziz recited:

"Verily we belong to Allah, and truly to Him shall we return." *(2:156)*

"But I thought he had recovered?" he asked.

"Yes ... I thought so, too," Badr said, his eyes scanning the ground, as if answers were hidden among the grains of sand. "That's why I didn't do anything when he left Fujairah."

"What do you think happened?" Abdulaziz asked, feeling a range of emotions he had not felt in a long time. The news of Rashid's recovery had made him feel like he had done something right with his life; sheltering Badr and introducing him to the jinns.

"I don't know, but ... it seems the jinni finally got to my friend, my brother!" Badr exclaimed, his voice raw with grief. "I just know that our Rashid is no more!"

"I know it's terrible to lose someone," Abdulaziz said. "Especially someone so young."

"I let him go...," Badr interrupted, as shame and sorrow gripped him. "But I should've known better."

"Known what?" Abdulaziz asked.

"I should have foreseen this," he replied, his voice rising abruptly. He seemed to be speaking more to himself than Abdulaziz.

"How could you have possibly foreseen this? You are not God," Abdulaziz said, but his tone was softer than usual.

"I should have known because he was so impulsive and unpredictable, and stupid!" Badr rambled, his eyes darting restlessly as he tried to make sense of what had happened.

"But we don't know how he died!" Abdulaziz said.

"I couldn't even attend the *salat-al-janazah*," Badr said, big teardrops rolling down his cheeks and travelling down his neck. "For the first time in life, I find my faith in Allah's justice wavering."

Abdulaziz gently placed his hand on Badr's shoulder.

"You know, once when I was younger, I was visiting a relative in a hospital in Kuwait," he said. "We overheard people in the next room say *'Alhamdulillah'* loudly. When we inquired, they told us that their loved one had just passed away, and they were celebrating because the Qur'an says:

"And the next life is certainly far better for you than this one." (93:4)

"In time, you might see Rashid's death as a release from his suffering."

"Do you mean he's better off dead than alive?" Badr asked, offended.

"Allah knows better," Abdulaziz replied. "As narrated in *Sahih al-Bukhari*, Prophet (PBUH) said, *'None of you should wish for death because of a calamity befalling him; but if he has to wish for death, he should say: O Allah! Keep me alive as long as life is better for me and let me die if death is better for me.'* "

"It can be hard to live a life without love and hope, watch the years go by uneventfully," Abdulaziz continued. "You start seeing life as the real tragedy and death as a blessing. To quote Gibran, 'And what is it to cease breathing, but to free the breath from its restless tides, that it may rise and expand and seek God unencumbered?'"

"I don't feel that way," Badr said. "Allah could have blessed Rashid with a better life."

"Death is a transition," Abdulaziz replied. "As Imam Husain (AS) said: *'Patience, O Children of noble (souls), because death is nothing but a bridge which takes you from difficulties and troubles to the vast Paradise and everlasting bliss. So, who among you would dislike to transfer from the prison of the world to the palace of the Paradise? But these enemies of yours will go from a palace to a prison and ever-lasting punishment.'"* Badr did not respond. They stood quietly, surrounded only by the roar of the waves and the scent of the salty sea, as Badr grappled with the weight of profound loss and unanswered questions.

"I guess I need to face the truth," he finally said, wiping his tears with the back of his hand.

"What truth?" Abdulaziz asked, emerging from his own contemplative silence.

"Something so dreadful has happened that life will never be the same again," Badr said. "It has all crumbled to dust."

"Is this the first time you've lost someone close to you?" Abdulaziz asked in a kind voice.

"Yes. He was like my brother. We were inseparable since school days. Why did this happen, Abdulaziz? We prayed so much for him."

"I don't know, Badr. But we must accept Allah's will," Abdulaziz said, his voice firm yet compassionate. "Loss is a part of life. As the Qur'an says:

'He is the One Who created you from dust, then from a sperm-drop,
then developed you into a clinging clot, then He brings you forth as infants,
so that you may reach your prime, and become old—though some of you
may die sooner—reaching an appointed time, so perhaps you may
understand Allah's power.'" (40:67)

"I understand what you are saying, but I don't know what to do," Badr replied.

"Rashid is at home with his Creator," Abdulaziz said. "There's nothing you can do now except pray to Allah to forgive Rashid's sins. Pray that the weight of his good deeds is greater than the bad ones. Forgive him if he has ever hurt you. Remember him for his good qualities. Give charity, *sadaqah jariyah*, in his name. You could donate to a hospital, a school or build a well perhaps, for continuous charity in his name. This might give you some relief. And over time, you may become friends with your grief. It will become a part of who are you and you'll feel like you have access to other realms."

"What do you mean?" Badr asked, feeling angry now. He knew Abdulaziz was saying all the right things to make him feel better. But he did not want to feel better. All he knew was that Rashid was dead and he would never see or talk to him again. Gone without a goodbye. But Abdulaziz continued, "When someone very close to you reunites with the Creator, you develop a connection with the spiritual world. You have always believed in it, but now you know in your body and soul that there is an afterlife, that heaven and hell exist, that there is a place where they rest and wait for you. They become a bridge between this world and the next."

"Maybe you are right," Badr conceded reluctantly, moving his feet away from the skeletal remains of a starfish. "Maybe someday I will find some sort of consolation in believing that I still have a connection with Rashid."

"You should rest now," Abdulaziz said. "Grief can be overpowering and consume you."

"But I can't rest! You don't understand what this means!" Badr exclaimed, his voice now loud enough to scare the seagulls away.

"What does it mean?" Abdulaziz asked.

"If Rashid did not recover, as we had assumed, it means Sheikh Omar failed. We all failed," Badr said, gasping for air.

"Well, sometimes, Badr ... Allah does not cure the mortal because it's their soul's time to leave. The timing of our deaths is predetermined."

"But God will not delay a soul when its time has come.
God is Informed of what you do." (63:11)

"No! I mean, I can't trust these remedies alone ... to heal Dana. I can't risk losing her. I've already lost Rashid."

"But what will you do?" Abdulaziz asked. "Go to another healer?"

"No, no ... I think I need to meet the jinns again," Badr said.

"The jinns? But why?" Abdulaziz asked.

"I think these jinns hold the key or can at least give me some clue about her possession before I leave," Badr said, suddenly standing up, his entire being bursting with energy.

"But, even if they do, how will you tell Dana?" Abdulaziz asked.

"I will go to her!"

"But I thought you couldn't leave the island?" Abdulaziz asked. "Let alone go to the US?"

"I don't know, but I will just have to find a way," Badr insisted. "If people just gave up so easily, no one would ever unite with the person they loved. You won't understand!"

Abdulaziz's face turned white.

"I am so sorry," Badr said quickly. "That came out wrong. It wasn't a jab at you in any way."

"I am sure it wasn't … I don't know … the jinns don't entertain human guests all the time," Abdulaziz said, frowning, but Badr interrupted him.

"Please, Abdulaziz. I just don't want to miss this opportunity. I might never come back here. And I'll probably never see the jinns again. Can you please take me to see them tonight?"

Abdulaziz was silent, his brow furrowed, as if he was deliberating on Badr's request.

"I know you've already done a lot for me. Gave me shelter here," Badr said.

"So, if the jinns say they can help, that means you'll be staying here a bit longer?" Abdulaziz asked, without letting him finish.

"Yes, I need some answers," Badr replied, casting a curious glance at Abdulaziz. Even in his present state of mind, he noticed a change in Abdulaziz's demeanour. He wondered if the man was trying to cover up the distress he must be feeling about being reminded of his lost love and of Badr's imminent departure.

"I will be forever indebted to you, Abdulaziz. Please!" Badr added.

"You are excessively devoted to Dana," Abdulaziz said after a few seconds, his expression troubled, his eyes not meeting Badr's.

"Yes. I can't imagine life without her."

Despite the internal turmoil he seemed to be struggling with, Abdulaziz looked at Badr and said, "Alright, I will speak to the jinns."

CHAPTER 34

*"So, surely with hardship
comes ease."*

(94:5)

Badr called Sultan from the grocery shop in Alhumriya, pretending to be a friend from college who lived in Ras Al Khaimah.

"Are you keen on having fish tonight?" he asked, his heart heavy. Sultan understood Badr's coded message and agreed to meet him.

Wearing western clothes and covering his face partially by placing a *keffiyeh* around his neck, Badr made his way to Umm al Quwain, the second smallest and least populated emirate.

Under normal circumstances, he would have loved the drive between Umm Al Quwain and Ras Al Khaimah. He considered it to be the most beautiful road in the country as it would cut into the beach side often, affording him the pleasure of watching the pristine waters and the sand dunes make love to each other. But today he was driving just within the speed limit. He wanted to reach the Nile Seafood Cafeteria as soon as possible. It was the only place he knew of in UAQ, frequented mostly by locals. He'd been there numerous times with college friends.

Crossing a group of young Emiratis, who were lounging outside, sipping on hot *karak* tea and laughing, Badr entered the small cafeteria. It was, as usual, filled with the fragrant aroma of warm curries.

Badr was surprised to see a couple sitting at one of the four rundown tables inside, enjoying a meal. Although there was no law restricting women from eating at this place, it was highly unusual. The Indian waiter was casting them a sly glance as they drafted a new chapter in their personal history, completely oblivious to his judgemental stare.

"You'll have the usual?" the waiter inquired as he continued to eye the couple with a mischievous grin.

"Yes, the usual," Badr replied curtly, realising that the sight of young couples courting each other freely, publicly, now left a bitter taste in his mouth. He also had little appetite for the cafeteria's special and his favourite dish: salted shark meat and calamari curry with a slice of lemon and green chili.

A wave of relief washed over him as Sultan entered, his weathered face etched with concern. Tears welled up in their eyes as they hugged and looked at each other, and at the empty seat beside them, paying a silent tribute to Rashid. Their lives felt colourless.

"How are you, *okhoy*?" Sultan asked, his voice emotional.

"Going crazy, *okhoy*," Badr replied. "Not being on his side. Not knowing what happened to Rashid. I know he had his share of flaws, but he still deserved a chance at life."

"Yes, he did," Sultan said, his gaze filled with their shared pain.

"Can you tell me what happened to him?" Badr asked.

"It was a harrowing night," Sultan replied. "I rushed to the hospital as soon as I heard that Rashid was injured and had slipped into a coma. But by the time I reached the ICU, it was all over. His brother handed me a paper with the flat ECG lines, *ya'ani*, confirming his death. When I walked towards Rashid's bed, he was already wrapped up in a white cloth. The colour of his face was changing when we took him for *ghusl*. And I can never forget the moment we lowered him into the ground, knowing he would soon blend into the earth."

"Death is not pretty," Badr said, trying hard not to visualise how Rashid must have looked when his heart stopped beating. "But what caused his sudden death?"

"I am not sure, *okhoy*," Sultan said, shaking his head. "His family hadn't seen him for a long time. They didn't know he was with you. And then one day he just came to Uncle's hotel and later a waiter discovered his body. They think he may have fallen and hit his head on something sharp. *Ya'ani* wrong angle. They are still looking into it to rule out foul play."

Badr felt a mix of anger, shock, and disorientation as he listened to Sultan.

"I was too disturbed to really pay attention to the investigation. I mean he's gone. Nothing is bringing him back. I just visit his grave often and pray for him," Sultan said.

"I wish I could accompany you," Badr said. "I didn't even get a chance to say goodbye, be part of the rituals. I realise now those things are important. It will take me a long time to even grasp the fact that he is no more."

Sultan nodded, teardrops quietly rolling down his cheeks.

"In retrospect, I think our month together was not so much about his recovery than a prolonged goodbye," Badr said, as Sultan wiped his face with a tissue. "But it all happened so fast I didn't even get a chance to tell him the stuff that had happened to me since the attack in the US."

"Oh, that reminds me," Sultan said, reaching out for his *ghaf* leather bag. "I was about to get in touch with you when you called me."

"To speak about Rashid?" Badr asked.

"Yes, of course, but also I have some news to share with you ... it might make you feel a little better."

"I doubt it. What's the news?"

"This is from your *Baba*," Sultan said as he handed a large, brown envelope to Badr. It contained a passport, several thousand dollars and some papers.

"What is this?" Badr asked, flipping through the unfamiliar passport.

"It's your nephew Essa's American passport. Remember, he was born there? Your *Baba* said you'll need to go to the US embassy, *ya'ani* you need to act as if you are Essa. They will need your fingerprints as luckily, Essa never gave his fingerprints. And you'll find all the necessary documents in this envelope, including an open ticket."

"But what if I get caught? Wouldn't that make things worse for me?"

"Uncle thinks this is the best available option. How long can you stay hidden on the island? Once you get this passport updated, you'll be able to fly out to any country. You should be safe in Europe," Sultan said.

Badr looked at the passport in his hand. This was it. His way out.

"I thought you would be more relieved," Sultan said.

"I am," Badr said. "I just need to do one more thing before I leave."

CHAPTER 35

———◆———

*"O believers! Seek comfort in patience and prayer.
Allah is truly with those who are patient."*

(2:153)

Abdulaziz withdrew into his own little world after Badr announced his intentions to leave the island sooner than expected. He spent the next couple of days brooding and smoking more packs of cigarettes than usual.

Badr felt remorseful about deserting Abdulaziz. He was the only human friend Abdulaziz had had in years, a connection to his past life. No matter how much Abdulaziz claimed to be a dead man or one of the jinns, Badr knew he was glad to have his company. Someone he could talk to about Azza and complain to about society's injustices. But Badr also knew his departure from the island was inevitable. He resolved to stick to his plan, promising Abdulaziz he would visit him once he had successfully reunited with Dana.

Abdulaziz shrugged off his sentimentality. "I have arranged for us to visit the jinns at the abandoned school, as you wanted," he said, changing the subject.

Feeling hurt, Badr gave up trying to get Abdulaziz to express what he was feeling. Later that evening, he followed him into a dusty, high-ceilinged classroom, with cobweb-draped corners and scent of aged paper; a stark contrast to the library they had previously been entertained in by the *Ulema*.

Akil, the leader of the *Ulema*, and his watchful tribe members, sat on mats, surrounded by dust motes dancing in the dim light. After exchanging greetings, Badr sat down on a *diwan* they had placed from him in the centre and started to recount his and Dana's story. He was very meticulous, fearing he might overlook a crucial detail that held clues to what had caused her plight.

Time slipped away unnoticed until the jinns became restless. Badr halted abruptly, realising he had started to repeat himself, and glanced expectantly at his audience.

Silence greeted him along with the whispers of wind travelling through the broken panes of the windows. Something felt off about this visit; the jinns looked solemn, disengaged, and restless. Like bored husbands at female-centric social events.

Badr stood motionless, waiting for someone to say something. Usually, Abdulaziz would jump in to help make his case, but today he also sat in a corner, scrutinising broken pencils, a faded ruler, and a slate, as though he had stumbled upon a hidden treasure.

Badr looked at Akil, who gazed back at him. He seemed unsure about how to respond and gently broke the silence. "Badr, we understand. But what do you need us to do?"

"Well … I was hoping you could help me uncover the source," Badr replied, ignoring the urge to shake the jinns and force them to react and act.

"What do you mean by the source?" Akil inquired.

"I mean, I want to uncover who is haunting Dana. Or who might have performed magic on her, who is responsible for her condition? Despite our best efforts, we haven't been able to pinpoint the source."

The jinns turned to each other, exchanging murmurs. Some retrieved scrolls from cylindrical containers, unfolding parchments adorned with intricate calligraphy, as if seeking answers within the ancient texts.

Badr stood by, trying to be best friends with patience and track time from an hourglass, as the jinns consulted each other and conducted their research.

"I don't think he can do much," Badr overheard Muhandis, the engineer-jinn remark.

Feeling a pang of frustration, Badr scanned the room and locked eyes with Muhandis.

"I came here with great hope," he said, his tone tinged with anger at Muhandis' dismissiveness. "I remember during our last meeting, you spoke of love surviving only when it's structured, when problems are solved with logic and rationality. Well, here I am, searching for a practical solution to my dilemma."

Before Muhandis could respond, Shaykh, a Sufi-jinn, broke the tension. "I think the words of Hazrat Inayat Khan may help you. He said, 'there can be no rebirth without a dark night of the soul,' one that dismantles all your existing thoughts and beliefs."

"And how does this dark night end?" Badr asked, feeling as though the jinns did not want to help him.

"There might be other avenues for her healing," Shaykh replied calmly.

"What other avenues?" Badr pressed, wanting to stamp his feet.

"Your relationship could be a source of healing," suggested Faylasuf, a philosopher-jinn.

"Yes, but ... that's not a solution ... there's no guarantee," Badr retorted sharply.

"We are not guaranteed anything in life," Faylasuf said, his voice carrying a serene wisdom that Badr found annoying. "The only thing you can do is paint the canvas of your life with love, which means loving them for who they are right now, with all their flaws and problems."

"That's why we say that love is unconditional. It is not convenient," Shaykh added.

"But perhaps you should consider the concept of synchronicity," Akil said thoughtfully. "It illustrates how life can align to bring us love in ways that feel destined."

"I cannot rely on destiny alone," Badr replied, remembering how he had relished these discussions, but tonight his patience for riddles was wearing thin. Still, he knew he couldn't afford to alienate the jinns—they had aided in Rashid's rescue, even if now it seemed that, like all the others, they were not in favour of his union with Dana.

"Why does love seem perpetually bound by pain?" Badr asked, breaking the uneasy silence that hung over the room.

"We understand your anguish," Akil said, coming close and laying a reassuring hand on Badr's shoulder. "But even if you knew who was haunting her, what would you do?"

"I might be able to help her," Badr murmured, though his confidence in his plan was dwindling quite fast,

Following Rashid's recovery, Badr had felt incredibly optimistic, but since his death, everything had spiralled downwards. He had come to the *Ulema,* expecting answers, but had only gotten more questions, more disappointments.

"*Salam* Badr!" he heard someone said.

"*Salam!*" Badr replied, turning around to find a tall and elderly *imam*-jinn, with a *tasbih* in his hand, walking towards him, the other jinns clearing the way for him.

"You are in the wrong place, Badr!" the *imam* scolded.

"What?" Badr asked, feeling attacked.

"Yes, indeed! When I heard you were at the school, I came straight here, from the mosque, to warn you."

"Warn me about what?" Badr asked, deciding the jinns were no better than humans.

"You need to know that interacting like this with the jinns is forbidden," the *imam* said, his tone stern.

"But I've been here before," Badr protested, seething with frustration at being treated like a defiant child.

The *imam* shook his head, looking grave. "Earlier we needed to conduct research on humans, and you needed our assistance, so we made an exception, but interacting further, without a specific purpose, would be considered a sin. You must leave immediately and seek Allah's forgiveness."

"But ... but I still need your help," Badr said, panic clawing at his throat.

"I know," the *imam* replied with a flicker of understanding in his gaze.

"You do?" Badr asked, wondering if the *imam* had been listening to his story.

"Yes," the *imam* replied, his expression softening. "I was present when you took Dana to Sheikh Ali's house."

"You were there?" Badr was astounded.

"Yes, we were there, a group of us, trying to help. You likely didn't notice anything amiss; you were so focused on Dana."

"I apologise," Badr said. "Even if there were signs, I wouldn't have recognised them. This is all so new to me. But why can't you help me now?"

"It's not a lack of willingness on our part," the *imam* clarified. "We simply cannot. Dana's situation is a mystery. That day, much like Sheikh Ali, we also could not fathom what was happening to her."

"What do you mean?" Badr asked, sick of hearing the same thing over and over again; how Dana's disease was undiagnosable.

"The sacred verses held no sway over her," the *imam* explained, his tone now compassionate. "It was unsettling. She seemed quite at home with whatever was oppressing her. As if Allah had sanctioned the presence of this unknown being. Like she had become one with that being."

A cold dread settled in Badr's stomach. He'd always sensed something was different about Dana's possession. Unlike Rashid and other victims of possession that he'd heard of, the changes in her behaviour seemed to be more subtle, non-violent.

"Are you trying to say she cannot be healed?" Badr asked, wondering what hope he had if even the jinns couldn't help him.

The *imam* sighed. "We don't know, Badr. But as Muslims, we believe any illness can cleanse the soul, erase sins, if we endure it with patience, prayer, and gratitude."

"But surely there's a cure, a way to extract her from this strange other world she involuntarily enters!" Badr pleaded.

The *imam* shook his head. "We're at a loss. This is beyond us. You won't find answers here, *abni*. Our knowledge is limited, a gift from Allah, but it doesn't encompass all the universe's mysteries. Only the Divine holds all the answers. Perhaps His other creations would have an answer."

"What other creations?" Badr asked.

"I think the angels might be able to answer you," the *imam* said.

"The angels?" Badr was baffled.

"Yes, the angels possess vast wisdom and dwell closer to the skies. They know more secrets of the universe than we do," the *imam* said.

"But how can I even meet an angel?" Badr asked.

"There is one inside the watchtower, guarding the gate to the sky, the gate that only the angels can use. But I doubt they would speak to a human," Akil said, looking grim.

"What am I supposed to do?" Badr asked, inhaling sharply.

"For now, you must leave. We need to attend to other important matters," the *imam* said in a firm tone, but his smile was sympathetic. "May Allah grant you peace, Badr. *Fee Amanillah*."

Turning a deaf ear to Badr's protest, the *imam* turned towards Akil and started to walk out with him. Badr could hear snippets of their conversation. "We need to speak with the new *Aljaysh* leader soon. He's trying to convince his tribe that the

Earth still belongs to them, like it did before Allah created humans. They want to regain their dominance. They plan to overpower the angel in the watchtower. We must get together soon and talk them out of it."

"Sounds like the jinn have their own twisted version of Samer," Badr thought, feeling bitter and disappointed at being dismissed so easily. Previously, he'd enjoyed the company of these jinns, appreciated their support. Now he felt like an outsider, an intruder.

He watched the *imam* and Akil walk away, their voices becoming distant while they remain immersed in deep conversation. The *Ulema* disbanded, taking with them his last thread of hope.

CHAPTER 36

*"'It was he who truly made me stray from
the Reminder after it had reached me.' And
Satan has always betrayed humanity."*

(25:29)

A labyrinth of nightmares, spun from the words of the jinns, kept Badr agitated for the rest of the night.

"Sheikh … sheikh … please wake up!" someone shouted, as he blinked against the harsh sunlight, his mind still foggy. He was struggling to recall whether Abdulaziz had roused him for *fajr* prayers.

"Sheikh," the familiar voice called out again.

"Maftoon?" Badr's voice trailed off as he shook his head, struggling to grasp the present moment. "Is that you? Where are you?"

"Yes, sheikh. It's me," Maftoon confirmed.

"But why can't I see you?" Badr asked, squinting, searching the empty space around him.

"The daylight is preventing you from seeing me, sheikh. You're not accustomed to seeing me at this hour."

"Ah … yes … of course," Badr murmured, confused by the change in his morning routine. "But why are you here in the daylight? Aren't you and the other jinns obligated to depart before *fajr*?"

"Indeed, sheikh. That's precisely why I'm here. We need your help!" Maftoon said, a hint of urgency in his voice.

"My help? What's wrong? What happened?" Badr asked, rubbing his eyes.

"The gate … we need to shut the gate … Abdulaziz did not show up today."

"What? Where is he?" Badr asked, not ready to deal with new challenges.

"We don't know," Maftoon replied grimly.

"Can't we wait for him? He might be at the cafeteria or fishing?" Badr asked, his voice wavering.

"At this hour? No, no, that can't be it. He is very punctual and has never missed a day since he became the gatekeeper," Maftoon said. "And time is not on our side, so we can't look for him right now. The gate must be closed very soon."

"Why?" Badr asked.

"Because the last time it remained open, war nearly engulfed everything," Maftoon said, his voice dropping to a grave whisper.

"But what can I do about it?" Badr asked, resisting yet another unwarranted distraction from his goal of escaping this unfortunate phase in his life. He was unprepared to take on a new responsibility, and not keen on helping the jinns since last night's debacle.

"You need to get the musk," Maftoon instructed, his voice filled with fear and urgency. "Seal the gate, just like Abdulaziz does."

Badr gazed into a vacant spot, where he assumed Maftoon was standing. His eyes travelled to the window and followed the flight of a crow as he deliberated on his next course of action.

"Please, hurry!" Maftoon pleaded when Badr did not move or say anything. Sighing deeply, Badr rose, reluctant to comply. His gaze scanned the room for the black bottle, which Abdulaziz usually handled as though it was made of precious stones. It took him some time to spot the bottle because it was wrapped in a piece of yellowish paper. The bottle sat on the side table next to Abdulaziz's meticulously made bed.

The sight of Abdulaziz's empty, tidy bed unsettled Badr. It was as if no one had ever slept in it.

"Something's clearly wrong again with the world today," he muttered under his breath, noticing how Azza's shrine was also gone.

"We have no time to lose," Maftoon's voice cut through Badr's jumbled thoughts.

"The musk," Badr managed to say as he grasped the bottle and untied the piece of paper wrapped around it, realising that it was a note from Abdulaziz. Following Maftoon's voice outside the house, he deciphered the hurried scrawl with some difficulty.

"Badr,

Sometimes, you become someone you thought you'd never be.

Sometimes, to get love, 'Azāzīl needs to become Iblis.

Abdulaziz."

Badr quickly dropped the note into his pocket, as if it was infected, realising that Abdulaziz wasn't just gone for the day. There was a high probability that he had left the island for good, abandoning Badr, his life and everything else.

"How could he just leave with a vague message? What is he planning to do? Where is he planning to go?" Badr wondered, feeling stung by what felt like unwarranted cruelty. Death from a thousand cuts."

"Abdulaziz, you aren't the man I thought you were," he said under his breath, mulling over his friend's cryptic words. It was hard enough to accept that Rashid had died, and now he had to consider the possibility that he would never see Abdulaziz again. He'd lost two important relationships within the span of a few days, sans any explanation.

> *"One of them said, 'Do not kill Joseph. But if you must do something,*
> *throw him into the bottom of a well so perhaps he may be picked up*
> *by some travellers.'" (12:10)*

He recited the verses as they reached Abdulaziz's rock by the shore.

"What now?" he asked Maftoon, wondering if running away was still a viable option, or if the jinns would hold him hostage till he met their expectations.

"Begin the ritual," Maftoon instructed, oblivious to Badr's misgivings. "I'll guide the jinns towards the sea. Remember, Badr, becoming the gatekeeper demands immense strength."

"What kind of strength?" Badr asked, but there was no response. Maftoon had hurried off to accomplish his mission.

It dawned on Badr that Abdulaziz may have left him without a warning because he needed someone to be the gatekeeper.

"Is that it?" Badr asked, looking at the rock, a surge of panic washing over him as he tried to recall the steps to close the gate. He knew he did not have Abdulaziz's monstrous strength.

With a shaky breath, he knelt by the rock and was about to draw *'Bismillah'* with musk when he froze outwardly. Inside, the numbness he'd been feeling since morning had been replaced by fury, surging inside him like a wildfire, sweeping away all his reasons and restraint.

No one had ever betrayed him before. He had certainly not expected it from a man who he considered a friend, a confidante and perhaps even a mentor of sorts.

"Abdulaziz, I had no idea you were so selfish," he muttered under his breath, staring at the sea with a melancholic longing to go back in time when the waves were content with just rising and falling.

"Maybe people were right about you. Maybe you are insane. I am the one who tried to give you the benefit of doubt, put you on a pedestal."

Badr felt foolish, realising he had mistaken Abdulaziz's silence for sorrow at his upcoming departure. He had been engrossed in making his own plans, without any consideration for Badr or how his life would be impacted. His voice higher than the waves, he recited:

"O believers! Do not betray Allah and the Messenger,
nor betray your trusts knowingly place no after."(8:27)

The betrayal felt ruthless, like Abdulaziz had used the sharpest knife to stab his already-punctured heart. One minute, the man was consoling and protecting Badr, keeping him company, helping him solve his biggest problems, the next he had dropped out of his life like he'd never existed. Their relationship felt like a figment of Badr's imagination.

"You're going to see Azza, aren't you? Where else would you go?" Badr asked as he threw a pebble at Abdulaziz's rock. "You'd rather stay with the ghosts of your past than care for the people in your life right now? And why should I be the gatekeeper? A role you just thrust upon me. You chose this life for yourself. I didn't!"

He took out Abdulaziz's note from his pocket, intending to crumple it and throw it away, but couldn't bring himself to do it.

"Rashid's death was a tragedy. But you made a choice, knowing fully well how badly, and deeply, your actions would hurt me," Badr said, shoving the note back into his pocket.

"Somehow, if even it's possible, your actions feel more hurtful than Rashid's death," Badr continued, looking angrily at the rock. "I know you do not owe me any explanation for your life choices. You didn't make any promises to me. It was I who foolishly assumed I was important to you. I didn't think the strength of a relationship was dependent on the amount of time you spent with a person. But now it seems like we never ceased to be strangers. You never really showed me who you are until now."

"I opened up to you and you left me stranded here as the gatekeeper. And these jinns, they're no better ... consumed by their own desires," Badr muttered, a raw, chaotic energy beginning to emerge from inside him.

"But isn't this what you do? When things get tough, and hard choices need to be made, you run away!" Badr said, as the energy travelled through his bloodstream and spread to all parts of his body. When it reached his brain, an idea began to take hold and grow bigger, stronger, until it had captured most of Badr's mind.

"Well, I don't need to accept the fate you have designed for me, like you're some kind of God!" Badr almost shouted. With a chilling resolve, he decided to set his new plan into motion.

"Maftoon?" His voice crackled, raw with shock at what he was doing. His actions seemed almost involuntary. Like a secret power he had just discovered was controlling him and not the other way round.

"Sheikh," he heard Maftoon said. "I came back to see what happened? The jinns are on their way out. Are you facing problems in closing the gate?"

"I need to speak to the *Aljaysh*," Badr replied, his tone assertive. "The other tribes can leave."

"But why? You are the gatekeeper now. You must close the gate and shield them and yourself from the consequences of defying the boundaries set by Allah," Maftoon said, speaking really fast now. "Otherwise, there will be chaos. They can attack humans, or worse, attempt to breach the heavenly gates, even challenge the angels!"

"I need to speak to them before I close the gate. Take me to them," Badr said, his voice forceful.

"Talk to them about what?" Maftoon asked, sounding anxious. "What has happened?"

When Badr did not answer, he said, "Well, the *Mashaikh* and *Ulema* are already out in the sea."

"What about the *Aljaysh*?" Badr asked.

"They're still on the island," Maftoon replied in a small, quiet voice.

"Take me to them!" Badr instructed.

"But..."

"I don't want to argue, Maftoon. It's very important that I speak to them before they leave."

Reluctantly, Maftoon directed Badr towards a dilapidated house close to the sea. "Nothing good can come of this," he insisted, but Badr ignored him.

"Please be quick with whatever this urgent matter is," Maftoon said. "And then, please guide the *Aljaysh* towards the sea."

Badr walked into the house, slowly but purposefully, as the sunlight obscured his view of the jinns inside. It was dark, so he left the door ajar and stood in the middle of a sunlit space. The room was warm and had the lingering scent of a recently extinguished fire.

A faint hum reached his ears as he stood in front of the encroaching shadows. "Badr?" a commanding voice reverberated through the room.

"Badr?" a commanding voice reverberated through the room.

"Yes," he said, trying to discern where the voice was coming from, but the gloomy room offered no hints. "Who ... who am I speaking to?"

"I am General Fairooz, the leader of *Aljaysh*," said the General, his voice harsh like the crackle of burning coal.

"I am honoured to meet you General Fairooz," Badr replied, suppressing his discomfort.

"What is it that you want from us?" Fairooz asked with a venomous authority, his presence overbearing despite his invisibility.

"I've heard of your plans to overpower the angels," Badr said, carefully choosing his words.
"I see," Fairooz replied. "Did the other jinns send you here to talk me out of it?"

"No, no. I want to help lead you to victory," Badr replied, trying to sound convincing.

"A human will help us?" Fairooz said with a derisive chuckle, and the room echoed with laughter. "And how do you plan on doing that?"

"You want to rule the *malayika*?" Badr asked, ignoring the mockery. He had vowed to do anything that would help him save Dana. Even tolerate obnoxious jinns.

"You're born of dirt. We're born with greatness. We believe the *malayika* and other creatures have lost their way. We will guide them, with Allah's permission."

"I am in awe of you and your vision for the world," Badr said, struggling to sound honest. "As the new gatekeeper, I could be useful to you."

"How so?" Fairooz asked, his voice a mixture of humour and scepticism.

"I could keep the gate open and divert the angel guarding the entrance to the watchtower," Badr said. "I won't be seen as a threat. Meanwhile, you could block the entrance and then capture the angel."

"Interesting ... and why do you want to help us?" Fairooz asked, sounding suspicious of Badr's motives.

"You saved my life when Rashid was taking me away in my car," Badr said. "I am grateful, and I want to return the favour, if you can guarantee the protection of me and my loved ones."

"Oh, how noble of you!" Fairooz said. "We love making our enemies bleed. Do you? It's a big undertaking. Are you ready for it? Is that the only reason? Because you feel indebted to us?"

Badr hesitated, unsure how frequently the tribes spoke to one other. If Fairooz had spies around, he would already know what Badr was after, and a lie could foil his entire plan.

"There is ... another reason," Badr replied, treading cautiously. "I need to ask the angel some questions. I fear that, even if he does speak to me, he might not give me the answers I need. But if you are victorious, you can make him reveal the truth."

"The truth about Dana?" Fairooz asked, with an air of smugness, as if ready to take advantage of Badr's weakness.

"Yes," Badr replied, irked, unsure of how things would play out. He could hear the other jinns talking amongst themselves.

"Can we trust him?" someone asked. "He comes from a world that is corrupt, decadent and in moral decline."

"But he's alone here and can't harm us in any way," another said. Their voices grew louder, their tone unpleasant, words increasingly offensive.

Badr moved back, trying to keep his anger in check.

"Enough!" Fairooz said, and the conversation shut down swiftly, as if the General had pulled the trigger on his soldiers.

Badr felt him move closer as he said, "Okay, Badr. I've decided to give you a chance. We can make a deal. We will go to the watchtower together. You will go up first and enter the tower. You will try to speak to the angel, gain his attention. Introduce yourself as the new gatekeeper and the angel might respond. Understood?"

"Yes," Badr replied. "And what will you do? I hear the angels have an eternal life. There is no death or decay for them."

"Yes, but they don't have a willpower either. Once we have captured and imprisoned them, they will have to do whatever we ask them to. So, we will block the entrance and capture the angel guarding the tower. Then, we'll obstruct the gate to the sky, to stop the angel from escaping and warning other angels. As we encircle and immobilise the angels, we'll get some time to execute the remaining part of the plan," Fairooz explained.

"The remaining part?" Badr asked. "Do you mean you will attack humans after that?"

"We might. But you and your loved ones will always be protected if, and only if, you follow all our orders. If you don't, if you take one wrong step, then nobody, not even Allah will be able to help you!"

"Fighting alongside you is my highest honour," Badr reassured him. "But will you get me the answers I need?”

“Yes, I will. Your unyielding spirit has impressed me,” Fairooz said. “I can recognise fellow warriors. Your eyes burn with the intensity of a thousand suns.”

Badr nodded and asked, “So what is the next step?”

“Let’s prepare for victory!” Fairooz commanded loudly, and the room erupted with applause and laughter.

CHAPTER 37

"Remember when you cried out to your Lord for help, He answered, "I will reinforce you with a thousand angels—followed by many others."

(8:9)

Hours later, Badr began an arduous and demanding journey, trekking towards the ancient Al Hamra Tower, with the *Aljaysh* marching close behind him, their presence palpable. He could now see their silhouettes under the warm orange sun.

There were about a thousand troops, wearing red uniforms and intricately engraved armours.

"Hungry wolves, ready to pounce on their prey," Badr muttered, as they moved closer to their destination. He looked up at the magnificent watchtower, made of coral and beach stone, mangrove beams and palm fronds. It rose majestically and ominously against the backdrop of the cloudless sky.

"Are you ready?" Fairooz asked, his voice menacing, his eyes fierce and defiant. He was watching Badr closely, as if trying to find any sign of mutiny.

"Yes," Badr replied, although his steely determination was wavering. The demonic energy, which had earlier pushed him to embark on his devious plan, was now loosening its grip.

As he admired the imposing and ethereal structure of the tower, he thought of how it had once successfully defended this town and survived almost a hundred years.

"You will enjoy being our recruit. We will surely outnumber them. Protect yourself from a rain of metal, bricks, and glass though. Expect the unexpected," Fairooz said, his lips curling into a sardonic smile. The hungry wolf appeared ravenous for the depth of flavours only the all-powerful could savour.

Badr nodded and started to climb the watchtower's steps slowly, feeling unprepared for the dangers that lay ahead. It had all seemed much simpler in his imagination. Now, closer to his destination, many questions appeared. "Can I really trust the *Aljaysh*? Why would they spare me and meet my demands after they capture the angel? Is this a suicide mission?"

"Am I no better than Samer?" he wondered. "He did things out of hate, while I am doing them for love. But will the outcome be any less destructive? What will happen to Al Jazirah and the world beyond it? If the angels can be defeated, what chance do humans have against an invisible enemy?"

Badr had now reached the top of the stairs and stood in front of the tower's dark brown wooden door, with partly broken hinges. The tower's exterior was a patchwork of faded hues and white circles. As Badr looked closely at this weathered canvas, he regained some mental clarity. Hearing faint sounds of footsteps behind him, he realised some members of the *Aljaysh* were slowly making their way up the stairs, ready to lay siege to the watchtower and ambush the angels.

With a determined push, Badr entered the tower's sunlit space below the observation deck, devoid of any occupants. Its walls seemed impenetrable.

Taking a deep breath, as if to usher in courage, Badr took out the bottle of musk he was still carrying with him. Uncapping it, he traced lines across the threshold and the window, hoping this would deter the *Aljaysh* from entering the tower and give him some time to put into action an alternative plan that had emerged.

The shouts and threats of the *Aljaysh* echoed in his ears, as they immediately realised what he had done.

With his terror intensifying, Badr closed the door and pressed his back against it. Desperate, he drew another line of musk on the window, though uncertain of its efficacy, and recited:

> *"And only believe those who follow your religion. Say, O Prophet, 'Surely, the only true guidance is Allah's guidance.' They also said, 'Do not believe that someone will receive revealed knowledge similar to yours or argue against you before your Lord.' Say, O Prophet, 'Indeed, all bounty is in the Hands of Allah—He grants it to whoever He wills. And Allah is All-Bountiful, All-Knowing.'" (3:75)*

With trembling hands and racing thoughts, he sank to the floor, seeking solace in the hope of God's help and the angel's arrival.

"If you're present, please communicate with me," he implored. "I need your help and guidance. Please!"

There was no response. "I know you are not supposed to speak to ordinary humans like me," Badr said. "But I have something very important to tell you. And I don't have much time!"

There was complete silence, only punctuated by the sounds of the *Aljaysh* settling outside the door. Badr anxiously paced across the space, trying to find some sign of where the angel might be. Each passing minute felt like an eternity until he detected a faint movement close to the light, entering through a small window on the opposite wall.

As if a floodlight had just been switched on, the sun slowly illuminated almost half of the space in front of Badr. He stepped back, shielding his eyes.

Gradually, his eyes grew accustomed to the bright light, to see a man, dressed in white robes, his head almost touching the ceiling, an intense radiance emanating from his form.

"I had to seek permission to converse with you, Badr," he said in a calm, authoritative voice. Badr felt some of his muscles loosen as the angel seemed more approachable than he had expected.

"We don't usually speak to the Almighty's other creations," the angel said. "But we want to know why you took the pains to come here today and seek our counsel."

"I am Badr, the new gatekeeper," Badr replied.

"I see. We were not aware of Abdulaziz's departure since he serves the jinns."

"He left unexpectedly, and I have inherited his role. But I simply desire an end to all of this," Badr confessed.

"Be more precise, Badr. Clarity is essential to obtaining the blessings you seek," the angel advised.

"I wish for this turmoil to cease," Badr exclaimed.

"What turmoil do you speak of? You must articulate your desires clearly and quickly, Badr," the angel urged.

"I refuse to become the gatekeeper. I don't want to be like Abdulaziz," Badr said, gathering his thoughts. "I need someone else to assume the role of gatekeeper."

"Understood. You have a free will and so we shall appoint a successor," the angel assured.

"I also demand the safety of my family," Badr stipulated.

"Safety and security are granted by Allah, *Al-Mu'min, Al-Muhaymin,*" the angel replied. "We simply worship Him and follow all His commands."

"But there is something else I want as well, and I've been told that you can help me secure it," Badr continued.

"What is it?" the angel asked.

"I need to know who is afflicting Dana, I love her, and need to know how I can save her," Badr pleaded. "No human or jinn has been able to help me."

"This matter exceeds my jurisdiction," the angel replied.

"I won't leave without an answer," Badr said feeling a rush of adrenaline, but the angel continued to look at him quietly, his face expressionless, offering no further explanation.

"I am not here alone. The *Aljaysh* are outside," Badr said in a low, menacing growl, changing his strategy.

"The *Aljaysh*?" the angel asked.

"Yes, they are armed and waiting for me to remove the musk so that they can take you hostage," Badr said, his hands clenching into fists. He hadn't come this far to return without answers. By rebelling against the *Aljaysh*, he may have just put his life in danger forever.

"If you don't tell me the truth about Dana, I will let them in," Badr threatened, knowing that the angel did not have the capacity for evil, and would not hurt him.

"They plan to not only attack you, but reign over the angels of Al Jazirah," he continued, annoyed that his words were not having any impact on the angel. "And do you think they will stop there?"

"Why do you think they would succeed?" the angel asked calmly.

"Why? Do you think your status makes you untouchable? That you'll just waltz out there with your celestial grace and they won't parade you around like a prized deer?" Badr asked, anger gripping him, as he started to move towards the door.

"Halt!" the angel exclaimed, stopping Badr in his tracks. Through the window, he could see shadows of the *Aljaysh* looming outside.

"Can you tell me who's haunting Dana?" he asked, taking another step toward the door. Life had already thrown him plenty of curveballs. Now he was determined to do whatever it took to get what he wanted.

"Please desist," the angel implored. "Wait here!" he said, then vanished, plunging the space into darkness. Badr reached for the wall and leaned against it, feeling anxious about the outcome of his actions, wondering whether he would be able to flee Al Jazirah, even if the angel complied with his request.

His fingers tapped a nervous tick on the floor as each minute dragged on endlessly. He closed his eyes and pictured Dana, the way she would smile for him and no one else, her blue eyes filled with trust. A warm sensation spread through him as he reflected on small moments of their relationship, and how he would feel when he stood in front of her again.

Light touched his face, and he opened his eyes to see the angel once again standing before him in the same spot.

"I have permission to convey the information that you seek," the angel announced, as Badr stood up and held his breath.

"We appreciate your brave gesture of preventing the *Aljaysh* from entering the tower," the angel said.

"So you have an answer for me?" Badr asked, feeling desperate. He was tense with the anticipation of what he might discover.

"Yes, I have an answer for you."

"Who is it?" Badr asked, each second feeling like a huge obstacle he needed to cross.

"This is unprecedented. What has happened to Dana."

"What do you mean?" Badr asked, his heart pounding.

"I can only tell you who is possessing her. But I won't be able to guide you further. Are you ready to hear it?"

"Yes! Please tell me!" Badr said, not sure his heart could bear the suspense any longer.

"Dana is haunted. I mean in the traditional meaning of the word," the angel said.

"I know that! Just tell me. Who or what has been possessing her?"

The angel looked into Badr's eyes with deep compassion, then replied, "Badr, it's one of your guardian angels."

CHAPTER 38

"And will provide for him from where he never expected. Whoever relies on God—He will suffice him. God will accomplish His purpose. God has set a measure to all things."

(65:3)

"Will you take me to the embassy?" Badr asked. He had called from a grocery store, located inside a fuel station, close to a major roundabout in Umm Al Quwain. "I have dropped my car at your friend's garage."

"Sure man. I am coming to get you," Sultan replied.

Badr hung up and wandered through the store's aisles, the previous day's events attacking his brain, as if pieces of glass and metal were still raining around him.

He did not know what was real anymore. What he had experienced in Al Jazirah or the part he was playing right now: a human waiting for his friend, engaging in ordinary activities.

The angel's revelation had been disconcerting, to say the least. Badr found it hard to believe that his guardian angel had been with Dana since the moment he had first met her. He was the reason she couldn't marry anyone else. He was the one who had caused her so much distress.

Now, with the truth revealed, Badr was at a loss. He did not know how to help Dana, if indeed there was a way to help. The angel had said such a thing had never happened before. Angels did not act out of their own free will.

"Surrender to the will of Allah," the watchtower's angel had advised, reciting,

"With Him are the keys of the unseen—no one knows them except Him. And He knows what is in the land and sea. Not even a leaf falls without His knowledge, nor a grain in the darkness of the earth or anything—green or dry—but is written in a perfect Record." (6:59)

Before Badr could have asked more questions, the *Aljaysh* had started blow a trumpet, signalling the start of war. The angel had once again disappeared, with a fierce confrontation erupting outside.

Through the window, Badr had seen red combatants rise in the air and clash with white, winged ones, surrounded by the campfires the *Aljaysh* had lighted.

The ground below his feet had been shaking violently so Badr had fallen into *sujood* and covered his ears, a futile attempt to keep out the deafening sounds that tore through the air. He had closed his eyes to the blinding flashes of white light and gripped the bottle of musk tightly, trying to steady his nerves. With nothing else to do but wait, he had reflected on how he had managed to withstand pain up until this point; prevented it from turning him into a beast. However, that day had been different. Lying in the dark, on the cold floor, he had tried to find solace in repeatedly reciting verses from *Surah At-Tawbah* (Repentance):

*"So fight them and Allah will punish them at your hands, put them to shame,
help you overcome them, and soothe the hearts of the believers—
removing rage from their hearts. And Allah pardons whoever He wills.
For Allah is All-Knowing, All-Wise." (9:14-15)*

Many hours later, the sounds of combat had finally faded into the distance and an eerie silence had enveloped the area. Badr had waited for the morning to arrive and after saying his *fajr* prayers, had finally mustered the courage to look outside. His eyes had met the quiet serenity of sunrise. The *Aljaysh* camps had vanished while the terrain appeared barren and undisturbed, with no spoils or signs of war.
Badr had left the tower cautiously and tiptoed towards the house he had once shared with Abdulaziz. To his surprise, he had found a cat sitting near the tree outside the house, its eyes closed, an expression of mourning on its face.

He had wondered if it was a jinn, but the cat had remained quiet, disengaged. With no time to waste, Badr had quickly changed into blue jeans, a white t-shirt, and a cap to conceal his face. Gathering his belongings, he had walked towards his car.
There had been a temptation to look back at the house and the place he had grown oddly attached to. But he had told himself that Abdulaziz did not deserve another moment of his consideration.

It was almost half-past nine when Badr and Sultan arrived at the World Trade Centre, also known as Rashid Tower, in Dubai. Sultan whistled as they walked towards a queue of over two hundred people outside the US consulate.

"They are here to apply for a visa," he whispered. "Most of them are Iranians. But since you are an American citizen, you can walk directly into their offices."

"*Baba* has done his homework," Badr said, impressed as he examined the contents of the large brown envelope in his hand. It had all the paperwork, his cousin Essa's birth certificate and attested copies of parents' passports. He was pleased to find a few Post-it notes in his sister Amena's handwriting, highlighting the important details he needed to keep in mind during his interview.

Badr felt nervous, nonetheless, as if a bomb was strapped to his chest and could detonate any moment now. With the recent string of bad luck he'd had, he could expect anything. Somehow it had felt easier to go to war on the island. He had felt strangely powerful. But here he was just an ordinary man trying to find his feet again.

As he waited outside one of the offices with Sultan, his mind drifted towards the future, one that was so hard to imagine because it was so different from the one he had planned.

If he passed through this final stage of his trial, he could expect diasporic loneliness for an unspecified amount of time, in a place where no one knew him, his family or his culture. Sure, he could embark on beautiful train journeys across Europe, find a job based on real skills but more fake paperwork, scrabble for connection with people who seemed familiar, even be friends with them, but it wouldn't be his home or his identity.

His family would be far away. He would be able to have only short phone conversations with them, call just to say he was doing alright so they wouldn't worry. Family occasions, like weddings and funerals, would pass without him, and he would miss the births of his nieces and nephews. To them, he'd just be some odd uncle who lived abroad for mysterious reasons.

Badr knew he would have gladly paid the price if the reward had been his reunion with Dana. But going to the US was also out of the question. It would mean more risks, more danger, based on what he had heard and read in the newspapers.

His face and name would be enough to cause alarm. He'd have to go through brutal airport security measures, feel humiliated when asked to step out of the queue for a thorough interrogation. He could be asked to strip down and to declare any affiliation with any terrorist organisation. Then, if he managed to survive all that, he'd still live in terror. At every knock on the door, he would think someone had arrived to arrest him. If they knew about his fake passport, they could use the Patriot Act or other new counterterrorism laws to detain him indefinitely.

Perspiration slicked his palms as he provided his fingerprints and then sat across from a young American, attired in a business suit with a name tag on his pocket.

Almost immediately, the unsmiling man who appeared to be the embodiment of every spy movie villain started to shoot questions at him.

Badr tried his best to answer with a mask of controlled calm, reminding himself of the odds he had stood against on the island.

Hours bled into a tense eternity, then came the unexpected. He was informed that his American passport had been successfully updated and he could leave.

"You can fly anywhere now," Sultan said, clapping his back and looking equally relieved as they exited the parking. "Just get out of here. You can go anywhere ... to London, Paris, or Singapore."

"Hmm," Badr replied, thinking about the distance between him and Dana. He wondered if she had forgotten him. Assumed he had deserted her. She had no way of knowing what had happened to him.

"So where will you head to Badr?" Sultan asked him as they entered Dubai Airport.

"It's Essa now, remember?" Badr said.

"Okay, okay. Got it. Where will you head to, Jesus?"

Badr did not laugh. A quick, furtive glance at the departure board sent a lump into his throat. There were several flights headed to New York. Dana was one flight away. Yet so unreachable.

"Munich, Rome, Paris?" Sultan asked, reading from the board.

"I think ... Munich ... I am familiar with it," Badr said. He did not feel as free and relieved as he had expected to. He seemed to be headed for another kind of prison, the kind which did not allow him to be near Dana or anyone else he loved.

Once Badr had bought a ticket and booked his hotel room in Munich, Sultan proudly said, "You know, you've been really brave, *okhoy!*"

Under usual circumstances, Badr would have cracked a joke. But he could not think of anything to say. The air was full of unspoken emotions, as they hugged each other. Badr could feel his heart aching as he watched Sultan walk away, thinking about how he'd wake up in a hotel all alone, have breakfast amidst a sea of strangers, constantly reminded of all he had lost and all that he was still missing. A caged lion hungry to achieve greatness in life, yet restricted by his circumstances.

His eyes followed Sultan, quickly moving through the sea of travellers, luggage trolleys and crying babies, but stopped at the glass exits. Across the glass, he saw a lean man in a white *kandura*, with a short ponytail and a wicked grin, waving goodbye.

CHAPTER 39

*"...the life of this world is no more than
the delusion of enjoyment."*

(3:185)

As Badr's plane ascended from the runway in Dubai, a clean-shaven Abdulaziz moved silently through the dark, swampy night, unnoticed and unrecognised.

With the top button of his *kandura* undone, his chest heaved with shallow, uneven breaths as he struggled to escape the relentless grip of guilt.

The rhythmic crashing of waves in Al Jazirah felt a world away, including the chaos that had engulfed the island when the first gatekeeper had fled.

He tried in vain to justify his actions to himself. Badr was more than capable of fulfilling the gatekeeper's responsibilities. And despite his numerous efforts, he didn't get the answers he was seeking. There was little chance he would ever reunite with Dana, given the number and magnitude of obstacles he had to face.

A bead of sweat trickled down Abdulaziz's brow, glistening momentarily before disappearing into the creases of his weathered face.

In seeking to make amends to Azza, he knew he had let Badr down —the one soul who had shown him kindness and understanding in years treated him like someone whose feelings truly mattered.

He knew in his heart that he hadn't been fair to his young friend. It wasn't in his nature to be selfish. But he had felt a compulsion to do the right thing by Azza. Burdened by regret and longing, he had been living like a ghost until Badr's arrival in Al Jazirah had reignited a spark of new possibilities within him. He'd realised he loved Azza as intensely, if not more, as he had when they were together.

He couldn't waste that kind of love, and he wanted to redeem himself. He had failed to do whatever it took to be with his childhood sweetheart the one person who had offered him the love so scarce at home.

He could be short-tempered when around other people but had never said a cross word to her. He could not say no to anything she wanted. Until the day that he did. Badr's unwavering commitment to Dana had opened his eyes to the chances he had let slip through his fingers all those years ago. He had tried to reason with Azza's father, hoping the man would understand how no one else could make Azza happy. But the man would not budge from his decision to marry her off to a wealthy suitor.

Abdulaziz, was young and gullible, so had accepted defeat. But now he knew he should have defied all rules and social conventions to fulfil his promises to Azza. He should not have run away from his feelings, from her and everything else he held dear in his life.

He imagined her, alone in her bedroom, a beautiful but sad bride, hoping till the very last-minute that Abdulaziz would show up. That he would take her away to a life of love and liberation, away from her greedy father and the stranger she was being entrusted to. How she must have yearned to bear his children and build a home full of happiness.

Nothing could now dissuade him from executing the twisted plot born of his desperation and despair. Neither the sacrifice of his friendship with Badr, the passage of fifteen years, or Azza's new life with her own family could deter him.

He did not feel it was wrong to pursue her. Their connection had never ceased to be. And if it was wrong, so was Azza's forced marriage all those years ago, he argued in his imaginary courtroom. The happiness of two individuals, who had never even hurt an insect, had been so easily sacrificed for the sake of wealth, status, and parental control.

Abdulaziz had been contemplating his reunion with Azza for some time, but Badr's decision to leave the island had propelled him into action. He had been hopeful the jinns would help delay Badr's exit. But when the jinns had been unable to help him, Abdulaziz knew there was nothing left for Badr to do but leave.

Under the neon glow of the silent streets, Abdulaziz now felt a tight pain in his chest. He had entered the Sharjah neighbourhood he'd once called home. Its unfamiliarity swept over him like a relentless tide, discovering wounds he had buried a long time ago.

He walked past his family's multi-storied villa, his childhood home, the embodiment of isolation, now dark and locked up, as if evil spirits and unseen devils were inhabiting the place.

It looked almost ancient beside the modern villas, an empty shell characterised by the indifference and rigidity that had defined most of his upbringing. But the spectre that haunted Abdulaziz the most wasn't inhabiting those walls. It was the spectre composed of uncontrollable laughter and dreams that had once woven the vibrant tapestry of his life. The parts of his life he had spent with Azza before she had been snatched away from him.

Abdulaziz had no doubt that Azza still loved him. But whether she would be willing to leave everything behind or not was a question he had been trying to avoid, jostling between hope and hopelessness, uncertain if he could withstand another bout of heartache. Without Azza, he had nowhere to go, no place to call home.

The joyful squeals of the children playing on streets nearby, was a bittersweet reminder of the times he and Azza had caused mischief. They'd ring doorbells and flee. Sneak into gardens to get their supply of tamarind that had fallen from trees or to collect pebbles for a game of *al-teela*.

The two had been inseparable. Even after puberty, when societal boundaries were harshly imposed, they had always found ways to tiptoe around their elders' disapproving eyes and steal precious moments in hidden nooks and corners of the neighbourhood.

They never discussed these acts of rebellion. To them, it was the most natural thing in the world, to be with the person who made them the happiest. It was as if both just understood that they belonged together.

There was never any formal proposal with grand gestures, but as they grew older, Abdulaziz had found himself pouring his heart out with poetry. He would blush and pretend to protest when Azza found poems tucked away in the pocket closest to his heart. He'd feel embarrassed but look at her like a starry-eyed fan as she would devour his words, her big smile a confession of how they uplifted her.

Now, accompanied by his silent screams and reminiscences, Abdulaziz entered a quiet and rather gloomy part of the street. His eyes instantly fell on a sandstone-coloured villa, a landmark that had been imprinted on his dreams. He stood on the same spot as he had on that terrible night, all those years ago, when Azza had arrived at her husband's home a beautiful, expressionless puppet, with her father pulling the strings tightly to prevent her from running away.

As Abdulaziz approached the modest, two-storey house, a fresh wave of bitterness hit him.

"I could have built a much nicer home for you," he muttered. "If only your father had given me the chance."

The man had been dead for quite a few years now, but Abdulaziz could not bring himself to forgive him.

As he drew closer to the villa, lots of toys—a tricycle, a football, a small doll, and pieces of a puzzle—were scattered over a neat green space in front of the villa. Signs of life built around children sent a tremor of fear through Abdulaziz, as he wondered if his fantasy was indeed misguided.

He slowed down, thinking about how he was going to dredge up the past and possibly disrupt Azza's life. But Abdulaziz could not let go of the flicker of hope that had appeared in his heart after all these years. It had made him feel alive again and spurred him on. He couldn't walk away without knowing, without offering

Azza a chance at a different life, one that included him. The Azza he knew would choose love over convenience any day.

As he stood on the green space and readied himself for what lay ahead, Abdulaziz could smell jasmine and remembered how Azza used to weave the flowers into her hair because he liked it. He smiled at the memory, then steeled himself for what lay ahead.

He rang the doorbell as a silent roar built up inside him. There was no response, so he rapped his knuckles against the wooden door in a pattern that felt both foreign and familiar. It was the special knock they had created to let the other person into their secret meeting places.

His heartbeat, once strong and steady, now faltered intermittently, a fragile rhythm on the verge of faltering into stillness.

The door opened slowly. A boy with curly black hair, who seemed to be around seven or eight years old, stared up at him with Azza's expressive eyes.

"*Salam*. Are you here to meet *Baba*?" he asked, with Azza's grin.

"Ah … Azza," Abdulaziz managed to say in a barely audible voice, a sense of affection for Azza's young boy mingling with the indescribable pain of seeing the offspring she'd had with another man. All the special moments in her life he had not been a part of began to cause a shooting pain in his arm. The boy looked confused by Abdulaziz's response, then ran inside, leaving the door slightly ajar.

Abdulaziz could only see a part of the foyer; a large, off-white wall covered with framed paintings. It seemed to be Azza's work. He was familiar with her style and brush strokes. But her style had matured. The brush strokes were bolder, the colours more evocative. She had moved on from calligraphy and painting horses, embracing abstract themes doused with melancholia.

Abdulaziz felt his heart stop as he continued to look at her art, not sure whether the feeling in his chest was joy or grief.

Inside, Azza hummed softly as she mended a shirt. Her son's sudden announcement of an unknown male visitor took her by surprise. No one else was home, so she quickly put on her *abaya*, curious to see who the caller was.

As she made her way towards the main door, an unsettling feeling prickled her.

She dismissed it as nerves; it was unusual to have visitors at this hour and her son would have recognised a relative or friend.

She looked through the peephole but could see no one. Hesitation held her back for a few minutes, but, telling herself that she was being stupid, she swung the door open.

The sight that greeted her left her gasping for air. Her mind reeled, refusing to accept what her eyes were seeing. In a daze, she moved forward and picked up a piece of paper that had fallen on the ground.

It read:

If they ask about me,
Say I adored you,
That you lived in my heart,
In your island I found solace,
In your haven, I survived.
And when I have died,
Tell them I was no hero,
That a demon I implied,
Haunting shadows I could not hide.
Your little child inside, I cherished, I protected,
Even as darkness pried,
And my soul, neglected, For love, I strived.
In whispers of night, And the dawn's early glow,
I held you tight, Though the winds did blow,
Against our fragile might.
If they ask about me, Let them know I was flawed,
But in you, I found beauty, A sanctuary awed,
It was only on your island that I thrived.

Azza sank down beside Abdulaziz, as he lay peacefully with a smile on his face and his pupils fully dilated. She had not cried since her wedding day. It had seemed she no longer had the glands that produced water for tears. But after fifteen years, all her emotions seemed to burst out in the form of uncontrollable weeping. She was not the quiet, polite, obedient housewife and mother anymore.

She cried loudly in pain, not caring if the neighbours heard her. Not worried that her husband might come home and find her grief-stricken over the death of her childhood sweetheart. It seemed like no time had passed between her wedding day and now. Despite having suppressed her feelings and memories for years, she immediately connected with her feelings for Abdulaziz; the way she would feel when they would listen to their favourite music, go on a drive, laugh, or simply sit together doing nothing. It had been so blissful. It had felt like home. She'd never found that feeling anywhere else.

Folding the poem in her hand, she tucked it in the pocket close to his heart, then held his right hand, stroking his long fingers, tracing the lines on his palm, an old friend she'd held on to often.

As she closed his eyes, her teary gaze drifted away from his limp body and became fixed on a painting, revealed by the open doorway.

It was the silhouette of a man and a woman holding hands, standing atop red and brown dunes, looking towards the vast expanse of sea before them.

CHAPTER 40

—◆———————◆———

*"And they carry your loads to distant
lands which you could not otherwise reach
without great hardship.
Surely your Lord is Ever Gracious,
Most Merciful."*

(16:7)

The flight to Munich took just over six hours, but for Badr, it dragged on endlessly as he finally had the time and space to acknowledge and feel all his emotions, think about all that had happened in the last few months, and the ordeal that had not yet ended.

Badr had no idea if he would ever return to life as he had known it before 11th September before he'd become acquainted with the other realms and mysteries of the universe. He had no awareness of who sat next to him on the flight, or what was served for dinner. Outwardly calm, a hollowness gnawed inside him, carved by the disquieting distance from his family, his shattered flying dreams, the shock of Rashid's death, estrangement from Abdulaziz, and above all, the truth about Dana.

His chest felt heavy with guilt and self-loathing as he thought about the war he had instigated on the Red Island, for purely selfish reasons, and how he had unintentionally harmed Dana, the one person he had never wanted to hurt in any way.

He'd always tried to do the right thing. Considered himself a good enough Muslim. But he'd realised it was easy to be good when life was good. But after being tested severely by God, he wasn't sure whether he had passed.

No make matters worse, there was no one he could share these thoughts with, no one who would understand. He was no longer the guy with a head full of dreams and a heart filled with innocent love.

It seemed that no matter what he did, no resolution presented itself. Answers led to more questions. In the days that followed, he sought solace in his hotel suite, but rest eluded him.

There were large stretches of time when he was neither fully awake nor asleep. Every act of relaxation only deepened his sense of fatigue. He would sit in the same spot for hours, in front of the television, with no recollection later of what he had watched. His body was weary. Too much of light, too much of sound, too much of anything, drained his soul.

A new kind of loneliness had set in. But one evening, he decided he'd had enough. He wanted to end his self-imposed solitary confinement, if only briefly. He had not left his hotel room for several days and decided to go for a walk.

The light evening breeze felt like a lifesaver. It quickly resuscitated him, bringing with it an unexpected wave of gratitude.

He strolled by shops, coffeehouses, and discotheques, watching strangers entering or leaving, chatting, and laughing. Their closeness and carefree lifestyle triggered a crying spell. He was about to run back to his hotel room to sob into a pillow, when the signage of an Islamic centre across the street caught his eye.

Badr was still praying five times a day, but lately it had felt more like a habit than a deep conversation with God, one he had previously looked forward to. He was in the midst of what he could only describe as a spiritual crisis. He paced outside the Islamic centre for ten minutes, uncertain if he wanted to go in. A kind, elderly woman smiled as she passed by him and opened the door. Badr decided to follow her inside.

He entered a large seminar hall, which was surprisingly swarming with people in well-fitted blazers and button-down shirts. Some held books on Islam in their hands. Most of them were listening intently to a German man, a recent convert to Islam and a devoted believer, who was narrating the story of his conversion and the teachings that had most inspired him.

Badr found a seat in the back row and looked at the multicultural audience, imagining what kind of stories and secrets each person was carrying, what had brought them here. He wasn't paying much attention to the lecturer until the man began discussing the life of saints and how some would perform *Salat-e-Istikhara* every morning, fully submitting to Allah's will and seeking His guidance in every aspect of life.

Badr had never really said these special prayers before. He'd heard of relatives and neighbours offering them when they were unsure about major life decisions, such as who to marry, which degree to pursue, or what job offer to choose. But he was hungry to do anything that would help him regain his sanity.

Thereafter, each morning after *fajr* prayers, Badr would perform two *rakat* and then, with deep sincerity, recite:

> *"It is out of Allah's mercy that you, O Prophet, have been lenient with them.*
> *Had you been cruel or hard-hearted, they would have certainly abandoned you.*
> *So pardon them, ask Allah's forgiveness for them, and consult with them in*
> *conducting matters. Once you make a decision, put your trust in*
> *Allah. Surely Allah loves those who trust in Him." (3:159)*

After completing the prayer, he would sit in quiet contemplation, his hands resting in his lap, his gaze fixed on the soft patterns of his grey prayer rug.

In the beginning, he found it difficult to concentrate, anger and sorrow blocking his mind, as if someone had placed a piece of black paper inside his brain due to which he couldn't understand or see anything properly.

He did not know exactly when, but his mind did grew quieter, and his body started to feel light. A profound sense of calm descended upon him, as if he knew that the guidance he sought was already on its way.

One day, as he was getting up from his prayer mat, the phone rang.

"Hello?" Badr whispered into the receiver, wondering if it was *Baba* checking up on him.

"Hello Essa!" It was Sultan. He called Badr at least once a week. Badr looked forward to these calls as Sultan filled him in on the latest updates related to his family and their mutual friends.

"And what else?" Badr inquired, once they had finished talking about who had gotten engaged or married, graduated, had a baby, or won a card game.

"What else?" Sultan repeated. "Well, I heard something odd a few weeks ago. It's been the talk of the town, but it's quite sad, *ya'ani,* I'm not sure if you'd want to hear about it."

"Don't worry. After all the crap I've been through, I can take it," Badr said. "I am bored out of my mind here. Just been applying for jobs. Please give me something else to dwell on."

"Well, you remember the guy everyone used to gossip about when we were kids?"

"What guy?"

"The crazy guy!"

"Abdulaziz?" Badr asked, his voice faltering. "Oh no, oh no, oh no," a silent scream rose inside him. He had scarcely begun to recover from the recent cascade of losses. The thought of Abdulaziz being hurt or in trouble bothered him. It melted away any residual anger Badr felt towards him.

"What has happened?" he asked, after a pause, feeling unprepared for a new horrifying twist in his life. He thought of all the catastrophes that could have befallen Abdulaziz. Perhaps a fight had broken out between Abdulaziz and Azza's husband, leaving his friend injured and humiliated. But shock paralysed him when Sultan recounted the tale of Abdulaziz's silent exit from the world at Azza's doorstep.

Badr had not expected to hear that Abdulaziz had taken his last breath a day after leaving the Red Island, as if he couldn't survive outside it anymore.

"*Okhoy*, I just remembered I need to do something urgently. I will contact you later. Bye," Badr mumbled and hung up, as intense emotions began to well up in his throat.

He drew the curtains and slid into bed, wrapping a warm blanket around himself, shivering, palpitating. He recalled how furious he had been with Abdulaziz for leaving him alone, without a single warning. It had taken him a long time to come to terms with it.

After leaving the Red Island, he had doubted if he would ever see Abdulaziz again. It had been difficult for him to accept that he still cared about the man, despite his deceit. He had felt some comfort in knowing he had returned to the world after all these years, and perhaps even changed the course of love and his life.

Badr had eventually let go of his resistance to what had happened, and realized how he would have never found the answers he was seeking had Abdulaziz not left his post and appointed him as the new gatekeeper. He had begun to think of Abdulaziz as less of a backstabber. He was no stranger to the fact that love could make people desperate. It could create differences with other loved ones. It could motivate people to do things they'd never think possible otherwise.

"I just wish it had all been worth it," Badr said out loud, as if expecting Abdulaziz to emerge and respond. But the only sound was the distant hum of the city.

As the clock ticked and the hours went by, Badr's preoccupation with Abdulaziz and his death moved to thoughts of his own mortality and his singularly isolated state. For the first time in his life, he felt completely unprotected, vulnerable, with no one to turn to. He looked in the mirror and saw an unshaven man, clad in a vest, staring back.

"Just like Abdulaziz, in his dishevelled state," he thought. The possibility, the inevitability of death began to take over his mind. His body tensed and eyes darted around the room, scanning the corners, as if at any moment the room would swallow him whole. He thought of Dana. How she might tie the knot with someone else while he stayed here, deteriorating internally, free from the dangers of the world he had left behind, but trapped, nonetheless. Transforming into a clone of Abdulaziz. Another Iblis.

CHAPTER 41

---

*"And one of His signs is that He created for you
spouses from among yourselves so that you may
find comfort in them. And He has placed between
you compassion and mercy. Surely in this are
signs for people who reflect."*

(30:21)

The air was full with the scent of vanilla candles as Badr stepped into his newly furnished master bedroom, its handcrafted furniture illuminated by soft, ambient lighting. He was happy with how the space had been designed to be both elegant and comfortable. But the decorative shades, the Persian rugs and everything else faded from his view as soon as his eyes rested on her petite form.

She sat like a princess on their grand bed, her fingers absently tracing patterns on the white silk sheets.

Today, he felt the discord dissolving. Not only because they were here together, with no boundaries to hold them back from one another, but also because a veil had lifted from his eyes.

Badr strode towards Dana. When their gazes locked, she quickly adjusted a cosy blue throw that was draped over her lap and said, "I was waiting for you."

A smile of nervous excitement played at her lips. At that moment, Badr had an epiphany: despite not having found a cure for Dana, her episodes had ceased since their reunion.

He stood close to her now, his demeanour relaxed, as she leaned against the bed's carved headboard, the movement making her pink lace dress slip off one shoulder. She flushed as Badr sat next to her, and with a mixture of affection and anticipation, gently caressed her bare shoulder.

He was savouring every moment, unwrapping secrets with happy awkwardness, realising how their connection created a protective, harmonious cocoon.

As his fingers grazed her arm, Badr wondered whether he was getting ahead of himself. But the more he pondered on this notion, the more he became convinced that this was the only viable explanation.

As he leaned in and inhaled the rich scent of the oud perfume lingering on her neck, his conversations with the jinns about love floated around in his mind. With his breath tickling her ear, he murmured, "So do you like this? Our version of *firdaws*?" She laughed softly, and then slowly, tenderly, her hands found his.

As their fingers intertwined, it all started to make sense to him. Angels did not have a free will. They could only carry out what God had ordained. The bond between him and Dana had been blessed and guided by divine influence. It was a journey he'd been meant to embrace. The angel, the haunting, had not been a curse, but a sign.

The exploration of love, the definitions he'd learned in Al Jazirah, had led him to this one truth: each person had a unique experience and definition of love. No two people could describe it in the same way.

As he closed the gap between him and Dana, Badr tried to create his own definition, "Perhaps our love is a sacred bond that transcends mere human connection."

"Love is a profound, transcendent force that enables you to do the unthinkable," he reflected, as his skin brushed against hers.

It dawned on him that it was their destiny to be together despite the hurdles. "It's like a holy gift, a reflection of the divine will, a purposeful union that aligns with a higher plan and spiritual truths. It's a manifestation of God's grand design for us to come together," he surmised.

"Perhaps the sacred nature of love infuses it with an inherent sanctity," he thought as their movements synchronised effortlessly into a comfortable rhythm.

With every new gesture of intimacy, Badr felt their bond deepening and being enriched. He knew what they had was not mere physical attraction or emotional connection, but a deeper spiritual alignment. With every curve and contour he explored with his hands, he realised there was no other explanation for how events beyond their control had ignited their love, tested, and transformed it.

His mind travelled back to that oppressive day in Munich, when he had received the tragic news about Abdulaziz. He had been on a rollercoaster of intense grief and then extreme fear, such that he had never felt before, not even during his time on the island.

He had been inconsolable and frightened like a child, until the next morning, when a *Surah* in the Qur'an had caught his attention:

> *"So she conceived him and withdrew with him to a remote place.*
> *Then the pains of labour drove her to the trunk of a palm tree. She cried,*
> *'Alas! I wish I had died before this, and was a thing long forgotten!'*
> *So a voice reassured her from below her, 'Do not grieve! Your*
> *Lord has provided a stream at your feet. And shake the trunk of this*
> *palm tree towards you, it will drop fresh,*
> *ripe dates upon you.'" (19:22-25)*

It was the story of Maryam, when Allah had instructed her to find food for Prophet Isa by shaking a date palm tree and had rewarded her for following His command by making the dates fall.

Some clarity had descended after Badr read the *Surah* several times. It had removed the fog clouding his mind. A few days later, he had boarded a flight to New York despite all the risks involved. He had gone with the conviction that his place was by Dana's side and nowhere else.

His arrival in the US had not been as horrific as he had imagined. He was able to leave unscathed, and within a few weeks, had been able to track Dana down at her aunt's place in Boro Park.

Everything had unfolded smoothly from then on. With her parents' blessings and the promise to get her the respect and acceptance she deserved as his wife, Badr had married Dana in a simple *nikah* ceremony. He had realised his family would have to accept Dana once they were already married if they wanted him to return home.

The distance had given him the unique opportunity to avoid weeks of strained silences and unnecessary bickering, and to restrict highly charged discussions, punctuated with barbs of "how-could-you" and "what-if-you-had-gotten-caught," to brief phone conversations.

As the months had passed, Badr's *nikah* with the Jew-girl had been begrudgingly accepted. Soon after, he had received the news he'd been eagerly awaiting. *Baba*, with the assistance of an Emirati royal, had cleared his name.

The turmoil was finally over. Badr could not believe he could finally go back. Finally, he could put his guard down, walk around and do whatever he wanted to. He could be seen in public with Dana without the fear of being judged.

Once back in Dubai, his family had insisted on throwing a lavish wedding reception, a public, face-saving declaration for the community that they were fine with Badr's choice.

Clad in a *bisht*, Badr had stood amidst his male relatives and friends, resplendent in crisp white *kanduras* and embroidered *ghutras*, greeting them with nose kisses and handshakes. The elders had offered words of wisdom and guidance for his marital life ahead.

In the women's section, Dana had sat with her sisters, looking radiant in her elaborate white wedding gown and diamond jewellery. She had watched the women gossiping around her in hushed tones, overhearing the words 'Jews' and 'eligible Emirati bachelors' often. But she had chosen to focus on the future she had planned with Badr.

CHAPTER 42

*"He is the Knower of the unseen,
disclosing none of it to anyone,
except messengers of His choice.
Then He appoints angel-guards
before and behind them."*

(72:26-27)

Despite his successful reunion with Dana and his safe return to the UAE, a churning disquiet had begun to brew within Badr. He often reflected on the time he'd spent on the Red Island, but didn't know who to share it with. Dana listened but could not relate. He felt foolish when he tried to explain to her all that had transpired, like it had not been real, a story he'd imagined to cope with distress. But parts of the island seemed to have woven themselves into his soul and fragments of him had been left behind.

One afternoon, as Badr sat in his garden thinking about Al Jazirah yet again, a sudden crash jolted him from his reverie. The sound, sharp and unexpected, had come from the shed.

He strode in and picked up the broken pieces of a plant pot, then searched for the source of the disturbance. As he glanced up at the wall shelves with gardening tools, a pair of deep blue eyes locked onto his, piercing through the dimly lit shed.

"Maftoon!" Badr exclaimed, as he turned around to switch on another light and make sure he wasn't hallucinating.

The sudden brightness confirmed Maftoon's presence, but he had quickly shifted to his human guise and was now sitting cross-legged on the grass.

"I'm delighted to see you again," Badr said, lowering himself onto the cold grass in front of Maftoon.

As he looked at his friend, Badr felt a sense of validation for his experiences on the island. But he was also reminded of his ongoing hesitation to get back into a purely human existence by taking up a nine-to-five engineering job again. He was unsure about how he would reconcile the world of jinns, angels, and the timelessness of Al Jazirah with his present life. Something inside him had changed so drastically and permanently that it was hard to imagine a life revolving around coffee break banter and farmhouse picnics.

Under Maftoon's silent gaze, Badr recalled their last encounter. He knew he had let Maftoon down, left him hanging with unanswered questions, joined the *Aljaysh* and started a war. Maftoon had every reason to be upset with him.

"I'm sorry I couldn't meet you before I left. I hope you understand why I did what I did," Badr said, a note of embarrassment creeping into his voice. "I realise now that my actions didn't serve your interests or those of the island, but I truly believed it was the only way to help Dana and leave my post on the island."

"It's fine sheikh," Maftoon replied, nodding.

"Abdulaziz, may Allah bless his soul, wanted me to be the next gatekeeper, but I had made no such commitments to him. I had made promises to Dana. I couldn't imagine living without her. And I don't believe there is greatness in suffering for love unless the object of that suffering is to unite with your beloved."

"Sheikh, you don't need to explain," Maftoon said. "Allah alone is *Hakam*. And no one on the island blames you for what you did. The *Aljaysh* would have probably found another way to attack the angels. Your interference and warning actually helped the angels emerge victorious."

"You are very kind and forgiving," Badr replied. "The best of jinns. But how did you come here? Are you even allowed?"

"I took permission," Maftoon replied. "I saw you at the graveyard earlier today."

That morning, Badr had visited the graves of Rashid and Abdulaziz, who were buried not far from each other. He made it a point to talk to them weekly, sometimes fighting with them for departing so soon. No one else seemed to understand him as they had, and the space left by their absence was only growing with time.

"Believe it or not, I kind of miss Al Jazirah," Badr confessed, wondering if Maftoon had overheard his conversations with his lost friends.

"You should try to move on from the island, sheikh," Maftoon advised, concern evident in his tone. "You're human; your place is in your world. The jinns and spirits have their own realms. You must let them go."

"But I ... I find myself more at ease with jinns and spirits now," Badr protested. "I feel restless around other people. I'm happy with Dana, but it seems like no one can grasp this other part of my life; who I became in Al Jazirah, the things I did."

"Most people in your situation would never go back," Maftoon said, and recited:

*'But We delivered him and those in the Ark,
making it a sign for all people.'"* (29:15)

"Allah has rescued you from all your difficulties and blessed you with everything you ever wanted. But I must take my leave now, sheikh. I've said what I came to say. The rest is up to you."

Badr felt a pang of disappointment. He wasn't ready for Maftoon to leave.

"Please wait," he said, trying to keep the conversation going. "I need to ask you something."

"What?" Maftoon asked as he stood up to leave.

"Before you leave, I must know about the island... How are Hakim and Talib? The *Ulema*? And who is the new gatekeeper? Has an angel taken over?"

"No, sheikh," Maftoon responded, shaking his head. "Not an angel. They have their divine duties to attend to and cannot stay or assume other responsibilities."

"Then, who has taken over as the gatekeeper?" Badr pressed, his curiosity piqued.

"A jinn?"

"No," Maftoon replied, his eyes glinting with a mix of mystery and gravity. "It's a woman."

"A woman?" Badr echoed, astonished. "In Al Jazirah? Alone? Surrounded by jinns?"

"Yes, sheikh, a young, beautiful woman," Maftoon said. "She arrived the very day you departed the island."

He recited:

> *"Then which of your Lord's favours will you humans*
> *and jinn both deny?" (55:13)*

"Is this a new person I need to rescue?" Badr wondered. He was ashamed to admit that the idea sounded appealing to him.

"But why was she there? Did she just come up to you and offer her services?" Badr asked. It sounded ludicrous, but he had come to expect the unfathomable, the unimaginable from the Red Island.

"I was on the quest to find a new gatekeeper when I sensed her presence. Soon, I found her, stumbling inside one of the houses, with a bag of clothes and some food items," Maftoon said. "Her face went ashen when she saw me. I tried to speak to her, but she panicked and tried to lock herself in a room, but I was too fast for her."

"Why was she scared of you? Did she know you were a jinn?" Badr asked, intrigued.

"No," Maftoon said with a hint of amusement. "She believed I was a human an undercover CID agent, sent to apprehend her and take her back to the city."

"Apprehend her?" Badr inquired, bewildered. "Who was she running from? Her family? Why would she resist leaving?"

"Yes, she was fleeing, but not from her family. She needed a place to hide," Maftoon confirmed.

"Hide from what?" Badr asked. This was hitting too close to home.

"She said she could not leave the country," Maftoon said.

"Why?" Badr's mind was racing. The strangeness of the situation bothered him. "What woman would be reckless enough to venture to the Red Island alone? Didn't she have anyone who could help her?"

"Apparently not. No family or friends here. In any case, she did not think they would like to protect someone who had committed a heinous crime!" Maftoon declared with a dramatic flair, clearly relishing Badr's shock.

"A criminal?" Badr asked. "Does the island really need more secrets? Another human disturbing the peace?"

"To tell you the truth, I have been pleasantly surprised by her strength. Every day, she fights with herself, with the devil inside her, and finds the will to live. But her devotion as the new gatekeeper is quite remarkable."

"But what has she done that is so terrible that she needed to self-exile herself in an abandoned ghost town?"

"She fears humans more than she fears jinns and other creatures," Maftoon said. "She was afraid to tell me why initially. But after I started taking care of her, bringing her food and other essentials she needed to survive on the island, I was able to gain her trust. She said I was her only friend now. Then, one evening, I found her weeping. I insisted she tell me, and it was then that she confessed."

"Confessed to what?" Badr asked, his heart pounding with uneasiness. Maftoon was a jinn, but as a human, Badr could not shield a criminal. He felt compelled to report her, remembering a verse from the Qur'an:

"O believers! Stand firm for justice as witnesses for Allah, even if it is against yourselves, your parents, or close relatives. Be they rich or poor, Allah is best to ensure their interests. So do not let your desires cause you to deviate from justice. If you distort the testimony or refuse to give it, then 'know that' Allah is certainly All-Aware of what you do." (4:135)

"She said she had taken a life," Maftoon replied, letting the gravity of her confession hang in the air.

"What?" Badr was stunned. His breathing quickened as a suspicion started taking root in the recesses of his brain cells. He had the nagging the feeling that he was somehow connected to this woman.

"Why did you appoint her as the gatekeeper then?" he asked.

"I know what you think, Sheikh," Maftoon said. "Allah has said in the Qur'an that if you kill someone, 'unless as a punishment for murder or mischief in the land,' it is like you have 'killed all of humanity.'"

"But who was her victim?" Badr asked, struggling to dispel the disturbing thoughts he had about the identity of this woman.

Maftoon fell silent for a moment, as if he could read Badr's thoughts. To Badr's astonishment, he confirmed his suspicions, saying, "She claimed she had taken the life of a man she loved more deeply than her own soul."

CHAPTER 43

◆———————·———————◆

"Fear is only for those who do wrong.
But if they later mend their evil ways
with good, then I am certainly
All-Forgiving, Most Merciful."

(27:11)

Every sunrise and sunset, she was a solitary figure against the backdrop of roiling waves. Her eyes, once bright with hope and love, were now permanently clouded with a deep, unshakable sorrow.

Leaning against rocks, she would trace the ancient symbols carved into their surfaces, her mind replaying the events that had led her here.

The man she had loved, whose poetry and hugs had once filled her heart with immense joy, was now haunting her. She could still see his face, the shock and pain in his eyes as she had struck him down. The memory was a dagger twisted deep within her chest, and the blood on her hands, though long washed away, seemed to cling to her soul. She had buried the crystal ashtray on the island, but would keep visiting its resting place.

No one had figured out what had really happened to him. Maybe they never would. But that wasn't the most important thing anymore. No matter where she went, she knew she wouldn't be free. She had condemned herself to an eternity of regret, guilt, and loneliness.

She sank to her knees on the cold, gritty sand, her hands trembling as she clutched her aching chest, tears streaming down her face.

"I never wanted this," she whispered to the wind, her voice cracking under the weight of her remorse. "All I ever wanted was to be loved by you."

She had hoped that by guarding the gate, she might find a way to atone for her sins, to make amends for the path she had taken in life. But each day, as the sun set and the shadows lengthened, the burden of her actions seemed to grow heavier.

She knew it would not be easy; atonement rarely was. Yet she clung to a flicker of hope that perhaps, in the endless expanse of the sea and the unforgiving vastness of the Red Island, she would find a measure of forgiveness.

GLOSSARY
OF ARABIC WORDS

A

Abaya—A traditional outer garment worn by women, covering the body from shoulders to feet.

Abni - My son; a term of endearment for one's male child.

Adhan - The Islamic call to prayer announced from a mosque's minaret.

Allahu Akbar - "God is Greatest"; a phrase used in Islamic prayers and expressions of faith.

Alhamdulillah - "All praise is due to God"; an expression of gratitude to God.

Al-teela - The term is less common and may refer to a specific cultural or regional context.

Ameerat-Quraish - The princess of the Quraysh tribe; a historical reference.

Ana - "I" or "me" in Arabic; used for self-reference.

Aqem alsalah - "Establish the prayer"; a command to perform Islamic prayers.

Asar - Afternoon prayer in Islam; also refers to the time of day when this prayer is performed.

As-salamu alaykum - "Peace be upon you"; a common Islamic greeting.

Astaghfar - "I seek forgiveness"; a plea for God's forgiveness.

Attar - A traditional perfume made from flower essences and essential oils.

Ayat - Verses of the Quran; individual lines or sections.

Ayat ul Kursi - The "Verse of the Throne"; a significant verse in the Quran for protection and blessings.

B

Baba - "Father"; also used affectionately for an older man.

Baklava - A sweet pastry made of layers of filo dough, filled with nuts and honey or syrup.

Barakah - Divine blessing or abundance.

Bedu - Nomadic Arab tribespeople; also known as Bedouins.

Bid'ah - Innovation in religious practices not established by Islamic tradition.

Biryani - A South Asian spiced rice dish often made with meat, vegetables, and saffron.

Bisht - A traditional Arabic cloak worn over the dress, often on formal occasions.

Bismillah - "In the name of God"; a phrase used before starting any task or activity.

Bokhour - A type of incense used for perfuming and purifying spaces.

D

Daal - A dish made from lentils; also refers to the lentils themselves.

Dhow - A traditional wooden sailing vessel used in the Arabian Sea.

Dua - Supplication or personal prayer to God.

E

Ekhty - My sister; a term of endearment for one's female sibling or close friend.

Enta 'umri - "You are my life"; an expression of deep affection.

F

Fajr - The dawn prayer in Islam; also the time of day when this prayer is performed.

Fee Amanillah - "In the protection of God"; a farewell phrase.

Firaun - Pharaoh; title of ancient Egyptian rulers, also used in Islamic texts to refer to the tyrant ruler of Moses' time.

Firdaws - The highest level of paradise in Islamic belief.

G

Ghaf - Forgiveness; to pardon or overlook someone's faults.

Ghusl - The ritual purification bath required before certain prayers and acts of worship.

Ghutra - A traditional headscarf worn by men, often in the Middle East.

H

Habibi - "My dear" or "my beloved"; a term of endearment.

Habibti - "My dear" or "my beloved" (female); a term of endearment.

Hala - A casual greeting meaning "hello" or "welcome."

Hakam - Judge or arbiter; someone who makes decisions in disputes.

I

Ilm al-sihr - The study of magic or sorcery; often considered forbidden in Islam.

Imam - The leader of prayer in a mosque; also a title for Islamic scholars.

Isha - The night prayer in Islam; also the time of day when this prayer is performed. compiled by the Islamic scholar Tirmidhi.

J

Jihad - Struggle or striving in the path of God; often misunderstood as only "holy war."

Jihad al-Nafs - The internal struggle against one's own desires and sinful inclinations.

Jihadist - An individual who participates in jihad, often associated with militant groups.

Juma'a - The Friday prayer in Islam; a weekly congregational prayer.

K

Kuboos - A type of Arabic bread, often flat and round.

Kufr - Disbelief or rejection of faith; the opposite of iman (faith).

Kurta - A traditional tunic worn in South Asian and Middle Eastern cultures.

L

La - "No"; used to indicate negation or refusal.

La Shukran - "No, thank you"; a polite way to decline something.

Laban - A type of fermented milk drink popular in the Middle East.

Luqaimat - Sweet dumplings made from flour and sugar, often served as a dessert.

M

Maghrib - The sunset prayer in Islam; also the time of day when this prayer is performed.

Mahram - A family member with whom marriage is prohibited; often a guardian in certain Islamic contexts.

Majlis - A council or gathering place; also refers to a formal meeting or assembly.

Malayika - Angels; spiritual beings in Islamic belief.

Ma'ashara - "Companions" or "fellowship"; refers to a group of people in some contexts.

MashaAllah - "As God wills"; an expression used to show appreciation or admiration.

Mehbash - A traditional Arabic coffee grinder.

Milcha - A type of traditional Arabic dessert or dish, depending on the region.

Miswak - A natural teeth-cleaning stick made from the Salvadora persica tree.

Motawa - An Arabic term that can refer to a religious police or enforcer of religious laws.

N

Nidaal - "Struggle" or "combat"; often used in the context of effort or battle.

Nikah - The Islamic marriage contract; also refers to the marriage ceremony.

O

Okhoy — "My brother"; a term of endearment for a close male friend or relative.

R

Rakat - Units of prayer in Islamic worship; each unit involves specific actions and recitations.

Regag - A type of traditional Arabic bread.

Rehal - A travel or prayer rug; also refers to a type of Arabic incense holder.

Ruqyah - Spiritual healing or exorcism using Quranic verses and supplications.

S

Sabah el noor - "Good morning"; a greeting meaning "morning of light."

Sabkhas - Traditional Arabic desserts or dishes, depending on the context.

Sadaqah Jariyah - Ongoing charity or acts of goodness that continue to benefit others even after one's death.

Saher - A term meaning "one who stays awake" or "watchman"; often used in a broader sense.

Sahera - "Enchantress" or "charm"; can refer to a woman who is captivating.

Sahih al-Bukhari - A famous collection of Hadiths compiled by the scholar Imam Bukhari.

Salam - "Peace"; also a common greeting meaning "peace be upon you."

Salat-e-Istikhara - A prayer for seeking guidance from God in making decisions.

Salat-al-Janazah - The funeral prayer in Islam performed for deceased Muslims.

Shams al-Ma'arif al-Kubra' - A well-known book on Islamic occult sciences and magic.

Shakshuka - A dish made from poached eggs in a spicy tomato and pepper sauce.

Shayla - A type of headscarf or shawl worn by women.

Shaytan - "Satan" or devil

T

Tawassul – using intermediaries in spiritual practices

U

Ummi - Mother

THE AUTHOR WOULD LOVE TO HEAR YOUR THOUGHTS ON THE RED ISLAND. SHARE YOUR REVIEW ON:

IF YOU WOULD LIKE TO LEARN MORE ABOUT THE AUTHOR: